Performing America

THEATER: Theory/Text/Performance

Enoch Brater, Series Editor

PERFORMING AMERICA

Cultural Nationalism in American Theater

Jeffrey D. Mason and J. Ellen Gainor, Editors

Ann Arbor

THE UNIVERSITY OF MICHIGAN PRESS

Copyright © by the University of Michigan 1999
All rights reserved
Published in the United States of America by
The University of Michigan Press
Manufactured in the United States of America
⊚ Printed on acid-free paper

2002   2001   2000   1999   4   3   2   1

A CIP catalog record for this book is available from the British Library.

Library of Congress Cataloging-in-Publication Data

Performing America : cultural nationalism in American theater /
    edited by Jeffrey D. Mason and J. Ellen Gainor.
        p.   cm.—(Theater—theory/text/performance)
    Includes bibliographical references (p.   ) and index.
    ISBN 0-472-10985-5 (alk. paper)
        1. Theater and society—United States—History—20th century.   2.
    American drama—History and criticism.   3. National characteristics,
    American, in literature.   4. Nationalism and literature—United
    States—History.   5. Pluralism (Social sciences) in literature.   I.
    Mason, Jeffrey D.   II. Gainor, J. Ellen.   III. Series.
    PN2266.5 .P47 1999
    792'.0973—dc21

                                                              99-6219
                                                                 CIP

Contents

PART TWO. NATION NOW

Jeffrey D. Mason

American Stages (Curtain Raiser)

When we decided to edit this collection, Ellen Gainor and I sought to explore the question of how America or "America" performs its own self-conception. (Throughout, I shall enclose "America" and "American" in quotation marks when I wish to signal theories, constructions, and attitudes in contrast with the actual space or nation, its people and their institutions.) The project led us to consider how artists and audiences inscribe "American," how those inscriptions both include and exclude potential constituents, how events and visions appropriate material into what may or may not be an essentialist view of "American," and how they foster the construction of "America" and contribute to American discourses. We accepted from the start that "American" is a formulation rather than a received truth—the very term, which we continue to use for the sake of convenience, arrogates a hemispherical designation for a single nation—so we approached our editorial task with a bias toward critique rather than acquiescence. In general, we aspired to learn something about the interaction between nationhood, as a way of establishing or articulating an identity for a people or a culture, and its expression on stage. The reflexive interactions between stage, nation, culture, and constituents, especially in so multifarious a country as the United States, seemed dazzlingly complex.

Underlying our overt agenda has been our interest in situating the theater as a product, an expression, and an integral constituent of its culture. Performances and para-performances persist in venues scattered throughout society, and any of them can employ and interrogate the discourse that permeates and drives the culture as a whole. The stage is only an explicit site for performing national identity, one that serves to focus the issues, rhetoric, and images found in the more general forums; its creative freedom and opportunity to take risks encourage attempts to develop, explore, test, and dispute conceptions of national character. In the performative arena, in the interchanges among artists and spectators, we can enact narratives of nation, whether ostensibly actual or openly speculative.

As a nation, America bears a special status and carries a unique burden. For more than two centuries, the United States has offered itself as the realization of the aspirations of multitudes, appropriating the halo of freedom and righteousness in spite of what seems, here at the end of the millennium, to be a growing chorus of resentful, accusatory, and critical voices. As the object of hope, "America" becomes a concept that transcends mere nationality, a symbol belonging not only to its citizens, but to those who yearn, no matter from what cultural tradition they may spring. It is what anyone might imagine it to be. Yet when immigrants' dreams harden into the everyday, ordinary reality of an actual nation, "America," as a symbol, becomes subject to interrogation. Who are "we"? Since this is a democracy, we might seek to define "we" in terms of the majority of the moment, but to do so is to strip and erase the corresponding minorities. How does "America" include and exclude? To what extent does it shape or is it shaped? The very ontology of America seems ambiguous, for if the nation evolves as it absorbs newcomers, then it would seem to have no reliable, discernible or even approximately stable being of its own.

American nationality is especially susceptible to performance, for insofar as the nation itself is the product of invention or design, its nationality is a consequence of imagination and an object of negotiation. An ordinary definition of "nation" involves commonality of territory, political system, law, language, ethnicity, traditions, and interests. Yet Ernest Gellner has argued that "nations are not inscribed into the order of things" but are, instead, the products of changing circumstances and of the willingness of the citizens to accept one another as sharing a community (49, 7). In other words, there is a choice to be made, an act of will. America is not organic, not a matter of essence, but rather the product of need and effort. Perhaps the hallmark of "America" is its broad capacity for self-invention and subsequent self-contemplation. Popular discourse tends to posit "America" as autochthonous, but it is, rather, the manifestation of design, an unfolding, proliferating narrative that is the product of generations of contributing authors. Sociologist Immanuel Wallerstein has described the maintenance of nationality, or of "peoplehood," as a function of history; indeed, such maintenance provides an important purpose for history, myth, or any discourse on the past, for "pastness is a central element in the socialization of individuals, in the maintenance of group solidarity, [and] in the establishment of or challenge to social legitimation" (78). In other words, the expression of a culture—the art, the music, the literature, the history, even the arrangement and decoration of our cities and homes, or the nature of our celebrations; or, to put it another way, the narrative and the ways in which we choose to shape our experience—serves to define, defend, and affirm a concept of nation.

Any contribution to the narrative both forms and depends upon some idea of "America," a notion that has broken loose from its original moorings. For generations, "America" appeared as a monoculture, smugly and comfortably homogeneous and unified, but even in the popular arena, this model has given way to a multicultural or pluralistic paradigm, reflecting widespread recognition of increasing ethnic diversity and the first signs of the waning of the white majority's hegemony. Trends in the academy have been more complex. Literary scholar Donald E. Pease has traced the history of American cultural studies from the myth-symbol school and its "metanarrative" to the more recent tension between new historicism and multiculturalism; he offers a critique of the latter methodologies and finds attempts to resolve their contradictions in the "postnationalist initiatives of the so-called New Americanists" ("New Perspectives" 23–25). Pease has described the "national narrative" as a means of creating a nation by constructing "imaginary relations to actual sociopolitical conditions" out of the supposedly universal ideals of the Enlightenment, a process that creates, employs, and fosters a specifically American "image repertoire." He argues that this "national narrative produced national identities by way of a social symbolic order that systematically separated an abstract, disembodied subject from resistant materialities, such as race, class, and gender" and so provided strategies for "the allocation of social empowerments" ("National Identities" 3–4). The American narrative is undeniably a product of desire and imagination, and part of what forms "America" is the sense that even history can be written as we will. In this vision, America is the land not of evolution, but of inspiration.

Ultimately, the narrative reflects the struggle over its ownership, an agon marked with questions: what is the narrative? how does it evolve? who can write it? who can read it? who can use it? The contenders grapple over control of the semiotic repertoire, over the consequent notion of nation, and over the ways in which "imaginary relations" will have consequences in the material world. To use a sign is simultaneously to appropriate it, to restrict its potential use, and to confine the concept at hand. In his critique of Frederick Crews' defense of "canonical mastertexts," Pease engages in what I regard as a struggle over "America" at one remove; that is, he contends not over the complex of signs and meanings and uses but rather over the principles, assumptions, and attitudes that vie to govern their study and therefore our understanding of them ("New Americanists" 3–19). To take up a position in such a discourse can be a political strategy, for to appropriate or pre-empt some portion of the national "character" is to forestall one's adversary from doing so. The tropes, phrases, and images of "America" form and re-form as they are used, and to employ them effectively can serve to shut out someone else's conception. To contribute to the national narrative becomes a political act, a matter of competition. More personally, each individual who participates in the contest establishes her or his own name and position in relation to all others; usage and advocacy mark identity, and the discourse turns on its authors.

The stage, then, becomes a site of this struggle, a platform where players and audience may enact conceptions of identity and community, where "America" becomes both the subject and the consequence of artistic, cultural, and social negotiation. To the extent that the stage deals in representation, it offers great power, for it brings the national narrative to life, possibly reducing experience within its narrow confines of time and space, but also illuminating its complexities and contradictions.

To so perceive the American theater is to remember a void in American theater studies. Those working in American literature can situate their work in long, rich debates over conceptualization and methodology, all in terms of the specifically American character of the experience. Yet there has been little attempt, if any, to theorize American theater or drama as such; there are no theatrical counterparts to such landmark literary studies as F. O. Matthiessen's *American Renaissance,* Henry Nash Smith's *Virgin Land,* Leo Marx's *The Machine in the Garden,* Annette Kolodny's *The Lay of the Land,* or Myra Jehlen's *American Incarnation.* In fact, Susan Harris Smith has devoted an entire study to the marginalization of American theater and drama in academia. Plays and their productions claim only a very little space in the discourse of American studies, no matter the decade or the methodology.

How might one theorize the American theater? In terms of colonization, of other cultures establishing themselves here, and then the emerging culture wresting away the initiative and appropriating from others? In terms of revolution, of the revision of received craft and sensibility? As a working-out of disparity or an affirmation of unity? As a mosaic essay on liberal individualism? As an epic on the ongoing response to an overpowering sense of mission that has traveled from its theological sources into secular ground? As a tale of cultural coming-of-age, of a journey from Edenic, pre-experiential innocence to a more mature awareness of the nation's place in history, perhaps interpreted as a fall from grace or presented within the transformation of landscape from garden to metropolis to cyberspace? As a meditation on the unabashed embrace of materialism in service of egalitarian ideals and a virtually sanctified free market system? As a resolutely optimistic interpretation of experience in terms of rights, privileges, and entitlements, in contrast to the sense of sorrow, loss, guilt, or struggle that, one might argue, marks such nations as Ireland, Germany, South Africa, and Korea? Yet there are challenges to any of these hypothetical proposals. Should Americanist theater studies focus on the written text, the drama, in acquiescence to the argument that the theater, in the senses of production, craft, technique, and the living event, seems to be trans-national, the artists, the practice, and the criticism traveling blithely across borders? Rather than treat theater (or drama) separately, should we instead join the Americanists and spur their swing away from "high" literature and toward a cultural studies that will include the stage, all in an attempt to encompass the cornucopian complexity of the underlying experience whose reality the Americanists seem to presume? Or should American theater studies eschew any such theorizing, instead arguing that to do so would be to select and simplify, or to allege patterns in chaos, in order to validate sweeping generalizations? Underlying such concerns is the case of history itself, of to what extent one can regard the present as a production of the past, a proof of evolution or of will, a situation explicable in terms of prior events that fall, even if only in the light of hindsight, into logical and even inevitable sequence, or, alternatively, of how persuasively one can assert the uniqueness of each moment in a flow so turbulent and complex as to seem virtually random. The American sensibility tends to claim two contradictory uses of history: to interpret the past, as Wallerstein explains, as a justification of the national mission and an infallible path toward the future, but also to dispense with the past and declare the first dawning.

Performing America will not answer all of these questions, but the following essays offer a variety of perspectives and suggest the intricacy of the debate. In traveling from colonial theater to queer theory, and in leaving the conventional playhouse to explore museums, Chautauqua, vaudeville, and pageantry, our colleagues present the American theater as a multi-dimensional tapestry, a set of responses to the performative impulse that permeate, penetrate, embrace, reject, convey, and speak to the American senses of nation.

REFERENCES

Crews, Frederick. "Whose American Renaissance?" *New York Review of Books* 35.16 (27 October 1988): 68–81.

Gellner, Ernest. *Culture, Identity, and Politics.* Cambridge: Cambridge UP, 1987.

Jehlen, Myra. *American Incarnation: The Individual, the Nation, and the Continent.* Cambridge, MA: Harvard UP, 1986.

Kolodny, Annette. *The Lay of the Land: Metaphor as Experience and History in American Literature*. Chapel Hill: U of North Carolina P, 1975.

Marx, Leo. *The Machine in the Garden: Technology and the Pastoral Ideal in America*. New York: Oxford UP, 1964.

Matthiessen, F. O. *American Renaissance: Art and Expression in the Age of Emerson and Whitman*. London: Oxford UP, 1941.

Pease, Donald E. "National Identities, Postmodern Artifacts, and Postnational Narratives." *National Identities and Post-Americanist Narratives*. Durham: Duke UP, 1994. 1–13.

———. "New Americanists: Revisionist Interventions into the Canon." *Revisionary Interventions into the Americanist Canon*. Durham: Duke UP, 1994. 1–37.

———. "New Perspectives on U.S. Culture and Imperialism." *Cultures of Unites States Imperialism*. Ed. Amy Kaplan and Donald E. Pease. Durham: Duke UP, 1993. 22–37.

Smith, Henry Nash. *Virgin Land: The American West as Symbol and Myth*. New York: Vintage, 1950.

Smith, Susan Harris. *American Drama: The Bastard Art*. Cambridge Studies in American Theatre and Drama 5. Cambridge: Cambridge UP, 1997.

Wallerstein, Immanuel. "The Construction of Peoplehood: Racism, Nationalism, Ethnicity." *Race, Nation, Class: Ambiguous Identities*. Ed. Etienne Balibar and Immanuel Wallerstein. 1988. London: Verso, 1991. 71–85.

J. Ellen Gainor

Introduction

In 1911, prompted in part by the tour of the Irish Players to the United States—but also crystallizing observations he had been making over time on the development of the nation's aesthetics—Theodore Roosevelt issued a call for distinctively American cultural representation. He mandated artistry no longer imitative of European models:

> The right feeling can be manifested in big things as well as in little, and it must become part of our inmost National life before we can add materially to the sum of world achievement. When that day comes, we shall understand why a huge ornate Italian villa or French château . . . is a ridiculous feature in an American landscape. . . . we shall use statues of such a typical American beast as the bison . . . to flank the approach to a building like the New York Library, instead of placing there, in the worst possible taste, a couple of lions which suggest a caricature of Trafalgar Square. (915)

Roosevelt's statements reflected the complex matrix, developing since the late nineteenth century, of America's move toward imperial expansion, on the one hand—particularly in the aftermath of the Spanish-American War—and solidified postcoloniality, with the championing of "native" over European culture, on the other.

Just five years later Randolph Bourne, one of the "young intellectuals" coming to prominence through journalism, decried the notion of America as a "melting pot," pointing instead to tensions between Anglo-Saxon influences and those of other originating cultures represented by America's more recently arrived immigrants. Bourne explains, "We shall have to give up the search for our native 'American' culture . . . there is no distinctively American culture. It is apparently our lot rather to be a federation of cultures" (91).

Roosevelt and Bourne serve, for me, as representative examples of the tension between the desire to codify American identity, largely through cultural expression, and the competing recognition that such uniformity may be neither desirable nor possible. During the period surrounding World War I—one of the key moments in United States history when national consciousness came to the fore—public statements about American identity appeared frequently in print media, expressing widely diverging perspectives on the issue. The debates were motivated by concern about the waves of immigrant arrivals as well as the strain of international conflict, both of which incorporated local as well as national fears over divided national loyalties. From any number of standpoints writers pondered what America had been, what it could become, and how to achieve these goals. American identity was increasingly a question rather than an assumption; essayists, artists, politicians, and others with opinions to voice shared freely their sense of the American national character. In this writing cultural expression began to emerge as one locus of American identity; cultural production both reflected and could shape the national ethos.

This heightened nationalist discourse actually echoed philosophies that had already been circulating in the country for almost three centuries. Countless groups and individuals in the United States since its colonial founding have looked to culture as a means to achieve hegemony, or to influence the population to embrace a given set of political, ideological, or social constructs deemed "American." That cultural expression should come to be one of the main conduits of American identity formation may seem ironic, given the Puritan tradition of distrust in many kinds of artistic representation. Still, the prevalence of artistic activity in what would become the United States from pre-Revolutionary times can be taken as evidence that America has always resisted a unitary definition; its colonists have always drawn upon a multiplicity of influences in their attempts to codify their identity. The editors of this volume note here an important issue even with the diction imbricated in this dialogue. In the present essay, as indeed in the collection as a whole, the terms "America" and "American" refer to the region and peoples of the United States of America. The authors and editors recognize that the very term "America(n)" is contested in its subsuming of geographical territory beyond the political boundaries of the United States. Our decision to employ these terms thus incorporates our understanding of the historical valence of their usage and indeed (we believe) calls that tradition into question, along with many of the other elements of what is "America" or "American."

One of our goals for this volume has been to demonstrate the role of theater in the construction of American identity. While "highbrow" critics like Bourne may posit a (perceived) weakness in the caliber of America's dramatic literature, for example, claiming it lags behind other demonstrations of American "genius" (91), other critics and practitioners have found theatrical performance to be a powerful ideological and cultural force. The power attributed to the theater may indeed be best measured by the strength of opposition to it; what Jonas Barish has called the "anti-theatrical prejudice" has thrived on these shores for over three centuries. While this bias against theater has dominated thought about its role in America, the essays in this collection suggest the impact, prevalence, and centrality of theater as an indomitable cultural force, despite moral opposition. Similarly, if the theater had no cultural resonance—if Americans did not gravitate toward performance as a central medium of self-representation—then we would not be able to trace the record of our national development as fully or from as many perspectives as we indeed can.

The authors included here demonstrate convincingly that developments in American theater over the centuries have paralleled events in American history: these contributors examine political debates brought to life, technological advancements used to enhance theatrical spectacle, social issues shared across the land in the eras before the electronic media could generate mass culture. As contributor Rosemarie K. Bank argues elsewhere, the very concept of America is a "performed trope" in the sense that our culture is always constructing and representing itself to itself as well as to others. Furthermore, we can follow the record of those key moments of national consciousness (or national crisis) through the emergence of performance forms addressing the strains on identity. Artists continue to redefine performance—to shape it to their needs—as they seek to use theatrical expression to convey their perspectives on nationalism. Finally, theater in the United States exudes an energy of oscillation; theater simultaneously reflects its concern with the broad political formations of its moment—particularly the evolving position of the United States as a world power—and the calculated construction of the country's citizenry (or inhabitants). We see, through performance, the dynamic relation between the individual and the surrounding society. The pieces in this collection demonstrate how American performance reflects the tensions in the positions exemplified by Roosevelt and Bourne; these essays particularize the shifting energies between the desires to codify American culture and identity and to create a dominant "native" culture but also to incorporate constant change.

The era of Roosevelt and Bourne is useful to us for another reason, however; the early decades of the twentieth century exemplify a historical period that scholars have explored for the rich and complex interactivity of culture and society that this collection also seeks to mine across more than two centuries. Recent scholarly works such as Adele Heller and Lois Rudnick's edited volume, *1915, The Cultural Moment,* demonstrate cogently how the arts directly responded to, and in turn had impact on, much broader political and social movements of that time. This particulate examination nevertheless mirrors the dynamic of other parallel moments in our national development. We can see through such in-depth glimpses the trajectory of our history, with connections across time as well as within a defined period. By pulling together essays that provide close readings of both moments in time and forms of cultural production, we seek to present an exploration of our nation's cultural history that is both synchronic and diachronic. While strong connections emerge between past and present, and artists clearly draw on their sense of history in their imagining of their own times, we eschew developmental paradigms for history that situate current events only by way of those that precede them.

In her essay on theater in post-Revolutionary America, Ginger Strand portrays convincingly the early, strong connections between American politics and the American stage—links evident throughout the pieces in this volume. Her analysis of the debate over theater's "ability to make or break republics" indicates the power attributed to the form in the new union and its role in the construction of American identity from the nation's inception. While the Federalists saw the hegemonic potential of theater for establishing their dominant ideology and creating a "vox populi," others saw the suppression of the theater as linked to free speech issues. Theater became a pawn within political debate and began to play out representations of political differences that have defined the country ever since. We may find it ironic that the theater itself once represented our political divisions, given the more recent turn to party conventions and related paratheatrical phenomena as the objects of performance study. Strand also throws into relief the realization that the post-Revolutionary theater initiated the culture wars still dominating our political discourse.

Rosemarie Bank shows how this idea of performing our evolving culture soon came to inform other sites such as museums. Now thought of as the repositories of high culture, hard scientific inquiry, or anthropological discovery, eighteenth- and early-nineteenth-century museums blurred the distinctions between documentation and entertainment. Through her examination of Native American Indian displays and trouping, Bank traces the evolution of museums as "archives" for cultural nationalism. She argues that "cultural performances" in this era "conserve the views of casual racism and ethnocide by normalizing them." Examined historically, such performances lay the foundations for the national and international representation of "America" and the evolving tradition of museum culture.

Kim Marra provides an interesting link to Bank's essay by showing how the actress was constructed as "savage" within the broader parameters of theater as a metaphor for the frontier. Not only does Marra posit performance as part of America's cultural landscape; she also sees gender roles (and role-playing) as integral to the metaphoric tie between the stage and the larger formations of exploration and adventure inherent in American identity in its expansionist phase. Marra introduces parallels between American industrialism and theater as big business, and points to the strong affiliations between American imperialism and its cultural representation.

Leigh Woods echoes Marra's findings on the ties between imperialism and theater in the realm of another performance venue—vaudeville—and expands upon them to demonstrate how this form refracted America's notions of nationhood during its most significant expansionist era. While recent scholarship has established the central role immigrant cultures played in the development and reception of this important popular performance medium, Woods takes a different tack here. His exploration of vaudeville looks not so much at the "politics" of the form but at the form as a political act. Examined carefully, vaudeville may, indeed, in its very structure of segmented performance, best represent the heterogeneity of the competing ideologies of the time. By importing and refiguring European stage stars, American vaudeville culturally "colonized" its former colonizers. This apparently anticolonial gesture stood cheek by jowl with images of jingoistic nationalism, internal colonization of indigenous peoples, and evolving representations of democratic pluralism in the vaudeville circuits.

A very different, but equally powerful, touring vehicle for disseminating political ideology developed with Chautauqua. Unlike vaudeville, Chautauqua attempted to homogenize American culture, to make it appear hegemonic for the masses by representing white, Christian, Anglo-Saxon figures as normative emblems of American history and society. While it achieved a goal of democratizing education and conveying some tokenist sense of ethnographic variety to communities all across the country in its display of sanitized folk culture, it also strongly controlled that representation, privileging images of the agrarian frontier at a moment when industrial expansion and a renewed emphasis on urban centers were actually beginning to control the politics and economy of the nation. Charlotte Canning vividly demonstrates the way Chautauqua began to commercialize American ideals, masking capitalist motives and ideological power behind a veneer of public service and pseudopluralism that has subsequently dominated most of our mass culture. Her essay also epitomizes the interplay between American society in its broadest sense and performance as *the* exemplar of the potential for cultural definitions of national identity. We see Chautauqua as an early example of mass culture being used to reinforce community identity but also as a force that can as strongly represent those within that community as those excluded from it.

American performance, in this key period of the late nineteenth through early twentieth centuries, is clearly marked by its concern with representations of the Other, a trope shared by "high" culture as well as popular theatrical expressions. David Krasner's essay on W. E. B. Du Bois's pageant *The Star of Ethiopia* resonates with many of the other pieces in this collection in its concern with this issue: here the construction of the African American as Other within American culture. Krasner clearly details how strongly Du Bois believed in the educative potential of theater to convey moral values to a community; furthermore, he shows how Du Bois used performance for revisionist purposes, to resist racially prejudicial ideologies coming to prominence in America. Yet Krasner also raises important questions about the power of cultural representation in our society. If we see all theater as community theater—in the sense that it is always created by and for some community, whether defined in terms of race, class, region, or religion—then we must also begin to ask how and if theater can transcend any given community. Even though Du Bois envisioned his pageant for black and white audiences, in the hope of educating both about the construction of racial identity in America, he had no control over who would actually see his work or who would benefit from its lessons. Furthermore, in his emphasis on a folk theater, Du Bois presciently pointed toward questions of high culture versus mass culture that were beginning to dominate considerations of the role of theater within America: who is the theater for? what kind of theater belongs with which segments of our society? how do we think about the different types of performance within our overall construction of American culture?

This belief in the communitarian force of theater, as Ann Larabee argues, also lay behind the work of the settlement houses, whose proponents espoused a "utopian vision of a civic America, unified in pluralism, run by benevolent institutions, and driven by public spirit rather than crass commercialism." By focusing on the complex and contradictory agendas surrounding immigrant culture in these institutions, Larabee turns our attention to a performance venue underrepresented in theater scholarship, especially given recent attention to multicultural concerns. She shows how these groups worked to achieve a leveling and a universalizing of difference within the immigrant communities by means of theatrical representations of the melting-pot ideology; this leveling in turn served the movement for a homogenization of American culture. The indoctrination of immigrant communities through settlement house activities emerges as one of the more insidious uses of theatricality. Yet Larabee's essay also reveals how, by comparison, these same social-constructionist concepts lurked only a bit less blatantly in many of the forms analyzed in this volume: vaudeville, Chautauqua, pageants, the legitimate stage, and other paratheatrical activities.

Larabee reinforces, but also puts a slightly more politicized spin upon, the point Banks makes about American identity as a performed trope: "The *citizen*," Larabee writes, "is a performative identity, constructed and deployed in social institutions that only grant agency to this type of actor." The sophistication of such scholarly readings demonstrates, ironically, one significant distinction between the cultural nationalism of our past and that of our present. While the scholars in this collection deftly provide theoretical frameworks through which we may newly understand theater history, the essays concerning more recent performance explicate how artists themselves now consciously grapple with theory and praxis, "then" and "now." Contemporary artists engage directly with their sense of history: do they have a place in it, and what is that place, given current notions of identity in America? Their calculated immersion in these issues highlights how contemporary art may be in dialogue with the past at the same time that it reveals its own agendas for the present and the future.

Robert H. Vorlicky further narrows the definition of what the theater has represented as the prototypical (and ideal) American in his analysis of the historical construction of the self as a white male: "His life was to be read and to be heard as the story of America." Vorlicky also makes the strategic connection between this presentation and the emphasis on individualism within the American mythos. Yet he also points out that the essentialized construction of American identity has changed in the past twenty-five years, such that representations of other genders, races, ethnicities, and sexualities have posed a challenge to the performance of that hegemonic image. The autoperformers whose work Vorlicky documents share the goal of many contemporary artists who overtly question the use of the theater as an ideological tool for the dominant culture.

Josephine Lee also demonstrates this struggle for a place in the American national identity through her exploration of contemporary Asian American theater. According to Lee, "The new challenges of self-representation for Asian Americans and other peoples of color are compounded in this age of multicultural initiatives: one must negotiate not just the search for visibility, but the managing of such 'hyphenated' identities as they become more visible." Lee identifies the representations of gender and ethnicity as the ground of conflict within this new dramaturgy: "Cultural nationalism becomes expressed through fixed, binary racial and gender oppositions, in which 'true' Asian American identity must be preserved against assimilation or contamination." Yet Lee argues that "the impulse of Asian American cultural nationalism to restore Asian American masculinity" need not be at odds with the goals of women's empowerment if each side recognizes the impact of stereotypes on the construction of both gendered and racialized identity.

Harry Elam and Alice Rayner expand this inquiry through their investigation of Suzan-Lori Parks, who "questions the fundamental myths and meanings of 'America' in relation to African American experience." Parks's mythopoetic inquiry into American history and its foundational tropes consciously inverts the margin and the center, simultaneously turning assumptions about race, gender, and culture on their heads. Elam and Rayner reiterate one of the dominant themes of this volume by pointing out that "Parks signals that 'America' itself is a theatrical and performative entity." As we gain greater historical perspective through the examination of such recent work as Parks's, we see contemporary artists echoing, or revising, concepts presented earlier in American theater. Parks's drama, with its sense of American culture as a museum of random artifacts, calls to mind the tradition documented in Bank's essay. We can also juxtapose *The America Play* to such pieces as Du Bois's pageant, for example, to see how the theater at different moments has participated in the cultural exploration of community concerns—whether that community be defined as a segment of society or as synonymous with the nation overall. Ironically, the same questions troubling Du Bois still plague artists today who are trying to use performance as a revisionist force: how do we reach a broad audience when our work—and now, with the advent of electronic media, even our medium—is perceived as "marginal" or "alternative"?

Although these issues are far from resolved, we might actually consider that the attempt to revise what has been perceived as already at the margins of mainstream American culture—for example, the theater of ethnic minorities in the United States—is really a sign of the continuing belief in the power of theater to effect social change. Tiffany Ana López shows how Cherríe Moraga's vision of the Chicana lesbian reconstitutes Luis Valdez's construction of his Chicano community, even as Moraga simultaneously engages with the relationship between Chicano/a culture and other social forces in the United States. Significantly, Moraga does not attempt to make her theater completely accessible to mainstream America, instead creating a theater that those outside her community must work to understand. This strategic shift marks a new moment for American theater—a time when artists hope to reach audiences beyond their immediate communities but not through any compromise with the representation of that community or of their artistic vision.

The success of Tony Kushner's *Angels in America,* on Broadway and on tour around the country and abroad, will no doubt quickly become "historical" for the very fact of its uncompromised representation of those whom the dominant culture portrays as marginal challenging the very notion of margin and center. The epic sweep of the drama, combining American history, the link between nationalism and religion, the construction of American identity, and an invocation for a new nationalism in Queer Nation, swirls together many of the major ideas of performance and national culture the essays in this volume address. David Savran sees part of Kushner's mission to "queer the idea of America," to overturn homophobia and jingoism in a utopian reconstitution of our society. The fact that Kushner chose the theater as his medium, and that this choice has proven so successful, renews belief in the potential for theater to speak to audiences all across our country—to draw them together in live, shared cultural expression.

One of the remarkable developments that these most recent theatrical works demonstrate is the American theater's return to a kind of postcoloniality, not unlike that of its foundational moments. Once again, communities within this country are using the theater to resist a dominant culture, to question its hegemonic hold, and to disrupt its attempt to define and control representation. We who study and work in the theater live amid the cries of its imminent demise or its irrelevancy to our times. We continue to think otherwise.

REFERENCES

Bank, Rosemarie K. "Meditations upon Opening and Crossing Over." *Of Borders and Thresholds.* Ed. Michal Kobialka. Minneapolis: U of Minnesota P, 1999.

Bourne, Randolph S. "Trans-National America." *Atlantic Monthly* 118 (July 1916): 86–97.

Heller, Adele, and Lois Rudnick, eds. *1915, The Cultural Moment: The New Politics, the New Woman, the New Psychology, the New Art and the New Theatre in America.* New Brunswick: Rutgers UP, 1991.

Roosevelt, Theodore. "The Irish Players: Introduction." *Outlook* 16 December 1911: 915.

PART ONE. NATION THEN

Ginger Strand

The Theater and the Republic: Defining Party on Early Boston's Rival Stages

In 1792, with Boston's 1750 antitheatrical ordinance recently upheld by the Town Council, William Haliburton published *Effects of the Stage on the Manners of the People; and the Propriety of Encouraging and Establishing a Virtuous Theatre: By a Bostonian.* In the pamphlet, the author not only advocates a legalized drama but proposes a theater to house it: a fourteen-sided building holding sixty-two hundred spectators, capped by a grand dome, surrounded with a piazza, and accessed by a lamp-lit, garden-lined coach road. All this grandeur, however, was not meant by Haliburton for the theater alone:

> Full half the building being reserved for the theatre . . . The first floor on one side, will accommodate the whole legislative assembly, in separate chambers, (with convenient offices and committee rooms adjoining,) where they may deliberate free from the noise of carriages, &c. (Qtd. in Clapp, *Record* 16)

Although he guesses that "some will object," putting plays and politicians under the same roof made perfect sense to Haliburton. The theater was a place designed to "suppress vice, and advance virtue": a perfect home for government. Not surprisingly, Haliburton's ideas did not take hold among Boston stockholders, who in the following year began work on the more modest Federal Street Theater (sometimes called Boston Theatre), but the fantasy theater outlined in *Effects of the Stage* was in many ways representative of ideals that drove Boston's—and the nation's—post-Revolutionary legalization of drama. The stage, proponents argued, did not erode republican virtue. Rather, it provided a paradigm for the good republic. Theater and politics, as Haliburton declares, were alike enough that they could share the same space.

The idealistic view of theater was relatively new. The pre-Revolutionary colonies were nearly uniform in their hostility to drama—in 1752, only Virginia and Maryland had not passed laws proscribing the presentation of plays (Wilson 13).[1] During the Revolution, the performance of plays was proscribed in most places by local law as well as generally by the Continental Congress. The ban was political: in addition to traditional moralism and the mistrust of anything British or "monarchist," antitheatrical legislation invoked a long tradition of thought that implicated theater in the downfall of republics. By "anesthetizing" the citizenry, the view went, theater prevented the active participation that was the mainstay of the republic.[2] As one representative put it in the Pennsylvania General Assembly's debate on the topic:

> The human mind can never be forcibly turned to several objects at the same time—if we suffer amusements to possess it here, it will be rendered indifferent as to the great object of our liberties. (*Pennsylvania Evening Herald*)

Debates over repealing the antitheatrical laws in the late 1780s thus focused on theater's assumed ability to make or break republics: supporters of the stage had to reenvision the drama as politically beneficial, rather than injurious. A well-regulated theater, proponents insisted, would expose vice, promote virtue, and instruct political citizens in their public role.

Yet what exactly was that role? In the 1780s, as increasing doubt about the factional public's ability to produce a unified voice led to the writing of the constitution, Federalists continued to employ the figure of theater to signify republican values.[3] For them, theater figured as a political formation central to their ideology: the creation of consensus out of America's multiple voices. Federalists made pro-theater arguments that reflected their political agenda. Theatrical representations, like political representatives, must select and refine utterances, harmonizing the fractured voices of the people into a unified vox populi.

In most major American cities, however, the arguments that prevailed in the fight to legalize the stage were not those of the Federalists. Instead, the language of civil liberty was invoked: government did not have the power to proscribe an amusement that had never been proven harmful. In Boston, the *Columbian Centinel* summed up the town meeting debate over theatricals:

> The morality, immorality; beneficial and pernicious effects of Theatrical Exhibitions—were largely discanted upon. In addition to which, it

was argued in behalf of the object of the petition, that the law in question was an infringement on one of the natural and unalienable rights of the citizen. This right was said to be, *That of promoting our own happiness, in any way not infringing on the happiness of another, or injuring the community.*

This approach neatly shifted the focus from the rights of the actors to the rights of the audience. It also partook of the very same libertarian, populist rhetoric employed by the incipient Republican opposition to the Federalists, often called Jacobins after their French counterparts.[4] Civil libertarianism paved the way for the reopening of the theaters, but it also heralded a new era of political partisanship that would influence the life of the stage as well as the republic.

Massachusetts repealed its antitheatrical laws in 1793. Despite the partisan cooperation that led to its legalization, the management of the Boston Theatre quickly became associated with the Federalist political persuasion. Manager Charles Stuart Powell was let go after two seasons and became the force behind the opening of Boston's second theater, the Haymarket, on 26 December 1796. Powell, as Clapp explains, "availed himself of the strong political antagonism which prevailed between the Federalists and so-called Jacobins to induce the latter to believe that the old theater was managed with a view of promoting political animosities" ("Drama" 363). Despite Justin Winsor's suggestion that Powell was simply rabble-rousing, the former manager was correct: the Federal Street Theater was Federalist, and the new Haymarket was even more decidedly Republican. The introduction of a theatrical opposition in Boston was not only concurrent with the formation of an American political opposition in the late 1780s and early 1790s, but the increasing partisanship of American politics was acted out nightly on Boston's competing stages.

The history of this competition demonstrates not only the political use of the theater itself, but also the mobilization of the theater metaphor in the creation of new political formations. Federalists were accused by the opposition of being closet monarchists and aristocrats. Republicans were depicted by their detractors as "mechanics"—craftsmen—bent on mobocracy. The factions differed over how large a role the "common man" should play in the actual workings of government. While Republicans advocated radical republicanism, the Federalists held to the cautiously selective representative democracy described in the *Federalist Papers*.

As two opposing concepts of the people's role in government took shape, two theaters fought a battle for the audience of Boston, much of which focused on the role the audience would play in the institution of theater. In architecture, management, choice of plays, and house rules, the two theaters represented two competing ideas about the "sovereignty" of the audience.[5] As party lines solidified, the new nation's struggle over the public's role in government was acted out as a struggle about the audience's role in the theater. Eventually, a wary compromise was reached, and the theaters divided up the year between them, but not before the stage had been implicitly acknowledged as a site for political self-assertion and display.

Boston's first legitimate playhouse, the Federal Street Theater, opened on 3 February 1794, with Henry Brooke's *Gustavus Vasa* and John O'Keeffe's *Modern Antiques* on the bill. Even before the plays began, however, the theater communicated its Federalist political leanings to the audience. The playhouse, designed by Charles Bulfinch, was divided into the traditional pit, gallery, and boxes. As Marvin Carlson has argued, "audience spaces have almost always reflected with great accuracy the class preoccupations of their society" (Carlson 135). The provision of separate boxes for aristocratic audiences is said to have become a standard theatrical feature in the late seventeenth century, following Benedetto Ferrari's 1637 design for the Teatro San Cassiano in Venice. As Carlson points out, the longevity of this architectural feature "was clearly due not to its usefulness for viewing the spectacle, for which such boxes are generally unsatisfactory, but for its importance in clarifying the social semiotics of the auditorium" (142). By the Georgian era in England, it was traditional not only to utilize separate seating and entrances in theaters—pit audiences often entered and exited through narrow subterranean passageways providing slow egress in the case of fire—but to highlight the implied social distinctions through the interior design. Southern notes that in most Georgian theaters, "the decoration of the house proper rises from the level of the stage where the lower boxes spring. Below that level is another world with which the design of the auditorium is quite unrelated" (30).

Theaters in early America do not seem to have diverged much from these traditions. In the burst of theater building that followed legalization, in fact, social distinctions seem to have been emphasized, as though to reassure upper-class audiences about the propriety of attending. Like the 1792 theater in Charleston, the Federal Street Theater emphasized implied social distinctions in the organization of traffic to and from the playhouse: a covered arcade for coaches on Federal Street supplied entrance to the boxes through a large lobby; the pit and gallery each had separate entrances without lobbies (Clapp, *Record* 19; McNamara 124).

Arrangements for the entire theater were designed to suggest that the audience in attendance would be genteel. Stockholders, Clapp assures readers, included "the most respectable citizens," and they retained control over all affairs of the theater, including repertory (*Record* 19). According to the agreement between C. S. Powell and the trustees dated 7 January 1794, they also enlisted the services of John Steel Tyler (brother to Royall Tyler) as master of ceremonies to ensure orderliness in the coach traffic and seating arrangements as well as "generally to arrange the whole etiquette of the auditory and to prevent or suppress all kind of disorder and indecorum" (qtd. in Alden 19). Robert Treat Paine's prologue for opening night, which stockholders had judged the best in a contest, assured the audience that the theater's offerings would be equally decorous:

> But, not to scenes of pravity confined,
> Here polish'd life an ample field shall find;
> Reflected here, its fair perspective view,
> The stage, the Camera—the landscape, you.
>
> (159)

The most obvious possible threat to this decorum was an unruly audience—a phenomenon not without political overtones. Clapp notes that the orchestra in the Federal Street Theater was allowed to take requests, a practice that led to members of opposing political parties in the audience attempting to drown out one another's airs. The habit had led to a riot in Philadelphia when the orchestra refused to play a request; with the master of ceremonies keeping close watch, no such disturbance resulted in Boston (Clapp, *Record* 22–23).

In addition to being kept under surveillance, the Federal Street audience was shaped in quite tangible ways: in its third season, beginning in November 1795 with John Steel Tyler replacing Charles Stuart Powell as manager, the Federal Street Theater raised its prices—for the "lower classes" of theatergoers. Boxes remained one dollar, but tickets for the pit were raised from three shillings ninepence to three quarters of a dollar, and the gallery price was doubled, from a quarter to a half-dollar. A prologue written for the opening of the new season and printed in the *Federal Orrery* declares the theater's political neutrality:

> Let Feds and Antis to our temples come,
> And all unite firm *Federalists in fun;*
> Let austere politics one hour flee,
> And join in free *Democracy of glee!*

Apparently, few were convinced. After his dismissal, Powell was able to take advantage of popular belief in the anti-Jacobin sentiments of the Federal Street Theater's shareholders and quickly began to enlist subscribers for a new theater. From its very inception, the Haymarket was designed as a more radically democratic institution. On its list of shareholders were many local mechanics, including three housewrights and a glazier who very likely took shares in payment for labor in the theater's construction (Stoddard 63). According to drawings and accounts, the design of the Haymarket, while still divided into pit, gallery, and boxes, did not maintain the dramatically separate entrances of the Federal Street Theater, and there were two galleries rather than one, allowing for more low-priced seating. In general the Haymarket was much more capacious than the Federal Street Theater, holding approximately 2,000 spectators, in comparison with the older playhouse's capacity of 1060 (Stoddard 65; Alden 12). Designed without the elegant architecture of its rival, the Haymarket was, as Brooks McNamara states, "obviously built to accommodate a large number of spectators and all other considerations seem to have been somewhat incidental." Interestingly, writing in 1969, McNamara reproduces all of the eighteenth-century sentiments about the Haymarket; pointing out its lack of "architectural sophistication" and the fact that its name reflected its location adjacent to an actual haymarket, he speculates that, although there are no reproductions of the interior, probably "it possessed an auditorium of no great taste or style" (128).

Powell's statement of purpose, printed in local newspapers, focused on the Haymarket's intended inclusiveness:

> The following arrangements shall be made for the ease, convenience, and general satisfaction of our Fellow Citizens.—The Pit shall be spacious, though to be able to admit them at 3s.—The Galleries on the same extensive plan.—The First Gallery, 2s3; where our citizens may go with their wives, or into the Pit, as in Europe.—The Upper Gallery 1s6.—These prices never to be altered; with an Annual Benefit for poor Widows and Orphans. (*Massachusetts Mercury,* 19 April 1796)

Public response to Powell's proposals was colored by political and economic loyalties. The Republican *Boston Gazette* printed letters from self-designated "common people" hailing the new theater. One letter writer, calling himself "a Tradesman of Boston," gives typical reasons for approving:

> I am highly pleased with the prospect of having a new Theatre established upon a cheap and liberal plan, that we Tradesmen can go with

our families and partake of a rational and pleasing amusement for a little money, and not be hunched by *one,* and the *nose* of *another* Aristocrat turned up at us, because we are Tradesmen. The present Theatre is an *imposition* on the Town—it is only a "School of Scandal" and *Aristocracy,* and of late the Slip Galleries are no better than BROTHELS—I conceive sir, that a Theatre may be conducted on a very different plan from the present one.

Federalists, on the other hand, treated the idea with scorn. An unsigned note in the *Massachusetts Mercury* sarcastically predicted that

"the *Liberty Theatre,*" which it is anticipated will rise by that name, under the auspices of the *Sons of Freedom,* it is presumed to pronounce, will be attended with many accommodating circumstances which have been wanting in *Boston:* In the first place, having two Galleries will give this advantage, that many respectable Citizens' wives will have an opportunity of going to the Theatre at a very inconsiderable expense and without being obliged to suffer the inconvenience . . . to dress for Boxes. The two Shilling Galleries in *London Theatres,* are generally frequented by the most opulent Citizens and their wives when they choose to go in dishabille. (15 April 1796)

Even before it was built, Powell's Haymarket Theatre was invested with an antiaristocratic aura, which drew both praise and scorn.

The Haymarket opened on 26 December 1796 with Mrs. Cowley's *Belle's Strategem.* The repertory included less Shakespeare but more pantomime and ballet than that of the Federal Street Theater, taking advantage of a French ballet troupe Powell had engaged. Some of the other plays produced by Powell were seen as straightforward bids to please Republican stockholders: Burk's *Bunker-Hill* and William Hill Brown's *West Point Preserved* (now lost) are most commonly mentioned in this respect. Other aspects of production at the Haymarket ensured the companies' appeal for a broader, less Anglophilic audience: in addition to seating more people, the size of the playhouse, with its extra level of galleries, provided ample fly space for "drops," so that spectacular scenery became one of the theater's main draws.

The capacity for spectacle was utilized by the play that became by far the biggest theatrical success at the Haymarket: John Daly Burk's patriotic *Bunker-Hill; or The Death of General Warren,* which played nine times in a season when only three other plays ran four times, and the vast majority were performed only once or twice. *Bunker-Hill* is a sprawling nationalistic spectacle, and central to its attraction for audiences were the elaborately produced battle scenes. Like the Federal Street Theater's opener, *Gustavus Vasa,* Burk's play tells the story of a hero called to lead his fellow citizens into combat against tyranny—a plot that played well in the young nation. But the two plays could not be more different, contrasting not only in style but also in their vastly different textual constructions of heroism. The audience-play relationships constructed by the two theaters were reflected in the citizen-leader relationships demonstrated by the two texts. *Gustavus Vasa* upheld the Federalists' political ideals; *Bunker-Hill* opposed that ideal with a radical Republican polemic.

Henry Brooke's *Gustavus Vasa* was an English Opposition drama, written in 1739 and promptly refused a license by the Lord Chamberlain's office under Walpole. Its historical subject—the liberation of Sweden from the Danish tyrant Christiern—has been read by critics (and clearly by the Lord Chamberlain) as straightforward political allegory,[6] but the general anti-tyranny message translated easily to the United States. Furthermore, the performance of a play well-known to have been censored in Britain was an act in itself, meant to signify the civil liberty enjoyed by American citizens after an era of English repression. The play is a model for the overthrow of tyranny, and as such it presents a specific political vision that accorded well with the Federalist position.

The action of *Gustavus Vasa* is nominally based on historical fact—Vasa's liberation of Sweden—but centers on two fabricated events added to the account. The first is Vasa's self-imposed exile as a laborer in the mines of Dalecarlia, a region in northern Sweden, and his subsequent revelation of his identity to the peasants he leads into battle. The second is Christiern's attempt to obtain Vasa's submission by holding his mother and sister hostage, resulting in Vasa's anguished decision to stand by as they are executed. Both situations serve to construct Vasa as exactly the sort of natural political leader central to Federalist political ideals.

The Federalist vision of the republic depended upon the virtue of the representative, as well as more practical measures, to purge public life of the dangers of individual interest.[7] Political representatives, as Madison optimistically predicted in *The Federalist* 10, would inevitably be men of "enlightened views and virtuous sentiments" who would rise to the top of public life (Rossiter 83–84).[8] Gustavus Vasa, in Brooke's play, is presented as exactly such a person. As the play opens, Anderson and Arnoldus—chief lord and ranking priest of Dalecarlia, respectively—are discussing the "stranger" who has appeared among the peasant miners. Despite the lowly condition in which Vasa toils, Arnoldus has no trouble recognizing his "wond'rous greatness" (5):

> Draw but the veil of his apparent wretchedness,
> And you shall find his form is but assum'd
> To hoard some wond'rous treasure, lodg'd within.
>
> (3)

Vasa's attempt to blend in with the peasant miners fails: "in servile weeds / But yet of mein majestic," he cannot help but betray his own nobility, even as he succeeds in hiding his actual identity (5).

Revelations of Vasa's distinctive leadership qualities structure the rest of the play. In his absence the Dalecarlians have no chance of escaping tyranny: "Never can I dare to rest a hope / On any arm but his," Anderson declares. Vasa's presence, however, will rekindle the "latent sparks / of slumbering virtue" in the Swedes, who, through "base fear, the laziness of lust, gross appetites" have allowed themselves to be oppressed (5, 11, 8). Vasa's repression of his own "gross appetites" demonstrates his complete freedom from the seduction of personal interests—a trait that would have been of particular value to the Federalists. The climactic scenes of the play are devoted to illustrating this aspect of the hero's virtue. Christiern tries to trick Vasa's friend Arvida into assassinating Vasa by declaring that Vasa had agreed to surrender if he could marry Christiern's daughter Christina. Arvida, in love with Christina himself, is shocked at the idea of Vasa "planning private scenes of happiness" (22). He becomes distraught enough to attempt to assassinate Vasa but cannot carry it out when he is faced with Vasa's implacable faith in his friend.

When at the end of the play Vasa also admits to being in love with Christina, he must renounce his own emotions and desires. His final speech declares him to be the perfect representative:

> —O I will
> Of private passions all my soul divest,
> And take my dearer country to my breast.
> To public good transfer each fond desire,
> And clasp my Sweden with a lover's fire.
>
> (62)

The ultimate test of Vasa's ability to elevate his country's good over his own, however, comes in the scene when Christiern tries to ransom Augusta and

Gustava, Vasa's mother and sister, in exchange for Vasa's submission. As Gustava clings to her brother and Augusta urges Vasa not to give in, Vasa nearly loses his resolution. When he quickly collects his senses, however— "So—we will to battle"—the onlookers express their amazement at his superhuman fortitude. "On thee we gaze," Anderson states, "As one unknown till this important hour; / Pre-eminent of men!" (51) In the course of the play, the fatherless Vasa sacrifices mother, sister, and lover. Stripped of any personal claims that could direct his interests away from his country— indeed, as the sister's name suggests, stripped of the personal side of himself—he becomes the perfect political leader.

The Boston published edition of Brooke's play announced itself as having "alterations and amendments as performed at the New Theatre in Boston." The changes made to Brooke's 1739 London edition were largely the deletion of profanity. References to "fiends," the spoiling of virgins, and a scene in which Christina contemplates the corpses of Augusta and Gustava were also deleted for Boston's more squeamish audiences. Most interesting, however, is the fact that, while the Dalecarlian "extras" are retained, most— but not all—lines assigned to individual Dalecarlians were cut. The most significant cut occurs in the final scene. In the English edition, Vasa's final speech is prefaced by the cries of his onstage audience. Sivard, the Dalecarlian captain, speaks first:

> *Sivard:* Oh General!
> *1st Dalecarlian:* King!
> *2nd Dalecarlian:* Brother!
> *3rd Dalecarlian:* Father!
> *All:* Friend!

It is only in the context of these lines that the opening of Vasa's final speech makes perfect sense:

> Come, come, my brothers all! Yes I will strive
> To be the sum of ev'ry title to ye;
> And you shall be my sire, my friend reviv'd,
> My sister, mother, all that's kind and dear;
> For so Gustavus holds ye.
>
> (62)

Although some Federalists did argue for the institution of hereditary offices and titles, most American audiences of 1794 would not want to label the perfect political leader a "king." The fact that these lines lay behind the ones actually spoken suggests that monarchism lurked behind Federalist notions of representation and government—a suggestion that many, by 1796, were beginning to think was true. In a letter to Philip Mazzei on 24 April 1796, Jefferson wrote that in the place of "that noble love of liberty, and republican government which carried us triumphantly thro' the war, an Anglican monarchical, and aristocratical party has sprung up" (Ford 8:238).

As an antidote to what many saw as Federalism's "aristocratic" leanings, John Daly Burk's *Bunker-Hill, or The Death of General Warren* premiered on 17 February 1797, during the opening season of the Haymarket Theatre. While the subject was on one level simply patriotic, its partisan politics were obvious. Following on the heels of the national debate over the Jay Treaty, which Republicans saw as an undeserved insult to France in its concessions to Britain, *Bunker-Hill* declared its party loyalties in its vilification of Britain and its covert compliments to France. The 1793 execution of Louis XVI, ambivalently supported by Republicans, could not have been far from the audience's mind upon hearing General Warren speculate that after America's example, "Revolutions '*will be so in use*,' / That kings, when they behold the morning break, / Will bless their stars for living one day more" (Moody 76).

Not only were party loyalties being shaped along pro-English or pro-French lines,[9] but the idea of a return to values represented by the American Revolution was itself a Republican motif. Philip Freneau, in the rabidly Republican *National Gazette,* published in 1793 a list of his own definitions for terms "commonly misunderstood," including "*Antifederalist:* a republican of seventeen hundred and seventy six" (Marsh 297). Burk's play was not unusual in presenting Jacobin ideas in the guise of Revolutionary patriotism. But it was singled out for censure. The new manager of the Federal Street Theater, John Williamson, wrote an angry letter to John Hodgkinson, manager of the Old American Company in New York. "You wish to be informed," Williamson began, "how we go on." His view of the situation was not bright:

> *We* have the opinion hollow as to the merits of the company, and the patronage of the "*better sort*." But the rage for *novelty* in Boston, and the prevailing Jacobin spirit in the lower ranks, are our strongest opponents. Two theatres cannot be supported. . . . They [the Haymarket company] have brought out a new piece, called *Bunker's Hill* [*sic*], a tragedy, the most execrable of the Grub Street kind—but from its locality in title, the burning of Charlestown and *peppering* the *British*

(which are superadded to the tragedy in pantomime), to the utter disgrace of Boston theatricals, has brought them *full houses.* (Qtd. in Dunlap 312–13)

Williamson's assessment of the play's dependence on spectacle is accurate, but *Bunker-Hill's* appeal to the "prevailing Jacobin spirit in the lower ranks" resided not only in its "peppering" of the British, but in its specifically Antifederalist construction of the tension between national loyalty and personal interest. *Bunker-Hill,* like *Gustavus Vasa,* pays tribute to the selfless patriotism of a national hero: General Warren, like Vasa, makes the decision to sacrifice personal happiness for the good of his country. But his reasons are very different from Vasa's, and as a hero he cuts a figure quite different from that of Brooke's Gustavus.

Burk begins by giving his working-class audience characters with whom they can identify: Warren's story is interspersed with a romantic love plot. The subplot concerns a British soldier, Abercrombie, who has fallen in love with an American farmer's daughter named Elvira after rescuing her from rape at the hands of his comrades. While he has serious doubts about the moral rightness of Britain's cause, Abercrombie is unable to resign his commission, as Elvira wants him to do, and retire to a quiet pastoral life in the United States. The reason he gives is his concern for his honor: "How would my friends in England feel to hear," he asks, "That in the teeth of danger I resign'd, / And on the eve of battle left the camp?" (74) Throughout the play, Elvira urges Abercrombie to leave the British army, but he refuses, even while he is critical of the values that prevent him from doing so. "Was I sure my conduct would be judg'd," he tells Elvira,

> By such as thee, so prudent and so pure,
> Long since decision would have crown'd thy wish;
> But as it is, when flimsy fashion rules,
> And guides the helm where honor should preside,
> 'Twere madness to so risk my reputation.

(74)

In choosing honor over personal happiness, Abercrombie is shown to be making the wrong choice. Honor itself becomes a function of "flimsy fashion," calling into question the value of public displays and thus of civic virtue itself. National loyalty, Burk suggests, is not an end in itself but must be qualified by a reasoned faith in the nation's moral accountability.

In contrast to Abercrombie, General Warren is held up as an example of appropriate civic virtue. When Warren first appears onstage, he is at home, responding to the news of the British defeat at Lexington. In a long soliloquy, he ponders whether he should volunteer his services in the war. His first thought is of the personal gain in doing so:

> And shall I then, inglorious, stay behind,
> While my brave countrymen are braving death
> To purchase glory; I too am fond of glory,
> And such a cause will make ambition, virtue.

He wonders whether military service is the only way to help his country, speculating that "by writing, I can help the public cause," but he immediately turns against this idea. In the following lines of the speech, he wavers between a sense of duty to country and the lure of family ties:

> No—Liberty will ne'er be woo'd by halves,
> But like the jealous female, must have all
> The lover's heart or none: but then again—
> I am not young, and feel beside, the ties
> Of family endearments; what of that?

Like Gustavus Vasa, Warren is tempted by his emotional attachments, and, just as Vasa does, he will reject the temptation. His decision to do so, however, brings to the foreground issues that had little effect on Vasa:

> The patriot should o'erleap all obstacles
> Which stand between him and his darling country;
> Not age, not sex, nor scarcely pain itself,
> Should be exempt from this important duty,
> But ALL before the sacred voice of country,
> When to her children she doth cry for succor,
> Should fly to her relief.

(75)

Warren, like Vasa, determines that the "darling country" must come before personal considerations. But it is not a personal call to arms that fires his patriotism; he is not, as is Vasa, his country's last, best hope. Rather, he is convinced that "ALL" should serve—in its egalitarian reasoning, Warren's pronouncement even suggests that "not age, not sex" exempts one from the nation's service. Gustavus Vasa is called to lead, Joseph Warren to serve; only later does a messenger arrive offering him a commission as an officer.

Even as he takes the leadership role of general, Burk's Warren affirms egalitarian values. As he joins Generals Putnam and Prescott in a review of the American troops, he steadfastly resists their attempts to label him preeminent, deflecting their compliments with a statement of equality:

> all our stations
> Are undetermin'd yet; this war will fix them,
> And candid history fearless will decide,
> Who best has serv'd his country; then my friends
> Let all of us so act that 'twill perplex
> Posterity to name the worthiest man.
>
> (77)

Even as he dies in battle, Warren refuses special treatment: in his dying speech he orders the grenadier who is carrying him off the field to flee the scene and save his own life.

Warren's high point as mouthpiece for the Republicans, however, is earlier, when he discourses with a British messenger from General Gage, who offers him clemency in return for deserting the American cause. Warren's answer is vituperative, demanding—"How comes he by the right to pardon me?"—and delivers a scathing condemnation of Gage's actions. The messenger, Harman, claims he cannot possibly return such an answer, since "at least his goodness calls for better language." The two then argue about the term "rebellion," by which the British refer to the war. Harman holds that English laws are so just and mild, " 'tis therefore rank rebellion, to resist them." Warren's reply surpasses the predictable tirade against monarchy by criticizing Parliament's control of the laws:

> know you not, good sir,
> All laws and usages are made to bend
> Before the *magic* influence of an act,
> And ordinance of your parliament.
>
> (80–81)

When Harman suggests that Warren's complaint must then be that Parliament infringes upon the king's prerogative, Warren dismisses Parliament as well:

Your parliament is not ours, nor shall be ours,
Why then presume to legislate for us?

Warren's subsequent ranting refers to kings as "the Manichean demons,
who undo / The good which heaven has done." When Harman makes one
final attempt to offer Warren "royal favor," the American general makes his
closing statement:

The man you speak to, holds himself as good,
Of as much value as the *man you serve,*
Ay: and of more, while he defends his country,
Than any *pamper'd monarch* on the globe:
All riches and rewards my soul detests,
Which are not earn'd by virtue: I prefer
One hour of life, spent in my country's services,
To ages wasted midst a servile herd
Of *lazy, abject, fawning, cringing* courtiers.
All future business 'twixt your lord and me,
Must be determined in the field.

(81)

Given the intense posturing of the scene, and the boastful threat of
the last lines, it is understandable why President John Adams, having been
invited to see *Bunker-Hill* in New York, is said to have told the actor
playing Warren, "Sir, my friend, General Warren, was a scholar and a
gentleman, but your author has made him a bully and a blackguard"
(Clapp, *Record* 55). Burk subsequently changed his mind about dedicating
his play to Adams and inscribed the printed text to the Republican Aaron
Burr instead (Seilhamer 363).

Burk's Warren is indeed something of a bully, a common man who
needs to argue politics with messengers and assert his equality with British
officers. But what would have angered the new Federalist president at least
as much is the implication that Warren's—and the Revolution's—rejection
of the British king was tantamount to a rejection not only of monarchy, but
of the English government's balance of power between the one, the few,
and the many—a political system that Adams was known to respect.[10]

In performing *Bunker-Hill,* the company at the Haymarket was offering
the public an American play, in contrast with the British opposition plays—
Gustavus Vasa, Cato, Venice Preserved—that made up so much of the early
American repertory. *Bunker-Hill'*s claims to Americanness lay not so much

in its nominally American authorship (Burk is said to have written it during his sea passage from Ireland), but rather in its specifically American setting, characters, and values. As such, it went some way toward answering the call that many—especially those of the opposition—were making for an American drama. Philip Freneau had complained in the *National Gazette* that theaters had for too long been the tools of monarchs and tyrants who wanted to prevent the people from thinking for themselves: "Regal conquests, and the struggles of regal ambition, the base plots of aristocracy, and the splendid feats of military butchers, are by no means proper subjects for an American stage, except only when held up as objects of public abhorrence and detestation" (6 March 1793, in Marsh 295). With its egalitarian political sentiments and reevaluation of American heroism, Burk's play can be seen as a step in this direction. The blow it struck, however, was not patriotic but partisan.

As the Haymarket Theatre gained success, the stockholders of the Federal Street Theater tried new means to fill their own house. On benefit nights, every possible ticket would be sold, and those remaining would be given away to anyone who would pledge never to enter the Haymarket (Clapp, *Record* 50–51). Those pledging loyalty were expected to stand by their promise. The ticket distribution literalized what was happening figuratively: American audiences attending plays at one theater or the other were themselves performing a manifestation of their particular political loyalties. They were using artistic preferences to mark themselves ideologically—a process that continues today, as Congress fights skirmishes over federal arts funding that is so small a percentage of the budget it would be insignificant, were it not a vital political display.

NOTES

1. See also Barish 8off.; and Richards 61ff.

2. I am indebted here to Silverman's overview of the postrevolutionary debate about theater and the republic (549ff.).

3. For a reading of the figure of theater in *The Federalist,* see Saks.

4. I shall use "Republican," with a capital "R," to refer to the incipient political party and signal the distinction from the broader term "republican," which refers to the tradition of political thought concerning republics. In their very early stages American political parties were neither overtly acknowledged nor clearly delineated. Writing to his friend John Wise, Thomas Jefferson explained that "both parties claim to be federalists and republicans" but that those of the government's party were usually described as "federalists, sometimes aristocrats or monocrats, and sometimes tories," while those of the opposition were termed "republicans, whigs, jacobins, disorganizers" (12 February

1798; qtd. in Sharp 174). It should be obvious that the Republicans of 1792 were very different from those of the late 1990s.

5. Audience "sovereignty" was in general much greater in the eighteenth- and early-nineteenth-century theater than in subsequent periods. Audiences reserved the right not only to talk among themselves and to performers but also to interrupt performances at will. The Federal Street Theater attempted a sort of control that would become more common later on, when, as Richard Butsch argues, "suppression of disturbance in (and out of) the theater by mid-century represented a rejection of the authority of the audience, an early stage in the depoliticization of the public sphere" (395).

6. For instance, see Loftis 150ff. Walsh argues for a less straightforward reading of the play's Opposition politics.

7. My understanding of the Federalist period has been shaped largely by Wood as well as Elkins and McKitrick.

8. While Madison's work in *The Federalist* contributed to the theory of Federalism, he himself became a Republican later in life, as Jefferson assumed leadership of that party.

9. Elkins and McKitrick explain that the French Revolution was, all along, "a major point of reference for domestic political partisanship, just as such partisanship was first publicly emerging" (309). According to Sharp, Republicans saw the Jay Treaty "as part of a sinister design to use British institutions and practices to subvert the republic" (114).

10. See Sharp 150–59.

REFERENCES

Alden, John. "A Season in Federal Street: J. B. Williamson and the Boston Theatre, 1796–1797." *Proceedings of the American Antiquarian Society* 65 (1955): 9–31.

Barish, Jonas. *The Anti-Theatrical Prejudice.* Berkeley: U of California P, 1981.

Boston Gazette 9 May 1796.

Brooke, Henry. *Gustavus Vasa: A Tragedy in Five Acts, Written by Henry Brooke, with Alterations and Amendments as Performed at the New Theatre in Boston.* Boston: n.p., 1792.

———. *Gustavus Vasa, The Deliverer of His Country, a Tragedy, as it was to have been Acted at the Theatre-Royal in Drury Lane.* London: R. Dodsley, 1739.

Butsch, Richard. "Bowery B'hoys and Matinee Ladies: The Re-Gendering of Nineteenth-Century American Theater Audiences." *American Quarterly* 46.3 (September 1994): 374–405.

Burk, John Daly. *Bunker-Hill; or, The Death of General Warren.* Moody 61–86.

Carlson, Marvin. *Places of Performance: The Semiotics of Theatre Architecture.* Ithaca: Cornell UP, 1989.

Clapp, William. *Record of the Boston Stage.* Boston: James Munroe, 1856.

———. "The Drama in Boston." Winsor 357–82.

Columbian Centinel 29 October 1791: 55.

Dunlap, William. *History of the American Theatre.* 2 vols. 1832. New York: Burt Franklin, 1963.

Elkins, Stanley, and Eric McKitrick. *The Age of Federalism.* New York and Oxford: Oxford UP, 1993.

Ford, Paul Leicester, ed. *The Writings of Thomas Jefferson.* Federal edition. 12 vols. New York and London: G. P. Putnam's Son, 1904.

Loftis, John. *The Politics of Drama in Augustan England.* Oxford: Clarendon, 1963.

Marsh, Philip M. *The Prose of Philip Freneau.* New Brunswick: Scarecrow, 1955.

Massachusetts Mercury 15 and 19 April 1796.

McNamara, Brooks. *The American Playhouse in the Eighteenth Century.* Cambridge: Harvard UP, 1969.

Moody, Richard. *Dramas from the American Theatre, 1762–1909.* Boston: Houghton Mifflin, 1969.

Paine, Robert Treat. *The Works in Verse and Prose of the Late Robert Treat Paine, Jun. Esq.* Boston: J. Belcher, 1812.

Pennsylvania Evening Herald 19 November 1785: 136.

Richards, Jeffrey. *Theater Enough: American Culture and the Metaphor of the World Stage.* Durham and London: Duke UP, 1991.

Rossiter, Clinton, ed. *The Federalist Papers.* New York: New American Library, 1961.

Saks, Eva. "The Staging of the Constitution, or, The Republican Masque of *The Federalist Papers.*" *Theatre Journal* 41.3 (October 1989): 360–80.

Seilhamer, George O. *History of the American Theatre during the Revolution and After.* New York and London: Benjamin Blom, 1968.

Sharp, James Roger. *American Politics in the Early Republic.* New Haven: Yale UP, 1993.

Silverman, Kenneth. *A Cultural History of the American Revolution.* New York: Columbia UP, 1976.

Southern, Richard. *The Georgian Playhouse.* London: Pleides, 1948.

Stoddard, Richard. "The Haymarket Theatre, Boston." *Educational Theatre Journal* 27 (March 1975): 63–69.

Walsh, Paul. "Henry Brooke's *Gustavus Vasa:* The Ancient Constitution and the Example of Sweden." *Studia Neophilologica* 64 (1992): 67–79.

Wilson, Garff. *Three Hundred Years of American Drama and Theatre.* Englewood Cliffs, NJ: Prentice-Hall, 1973.

Winsor, Justin. *The Memorial History of Boston, 1630–1880.* 4 vols. Boston: James R. Osgood, 1883.

Wood, Gordon. *The Creation of the American Republic, 1776–1787.* 1969. New York: W. W. Norton, 1993.

Rosemarie K. Bank

Archiving Culture: Performance and American Museums in the Earlier Nineteenth Century

We live in the era of *Omnium Gatherum;* all the world's a museum, and men and women are its students.
                              —Robert Kerr, *The Gentleman's House* (1864)

Cultural values are gathered in many spaces: in libraries, in theaters, in museums, in parades—indeed, it is difficult to conceive of a site where culture does *not* accumulate, from individual bodies to readings of the heavens, from the oldest of life forms to cells born in this breath of time. It was customary to think of the United States in the late eighteenth and earlier nineteenth centuries as a new nation in a new world, yet it constructed itself in part of old and in part of new cultural ideas. These ideas were performed in and through both theatrical and nontheatrical, animate, and inanimate sites, in what I have elsewhere called theater culture, but want here to examine in the context of some of the values that informed cultural preservation and exchange in America between 1786 (the founding of Charles Willson Peale's Museum of paintings and natural history) and 1850 (the dispersal of the museum's collections by P. T. Barnum and Moses Kimball). This essay will highlight some performances during these years in nontheater locations devoted to collecting and arranging cultural objects (specifically, museums and galleries), which became the scenic backgrounds for enactments by humans functioning as performers, directors, and audiences.

Beginning in 1776, Charles Willson Peale began to follow "the painter's trade-practice of keeping a small picture gallery" (in the outbuilding to his Philadelphia home) that specialized in portraits of distinguished men of the Revolution. In 1786, the exhibition space was redefined in advertisements as a "Repository for Natural Curiosities," with preserved animals, fossils, and minerals augmenting Peale's paintings. As significant as the transition from picture gallery to museum was its move out of Peale's home in 1794 and into Philosophical Hall, headquarters of the fifty-year-old American Philosophical Society. Association with this most august body—

Peale was a co-curator of the society from 1788 to 1811—secured the museum's status as a prominent intellectual/academic activity. That standing was transformed into "an identity as a national institution" in 1802 when Peale moved part of the burgeoning collection into the upper floors of the Pennsylvania State House (Independence Hall). Thomas Jefferson regarded Peale's as the premier museum of its kind in America and, beginning in 1805, directed specimens from the Lewis and Clark expedition to it. Given donations of this character, Peale labored throughout his life to define his museum as both "national" and "educational," a status affirmed by its identity, until 1811, as a continuing part of intellectual activities at Philosophical Hall (Brigham 1–17; Sellers).

Although Peale believed his museum had a crucial part to play in creating "a universally educated public," he contextualized instruction in "useful knowledge" as a form of "rational amusement." The alliance of knowledge with entertainment in Peale's advertisements of the museum followed the lifting of the Philadelphia theater ban in 1789; indeed, the Philosophical Hall–Pennsylvania State House buildings stood in proximity to Rickett's Circus, the New (Chestnut Street) Theater, and Oeller's Hotel in Philadelphia (where concerts and balls were held). Peale cultivated the audience for entertainments by keeping ticket prices competitive, by offering season subscriptions to wealthier patrons and evening hours on Tuesdays and Saturdays as a convenience for working men and women, and he particularly encouraged attendance by women. In addition to touring the collection, museum visitors could hear regular evening lectures about natural history and other subjects of interest, have their silhouettes taken, or watch the operation of new inventions and technologies. Under the management of Peale and his son Rubens, after 1811 (and particularly after incorporation as a joint-stock company in 1821), the museum expanded performance to include human curiosities and amusements of the sort emphasized in the 1840s by Kimball in Boston and Barnum in New York. So pronounced and disreputable would the entertainment element become in museums that, well before the Civil War, learned societies retreated even "from public exhibitions and the collection of antiquities other than books and paintings" (Kulik 5–6; Brigham).

Historians of the American theater have long been aware of the alliance that operators of theaters and other public places of exhibition in the eighteenth and earlier nineteenth centuries attempted to forge between instruction and amusement; indeed, arguments joining the *dulce et utile* are centuries old, even ancient. What is significant about the museum as a site for cultural performance in the United States at the time is the classification system that informed the organization of museums like Peale's and its locating of human figures. In this regard, U.S. practices in part looked back toward the sixteenth and seventeenth century *wunderkabinett* or *kunstkammer* of Europe, in its jumbled collection of rocks, plants, animals, and human artifacts (fig. 1). These collections of earthly marvels (often including Amerindian materials from the New World—pre- and post-Columbian headdresses, masks, weapons, jewelry, wampum, belts, canoes, and baskets) were gathered for their oddity rather than representativeness and certainly for their uniqueness, which gave status to the collector (Feest and King). *Wunderkabinetten* were arranged without scientific plan, as, for example, by color or size or as minerals with minerals, plants with plants, and so on, without further divisions (Bank, "Meditations"; Doggett).

The reorganization (indeed the "birth") of the modern museum in what has been called "the long nineteenth century" (1789–1920) was significantly influenced by the Swedish botanist Linnaeus, who developed a system of classification in the 1750s for all the phenomena of the natural world, including humans, consisting of a genus and species name for things and division by classes, orders, and genera (subsequently also phylum, family, and subspecies names) (Fisher; Preziosi; Barber 49–50). Charles Willson Peale was a convinced Linnaean, as were the scientists of the American Philosophical Society and Thomas Jefferson (Barber 157–58; Brigham 58). Although not a naturalist by training, Peale approached "natural curiosities" scientifically, including the display of nonnatural things, such as waxworks, stuffed monkeys dressed in clothing, and a live five-legged cow. He had the museum's collection catalogued according to the Linnaean system in 1796 by Palisot de Beavois, a French naturalist. In this, Peale's was in advance of the British Museum and consistent with the founder's view—and that of most educated people of his day—that "proper modes of seeing" contributed to a natural theology of design by God and use by humankind. The hierarchical character that such a view of the world (and of museums) bestowed upon the nineteenth century has been much discussed by scholars and is prominently on view in Peale's often-analyzed 1822 painting *The Artist in His Museum* (fig. 2) (Kulik 3–5; Barber; Rigal 34–38; Brigham 2–4, 47–48; Sellers 246).

The hierarchies evident in Peale's self-portrait in his museum can be read from many angles, for example, vertically (Peale the naturalist lifting the curtain to gesture to patriots and birds in the heavens, fossils in the ground, and an emblematic man in the middle), horizontally (the class, age, and gender hierarchies of patrons in the middle ground suggesting "a recapitulation of Lockean/Linnaean epistemology" either in the balance of sense

FIG. 1. "Title page to Ole Worm," *Museum Wormanium* (Leiden, 1655). (Courtesy of the Houghton Library, Harvard University.)

perception, reason, and wonder or in the progression from religion-dependent woman to scientific, independent man), and in depth (Peale in the foreground mediating audience perceptions, the one creator of the collective view, self-deprecatingly reverenced by a stuffed turkey—the would-be national symbol of Philadelphia scientist/patriot [and American Philosophical Society regular] Benjamin Franklin—yet lord over a taxidermy kit and painter's palette and, through them, the patrons in the background). Peale's painting takes some license with the ground plan of that portion of the collection housed in Independence Hall (depicted more representationally in his and Titian Ramsey Peale II's 1822 watercolor *The Long Room*), which displayed stuffed birds and their innovative "painted backgrounds (instead of the white ones common in Europe)" (Kulik 5; Brigham 44–47).[1] The mammoth skeleton, lurking behind a curtain in Peale's self-portrait and heavily referenced by the bones in its foreground, had been unearthed in New York state in 1801 and excavated by Peale, with funding from the American Philosophical Society and the newly inaugu-

FIG. 2. *The Artist in His Museum* (Charles Willson Peale, 1822).
(Courtesy of the Pennsylvania Academy of the Fine Arts,
Philadelphia. Gift of Mrs. Sarah Harrison [The Joseph Harrison,
Jr., Collection].)

rated Thomas Jefferson (Sellers 143, 147; Rigal 18–19). The subsequent
display of the nearly complete fossil skeleton (which has survived flood, fire,
and world war to be viewed at the Hessischen Landesmuseums in Darm-
stadt) brought Peale "popular and scientific acclaim, doubling the museum's
revenues" (Rigal 18). Indeed, the misnomer "*mammoth* entered the political
lexicon of the time, in association with the social and economic policies of
Jefferson and his supporters," and became an emblematic "American" word
for national enterprises as varied as global voyages and producing large
cheeses (Rigal 19).

Peale memorialized his "mammoth" family and the "mammoth" expedition in his painting *Exhuming the First American Mastodon* (the correct

nomenclature), completed in 1808 and hung in "the Mammoth Room" (Rigal 18), as the space in Independence Hall was christened in 1811 when the mastodon skeleton was moved there from Philosophical Hall. This room led from "the Long Room" via an entranceway lined with Native American artifacts. The liminal space between the two rooms was purposive, since the Mammoth Room housed the museum's aboriginal costumes and implements and exhibits from the Lewis and Clark expedition, the centerpiece of which "was a wax model of Meriwether Lewis wearing the buckskin costume given him by the Shoshone chief Cameawait" (Brigham 128). Donors had given and Peale had purchased Indian artifacts since the eighteenth century; indeed, with no government repositories for them, Peale's Museum was often the recipient of materials taken in military campaigns (Anthony Wayne's to Ohio in 1795, for example) or obtained through gift or trade (Sellers 252–54). In 1797 Peale had mounted an exhibit of ten wax figures and portraits of Red Pole and Blue Jacket, principals in the [Old] Northwest Territory Wars who, in 1796, had met tribal enemies, also touring the museum, and concluded a peace with them on Peale's premises (Sellers 91–94; Brigham 126–29). In years to come, though no longer housed in Independence Hall, Indians touring Peale's Museum (as Black Hawk did as a prisoner of war in the summer of 1833) could contemplate the archiving of tribal people as art and artifact. As Black Hawk's presence proved, living or dead, Native Americans and Native Americana drew crowds.

It is not possible to determine how many wax figures were in the two sites where Peale's collection was located at the time of his death in 1827. It is certain that, despite his devotion to science, he collected and exhibited the nonnatural, and he offered entertainments, the former hidden in a tower room in Independence Hall, the latter offered in the main lecture room and varying from child prodigies to musical evenings to demonstrations of experiments and technologies to lectures about natural science (Sellers 216). Today this may seem fare too rational for amusement, but in the antebellum decades all the world appeared to be gathering and displaying the fruits both of collecting and classifying (Barber, chap. 11). Of significance is the normalizing process at work that locates living cultures in monuments to the inanimate and hierarchizes them with extinct species.[2] Peale positioned himself as the director and designer of this brand of theater culture, for which his patrons were the performance's participating audience. In the years that followed Peale's death his sons and others would follow his "national" precedent in transferring the normalizing and hierarchizing processes to entertainment. In this, one sees less the "degrading" of museums and science by the theatrical (as has often been argued) than the transference of cultural "archiving" from museums and galleries to performance. A few examples of these archiving processes with respect to performances by and of Native Americans and Native American artifacts may be illustrative.

As it became clear that the collection at Peale's Museum in Philadelphia would never be acquired or supported by the federal government, Peale's sons began to branch out. Rembrandt Peale opened a museum in Baltimore in 1814 (just as the British began to attack Washington, DC), which limped on under various managements until the collection was sold to P. T. Barnum in 1845. After managing the Philadelphia Museum for some years under his father's shadow, Rubens Peale opened a museum of his own on Broadway in New York City, facing the park and City Hall. (He chose for his debut 26 October 1825, the date of the city's gala celebration of the opening of the Erie Canal.) Rubens Peale presided here for more than a decade as a popularizer of scientific discoveries and a manager of theatrical attractions. The aftermath of the panic of 1837 sent him steadily bankrupt until, in 1843, the New York museum was taken over by Barnum. Like their progenitor's museum, Peale's sons' establishments sought to retain the scientific and educational character of the original, excusing (as the Philadelphia museum did) live animal exhibits in 1812 or "catchpenny shows" in 1819, the display of Siamese twins in 1829 or "the Virginia Dwarfs" in 1835, as instructive. Amusements increased when the Philadelphia Museum moved to an arcade (1827–37), a site shorn of either the national associations of Independence Hall or the scientific ones of the American Philosophical Society and flatly allied with commerce. There, the conflation of Black Hawk and the Virginia Dwarfs as museum "exhibits" converted both simultaneously into performances and into collected, commodified curiosities (Sellers 222, 249–50, 305–6).

The association between museums and performance became a national (and then international) one during these decades, as collections other than the three Peale museums reflect, not in achieving the federal (or even local) support that eluded Charles Willson Peale, but in carrying the association of performance and archive to frontier regions and, finally, abroad. Daniel Drake, for example, organized the Western Museum Society in Cincinnati in 1818, an enterprise that involved John James Audubon as taxidermist, the sculptor Hiram Powers as modeler of wax figures, and naturalist Joseph Dorfeuille as creator of a mechanical spectacle known as *Dorfeuille's Hell*. It is in the career of George Catlin, portraitist of North American Indians, however, that the museumizing of performance reached further development, in looking back to earlier forms of diplomatic and commercial cultural exchange and joining these to an archive. Catlin exhibited at the Academy of

Fine Arts in 1821 and lived in Philadelphia until 1825. During these years, he was inspired by an Indian delegation passing through the city and had ample opportunity to study Peale's collection of Indian artifacts. In 1830, and for the next six years, Catlin traveled the trans-Mississippi west, sketching and painting Indians and tribal life and collecting artifacts. In the fall of 1837, he began to exhibit his "Indian Gallery" in New York, and, in 1838, in Washington, DC. Catlin, like Charles Willson Peale, a portrait painter and accidental naturalist, was determined to become a history painter of "the finest models in Nature, unmasked and moving in all their grace and beauty," the "savage Indians" of North America. The reading of history that emerged from this calling produced an erasure within the museum/art gallery of the separation between artifacts in glass cases or on wax effigies and performances in lecture halls (Sellers 250–51; Truettner 12–15).

In 1801, the Peales invited a dozen guests to join them for dinner *inside* the mammoth skeleton that had just been installed in Philosophical Hall. Fortified with food and drink, the guests were serenaded by John Hawkins's new Patent Portable Grand Piano, and choruses of "Yankee Doodle" and other songs punctuated patriotic toasts (Sellers 147; Barber 156). George Catlin was five when this gathering took place, but he very well understood, as he opened his own Gallery, the benefits that performance could add to a celebration by distinguished guests. Embodying the historical mission of preserving Indian culture (Truettner 13, 36), Catlin moved from presentation to representation, promoting his Indian Gallery via entertainments such as the one Philip Hone described on 6 December 1837:

> I went this morning by invitation of the proprietor, Mr. Catlin, to see his great collection of paintings, consisting of portraits of Indian chiefs, landscapes, ceremonies, etc., of the Indian tribes, and implements of husbandry, and the chase, weapons of war, costumes, etc., which he collected during his travels of five or six years in the great West. The enthusiasm, zeal, and perseverance with which he has followed up this pursuit are admirable. I have seldom witnessed so interesting an exhibition. Among the invited guests were Mr. Webster, some of the members of the Common Council, the mayor, and some of the newspaper editors. We had a collation of buffaloes' tongues, and venison and the waters of the great spring, and smoked the calumet of peace under an Indian tent formed of buffalo skins. (Hone, qtd. in Nevins 1:290–91)

In the United States, Catlin's collection blended paintings with natural history exhibits in a show format in which the paintings were exhibited and explained one at a time against a backdrop of Indian artifacts. When Catlin took his eight-ton Indian Gallery to England and opened it to the public in 1840, he entered further into the domain of the performative. The staging site was Egyptian Hall, a popular London entertainment and museum facility. The paintings—some five hundred of them—were hung on the walls, and a Crow tipi twenty-five feet high was erected in the center of the room, ringed by several thousand Indian costumes, weapons, and artifacts. By the fall of 1840, in an effort to bring in patrons, Catlin had begun to illustrate his text with *tableaux vivants* that, according to Catlin's letters and travel notes, featured twenty white men and boys (some of whom evidently impersonated Indian women), dressed, barbered, and painted as Plains Indians, in staged re-creations of (according to a broadside) "warriors enlisting," a "council of war," a "war dance," a "foot war party on the march," a "war party encamped at night," an "alarm in camp," a "war party in council," "skulking," "battle and scalping," a "scalp dance," a "treaty of peace," and a "pipe of peace dance." On Thursday evenings, to attract women visitors, the museum's tableaux were "descriptive of Domestic Scenes in Indian Life in times of Peace; representing their Games—Dances—Feasts—Marriage Ceremonies—Funeral Rites—Mysteries, etc." (Catlin 1:95; and Roehm 206).[3]

In the spring of 1843, Catlin entered into partnership with Canadian showman Arthur Rankin, then touring a troupe of nine Ojibway through England. The performance/art combination proved far more popular than Catlin's white Indians had been, and the Ojibway continued to perform into 1844, when competition from Barnum's Tom Thumb and increasing criticism of the Indians' behavior and their exploitation by Catlin and Rankin brought declines in revenue. The partners fell out, and Rankin reassumed sole management of the Ojibway. Catlin's fortunes were saved when, in August 1844, a party of sixteen Iowa Indians, under the management of G. H. C. Melody, arrived in London. Barnum had recruited them for the Egyptian Hall, where, he writes, "Mr. Catlin on our joint account" exhibited them (Altick 380; Saxon 27–28; and Fitzsimmons 87–89). Catlin drummed up interest in his Indian Gallery by repeating the sightseeing techniques he had used with the Ojibway, by showing the Iowa at private gatherings (such as a breakfast with Disraeli), by taking them for exercise on Lords' Cricket ground, and by encamping them at Vauxhall Gardens (where horses could be added to the show) after the Egyptian Hall run ended. A provincial tour followed through England in the winter of 1844–45, during which two of the Iowa died of illness. In April 1845, the Gallery left for Paris (Mulvey 253–75).

Initially, success greeted Catlin's ventures in France. The French press acclaimed the Gallery, and Louis Philippe received the Iowa at the Tuileries. Prominent authors supported Catlin's attempts to sell his paintings to the French government, and his entries into the Salon of 1846 were subsequently praised. But the Iowa did not thrive, and, following a death in their party, they returned to the United States in the summer of 1845. Their place was soon taken by a group of eleven Ojibway who had been performing in England with some success since 1843, meeting the archbishop of Canterbury, the duke of Wellington, and even Queen Victoria. In France, the Ojibway pleased Louis Philippe sufficiently to prompt him to offer Catlin a room for his gallery in the Louvre. At the close of its exhibition, Catlin's troupe began a November 1845 tour, at the invitation of the king of Belgium, to Brussels, Antwerp, and Ghent. In Brussels, eight of the Ojibway came down with smallpox. Two died, and the others had a slow recovery until January of 1846, when the Ojibway left Catlin. They did not, however, leave Europe, but traveled to the German border and returned to Britain, where further touring may have contributed to the deaths of five more of the party. Reduced to commercial management as a sideshow, the surviving Ojibway left England for the United States in April of 1848, after a five-year absence from their homes.[4]

The trouping Ojibway and Iowa who brought Catlin's Indian Gallery to life in the 1840s did much that was similar, in the way of cultural exchange, to what Indian diplomatic delegations and what the Bureau of Indian Affairs would come to call "show Indians" had done in the United States and Europe for centuries. The same mixture of politics, business, science, entertainment, and curiosity typifies these exchanges, and the same elements of exploitation, imitation, representation, preservation, and commodification characterize them. Catlin's reputation as an artist and naturalist did not fully recover, in scientific and fine arts circles, from his association with showmen, but the link between museums/galleries and performance had been forged. Performance as a form of cultural archiving in theatrical history is evident, to be sure, in the surge of "Indian plays" in the 1830s and 1840s, but it is also evident in the Yankee and frontier characters of these and earlier decades and in the staged Negro and the Bowery B'hoy and G'hal. These white dramatizations of "national" and "native" types lay claim (as I have elsewhere argued) to "authenticity," but it is in the reproduction of those disenfranchised in U.S. society in the antebellum decades that cultural authenticating processes are most exposed. Archives played a strong role in the development of these processes in American culture and in their appropriation by the American theater.[5]

George Catlin remained in Europe until the revolutions of 1848 forced him back to London, where, in 1852, he was imprisoned for debt and his gallery sold (Truettner 53). The fate affecting Catlin's Gallery also befell Peale's Museum in Philadelphia. In 1838, the collection moved from the arcade to a newly erected building containing "a stage for an orchestra" at one end of the new museum's main hall. Once again, lectures ran in tandem with child prodigies. Composer/conductor Francis Johnson's Negro band appeared, E. L. Davenport offered his Yankee impersonations, and vocalists and "the Belgian Giant" vied for audiences with the latest in natural history research. In 1843, a committee appointed to examine the museum's affairs on behalf of its stockholders attributed its woes to

> the injurious effects resulting from the morbid excitement produced by a series of entertainments catered to the public taste in 1839 and 1840, and at a subsequent period continued in, on a more reduced scale both as regards the means employed and the receipts realized. Public opinion, at all time and under all circumstances Omnipotent, has decided that the departure from the legitimate objects of the Company could not be sustained and the converting into a concert room of a receptacle for the works of Nature and Art, and for which purpose alone it was reared and nurtured by its illustrious founder, was sufficient cause for the withdrawal of the patronage formerly so liberally bestowed by our most influential citizens. (Sellers 299)

True to the credo that led the taxidermist at Peale's in 1842 to expose the Kimball-Barnum "Feegee Mermaid" as a hoax created by joining a monkey and a fish, Peale's heirs struggled to create a firm financial foundation for their tottering collection. The museum building was sold in 1843, forcing the collection into high rent (Sellers 299–308). In 1845, Peale's grandson Edmund (freshly capitalized by having sold the Baltimore collection to Barnum) bought the Philadelphia collection at auction and moved it into a former Masonic Hall at Chestnut Street near Seventh. The building had a fully equipped theater but no regular company. Instead, manager John Ellsler engaged Joseph Jefferson, John Sefton, John E. Owens, and other stars when they were at liberty, filling in between plays or one-man shows with "Ethiopian Harmonists" and similar light entertainment. Following Barnum's and Kimball's leads in having no bar and refusing admittance to prostitutes, contemporaries remembered the last Peale's Museum as a "moral house."[6]

With that combination of cooperation and competition for which he is infamous, Barnum, with all that he represents as part of the process of archiving culture in the United States before the Civil War, formally linked the elements of showmanship that science found most objectionable to those that the naturalist-artists Peale and Catlin had taken as their historic mission to their national culture when, in 1848, Barnum "lent" Peale's Museum General Tom Thumb while Choc-chu-tub-bee, an Indian "chief," who performed on "the one-keyed Flute, Fife, Flageolet, Castanet, and Saucepan!" as his wife sang accompaniment, appeared at Barnum's own Philadelphia venue. It was a linking that forecast the end of Peale's Museum. Sometime in 1849, Barnum bought Peale's remaining collection for himself and Moses Kimball, and in the next year he dispersed it to Boston, Barnum's Museum in New York, and to his museum in Philadelphia. In 1851, Barnum sold out the Philadelphia venture, a few months before the building and everything in it were destroyed by fire. In 1865, a similar fiery end befell Barnum's New York operation and all that it or his Philadelphia venues had contained of irreplaceable natural and cultural objects. The laggardly U.S. government did no better, indeed worse, when it came to preserving the national (and international) treasures that it began to gather from government agencies in 1840, in an attempt to satisfy the conditions of the Smithson bequest for a national museum. Objects that escaped the Smithsonian fire in 1865 (including those confiscated or seized from Peale's) were left to molder under a museum coal bin until 1899, nor did a national art gallery materialize until the Harriet Lane Johnson bequest of 1906 (Sellers 298, 332). Catlin's collection fared as badly. Bought by an American industrialist, the Indian Gallery deteriorated in a Philadelphia boiler factory from 1852 until the collection was finally acquired by the Smithsonian in 1878 (Truettner 135–37). Kimball's portions of Peale's collection did somewhat better, passing from Kimball to the Boston Museum in 1893, and from Kimball's heirs in 1899 to Boston's Society of Natural History and Harvard's Peabody Museum (Sellers 309–13, 333).

London's 1851 "Crystal Palace" Exposition in many ways wrote both a coda to and a new beginning for cultural archiving in the United States. As I have noted elsewhere, the soon-to-be-bankrupt Catlin supplied the Crow tipi and manikins displaying Indian dress that formed (with Hiram Powers's marble statue *The Greek Slave*) the central cultural display of the American wing of the Exposition. Peale's legacy was also reflected in the Crystal Palace. John Hawkins, who had dined inside the mammoth in 1801 and entertained fellow guests with his patented piano, settled in England. In 1853, his son, a sculptor and anatomist, feasted (with Richard Owen and other scientists) inside a model Iguanodon in the Crystal Palace, itself removed from Hyde Park to Sydenham, where it supplied "useful knowledge" and "rational entertainment" to millions of visitors until its destruction by fire in 1936 (Sellers 333–34). Barnum was in evidence in the Crystal Palace year, of course (his presence "always ominous of business," as the London *Times* quipped), and, by 1853, involved in a "Crystal Palace" scheme in New York (Bank, *Theatre Culture* 176–83). Yet, for all his hustle, Barnum's day had but a short time to run. The "American Museum" he built in New York at the end of the Civil War never achieved the popularity of the burned museum it replaced. A *New York Times* editorial argued in 1868, two weeks after Barnum's second establishment burned, that America needed "a museum without any 'humbug.' " In less than a decade (1877) the American Museum of Natural History in New York opened its doors, fulfilling part of the lifelong dream that Charles Willson Peale and George Catlin had so long vainly pursued.

The archiving process in U.S. museums and galleries in the decades before the Civil War normalized and hierarchized the natural world according to the "scientific" principles that informed it. One of these classified and hierarchized cultures in a way that allowed the Linnaean Peale, in 1805–6, to liken a stuffed orangutan in his museum to "an old Negro" and Catlin and his white performers to troupe (and trope) "the vanishing Indian" in 1840 (Brigham 130, 193 n. 13). Alerted to the casual racism and ethnocide such archiving processes can produce, spectators become sensitized to the ways in which cultural performances conserve these views by normalizing them. At the same time, newborn forms of performance develop out of such normalizations and themselves become inhabited constructs. In this way, for example, "show Indians" like the Iowa and Ojibway in Catlin's Gallery and white and Indian Wild West shows come to be, and the tipi and buckskin dress to represent, "America" on the international scene. More than "humbugging" natural and cultural history, these inhabited forms appropriate and redistribute archived culture and cultural performance—as the National Museum of the American Indian in New York and in Washington, DC, is doing—in ways that can already be marked in the United States, for better and for worse, in 1850. The concept of "theater culture" invites us to examine these processes and their accumulation in performances inside museums and galleries as well as the presence of archived culture in performances outside them.

NOTES

Research for this essay was supported by a National Endowment for the Humanities Fellowship and by a grant from the Phillips Fund for Native American Studies of the American Philosophical Society.

1. See Sellers's color reproduction of the painting (121) and the floorplan (217).

2. Regarding normalizing constructs, see Foucault.

3. For a description of Catlin's presentations in the United States and a broadside, his fortunes in London and a broadside, see Truettner 36–38 and 41–44. Altick (275–79) explores Catlin's activities in London in the 1840s. For previous discussions of Catlin, see Bank, *Theatre Culture.*

4. For the number of Iowa, I am using Truettner's figure rather than Mulvey's. Mulvey (49) corrects Truettner concerning the fate of the second party of Ojibway in that the Indians did not immediately depart for England. In 1848, both Catlin and Maungwudaus, the leader of the second Ojibway troupe, published accounts of their tours; the latter's appears in Peyer 66–74.

5. Although he claimed to be chastened by the deaths of the Indians in his company, Catlin is reported to have had Iroquois in his show in 1851, the year of the Crystal Palace Exhibition in London (Altick 463; and Bank, *Theatre Culture* 178–81).

6. Regarding some of the problems surrounding the "prostitutes in theaters" issue in America in the nineteenth century, see Bank, *Theatre Culture* 128–38.

REFERENCES

Altick, Richard D. *The Shows of London.* Cambridge: Harvard UP, 1978.

Bank, Rosemarie K. "Meditations upon Opening and Crossing Over." *Of Borders and Thresholds.* Ed. Michal Kobialka. Minneapolis: U of Minnesota P, 1999.

———. *Theatre Culture in America, 1825–1860.* Cambridge: Cambridge UP, 1997.

Barber, Lynn. *The Heyday of Natural History, 1820–1870.* New York: Doubleday, 1980.

Brigham, David R. *Public Culture in the Early Republic: Peale's Museum and Its Audience.* Washington, DC: Smithsonian Institution, 1995

Catlin, George. *Catlin's Notes of Eight Years' Travel and Residence in Europe.* 2 vols. London: n.p., 1848.

Doggett, Rachel, Monique Hulvey, and Julie Ainsworth, eds. *New World of Wonders: European Images of America, 1492–1700.* Washington, DC: Folger Shakespeare Library, 1992.

Feest, Christian. "Mexico and South America in the European *Wunderkammer.*" Impey and MacGregor 237–44.

Fisher, Philip. "Local Meanings and Portable Objects: National Collections, Literatures, Music, and Architecture." Wright 15–27.

Fitzsimmons, Raymund. *Barnum in London.* New York: St. Martin's Press, 1970.

Foucault, Michel. *Power/Knowledge.* Trans. Colin Gordon et al. New York: Pantheon, 1980.

———. *The Order of Things.* New York: Vintage, 1973.

Impey, Oliver, and Arthur MacGregor, eds. *The Origins of Museums: The Cabinet of Curiosities in Sixteenth- and Seventeenth-Century Europe.* Oxford: Clarendon, 1985.

King, J. C. H. "North American Ethnography in the Collection of Sir Hans Sloan." Impey and MacGregor 232–36.

Kulik, Gary. "Designing the Past: History-Museum Exhibitions from Peale to the Present." *History Museums in the United States.* Ed. Warren Leon and Roy Rosenzweig. Urbana: U of Illinois P, 1989.

Mulvey, Christopher. "Among the Sag-a-noshes: Ojibway and Iowa Indians with George Catlin in Europe, 1843–1848." *Indians Abroad*. Ed. Christian Feest. Aachen: Rader Verlag, 1987.

Nevins, Allan. *The Diary of Philip Hone, 1828–1851*. 2 vols. New York: Dodd, Mead, 1927.

Peyer, Bernd, ed. *The Elders Wrote: An Anthology of Early Prose by North American Indians, 1768–1931*. Berlin: Reimer Verlag, 1982.

Preziosi, Donald. "In the Temple of Entelechy: The Museum as Evidentiary Artifact." Wright 165–71.

Rigal, Laura. "Peale's Mammoth." *American Iconology: New Approaches to Nineteenth-Century Art and Literature*. Ed. David C. Miller. New Haven: Yale UP, 1993.

Roehm, Marjorie Catlin. *The Letters of George Catlin and His Family: A Chronicle of the American West*. Berkeley: U of California P, 1962.

Saxon, A. H. *Selected Letters of P. T. Barnum*. New York: Columbia UP, 1983.

Sellers, Charles Coleman. *Mr. Peale's Museum: Charles Willson Peale and the First Popular Museum of Natural Science and Art*. New York: W. W. Norton, 1980.

Truettner, William H. *The Natural Man Observed: A Study of Catlin's Indian Gallery*. Washington, DC: Smithsonian Institution, 1979.

Wright, Gwendolyn, ed. *The Formation of National Collections of Art and Archaeology*. Washington, DC, and Hanover, NH: National Gallery of Art and the UP of New England, 1996.

Kim Marra

Taming America as Actress: Augustin Daly, Ada Rehan, and the Discourse of Imperial Frontier Conquest

Daly must have been a great actor who could not act. He was rough and uncouth, with harsh utterance and uncultured accent; a singer without a voice, a musician without an instrument. But in Ada Rehan he found his means of self-expression; Ada Rehan with her quaint charm, her voice of music, her splendid presence and her gentle good nature which he could mold to his will.

—W. Graham Robertson, costume designer for Daly's Theatre

A statue of solid silver, eight feet in height, costing $50,000, and standing upon $250,000 worth of gold compressed into a pedestal, will be one of the exhibits from Montana at the World's Fair. The pedestal will represent the largest lump of gold ever seen. Miss Ada Rehan, the actress, has been asked to pose as a model for the work, "as she is one of the finest types extant of American physical womanhood," to quote the words of the directors of the Montana exhibit.

—1892 newspaper clipping, Ada Rehan Scrapbook

No apology is needed for giving an account of the man who lifted the American stage from a very low estate to a position of great dignity, and gave the dramatic art of his own country a first place in two continents; and who did all his life work with such courage in the face of obstacles and such steadfastness in pursuit of a single purpose, that the history of his career must give heart to every self-reliant, intelligent striver in every business of life.

—Joseph Francis Daly, preface to *The Life of Augustin Daly*

In the annals of theater history, Augustin Daly (1838–99) holds the status of first American *régisseur,* or autocratic producer-director. Employing methods analogous to those of seminal European theatrical autocrats, Richard Wagner and Georg II, Duke of Saxe-Meiningen, Daly made each stage presentation a realization of his own singular vision. Like Wagner, he believed his vision would edify both theater and society, and, like Saxe-

Meiningen, he invoked the posture of state authority to enforce its realization. Company members addressed him as "Governor," while less flattering commentators compared his regime to that of a Napoleonic dictator, Roman emperor, military commander, martinet, and mounted despot driving his company with whip and spur. With his authoritarian methods Daly exceeded earlier managers in his attempts to control the anarchy and disrepute associated with the unruly audiences and itinerant stars who had dominated much antebellum theatrical activity. In so doing, he achieved an unprecedented level of "civility" and artistic unity in stage production in the United States, set the mold for later autocrats, and thereby contributed instrumentally to the modernization of American theater.

Historians have related the advent of Daly's enterprise to a variety of phenomena, including the growth of an urban bourgeoisie desirous of more genteel, controlled entertainments; the growth of theater as big business and the organizational and economic pressures of the star system and the long run; and naturalistic aesthetics demanding greater integration of production values (McConachie 231–57; Wilmeth and Cullen 5). Into this matrix of factors I would like to read larger discourses of American nationalism ascendant during the period as productive of theatrical autocracy. Just as Wagner and Saxe-Meiningen's enterprises can be linked to the German unification movement of the late nineteenth century, so Daly's can be linked to the rising wave of U.S. expansionism led by Northern industrialists in the decades following the Civil War. Whereas Wagnerian opera actualized the German national myth of a collective *volk,* Daly's theater actualized the American national myth of bourgeois individualism, or the so-called success myth, the fierce pursuit of which marked the Gilded Age. Corresponding with his closest confidant and frequent collaborator, his brother Joseph Francis Daly, Augustin Daly asserted: "I have the will and disposition to ride over every puny obstacle" (Daly and Daly, 15 January 1865). He revealed his admiration of one of the success myth's premier exponents when he compared himself to "an officer in Carnegie's steel works" (qtd. in Felheim, "Career" 524). After opening his first theater in 1869, he again invoked the image of a captain of industry: "I went upon the stage and felt as one who treads the deck of a ship as its master" (qtd. in J. Daly 88).

As pursued by titanic individualists like Carnegie, the success myth fostered the mutual aggrandizement of self and nation by imperial capitalist means. American nation and American empire were symbiotic—if not synonymous—formations, and the national mythos promised individual citizens the right to prosper by reproducing in microcosm the tropes of their nation's imperial formation (Van Alstyne 9; Trachtenberg 84–85). Bourgeois selfhood and white, Anglo-Saxon, Protestant nationhood alike were forged and ennobled through the conquest, cultivation, and possession of "Othered" territories and the display of power and wealth in the form of "finished" goods (Jennings 15). With increasing fervor in the second half of the nineteenth century, the interests of American private and public empires coincided in a matrix of mutually reinforcing discourses.

My analysis of how Daly's theater reproduced signal tropes of American empire building proceeds from Bruce McConachie's discussion of the impact of the autocrat's status as an *arriviste* on his ambitions and managerial policies. As the disadvantaged son of Irish Catholic immigrants, Daly wrestled with anxieties of inferiority and inauthenticity in his efforts to join the ranks of a business-class patriarchy bent on consolidating its power. Noting that actresses who defected from his company threatened Daly's masculinity, McConachie identifies the gender as well as class and race/ethnic dynamics of his struggle (204–10). I extend McConachie's analysis thematically and chronologically by positing that Daly's enterprise proved assimilationist in intent and imperial capitalist in method. For Daly, theatrical gentrification and, in particular, the "taming" of purportedly savage actresses provided the chief means of overcoming his denigrated Old World heritage and acceding to American manhood. This essay examines tropes of conquest at play in Daly's relationships with his leading ladies, especially with his most famous protégé, Ada Rehan, and then shows how nationally constitutive myths of bourgeois individualism and empire were imbricated in his and Rehan's definitive 1887 production of *The Taming of the Shrew*.

To demonstrate the self- and nation-forming efficacy of Daly's conquests of actresses, I begin by situating his enterprise amid three interlocking discursive traditions that conflated women's bodies with nature and savagery: frontier imperialism, evolutionary theory, and bourgeois antitheatricalism. As historians such as Richard Van Alstyne have shown, policy makers since the nation's founding have conceived of the United States as an *imperium,* a dominion or sovereign state that would expand and strengthen on the assumption that the continent belonged as of right to those who could colonize it (1–18). Frederick Jackson Turner, perhaps the preeminent author in this long tradition, saw this imperialism as the essence of nationhood, arguing that both America and Americans developed through progressive encroachments of "civilization" into "savagery" on the Western frontier (Turner, esp. 3–5; Smith 3–4). Premised on the classical (Aristotelian) paradigm that gendered male the active, ordering principle, and gendered female the chaotic, primitive matter for the male principle to work upon, this discursive tradition made woman the alpha and omega of American

individual and national transformation. The white, European pioneer escaped a tyrannical motherland to seek freedom and fortune in a wilderness
figured as a woman's body ripe for possession. Annette Kolodny suggests the
image of virgin land may have been formulated to diffuse the emasculating
specter of terrible nature, awesome and beautiful, but also "dark, uncharted,
and prowled by howling beasts" (9). She argues more centrally, however,
that a vexing ambivalence inhered in the abundance of the virgin land itself.
Approaching her as mistress, the pioneer, through the penetration of settlement, turned her into mother, inducing regeneration and extracting nur-
turance and riches, but at the same time reconstellating archaic male fears of
maternal power in a New World context (71). The threat of emasculation
posed by constructions of either a "savage" wilderness or an immolating
maternal plenitude fueled increasingly aggressive male assertions of control
over both feminine nature and actual women, coupled with growing nostalgia for lost paradise (132–33).

Ironically, these responses to perceived female threats to male autonomy themselves gave rise to a further danger with feminine connotations,
the threat of "overcivilization." Industrial expansion spurred the growth of
cities, which, while lauded as progress, also conjured more specters of savagery and devourment. As Thomas Jefferson had warned: "When we get
piled up upon one another in large cities, as in Europe, we shall become
corrupt as in Europe, and go to eating one another as they do there" (qtd. in
Muccigrosso 122). For many white, middle-class men, urban women contributed to the threat. If rigid control of female deportment and investiture
of moral authority and duty in Victorian housewives were intended to
contain their sexuality, these gender prescriptions resulted in fostering an
alleged conspiracy of domestic tyrants to inhibit the individual freedom of
husbands and sons (Norton 53). Such constructions of overcivilization com-
pelled male escape into the wilderness for renewal and reassertion of autonomy, restarting the self- and nation-forming processes of converting "savagery" into "civilization" and overcoming maternal power both behind on
the homefront and ahead on the frontier (Pugh 59, 86).

The absorption of the work of Darwin and his disciples into U.S.
culture in the second half of the nineteenth century reinforced the prevailing discourse of frontier conquest with further implications for dominant
gender ideology. Controverting prior assumptions that white, European
man, created in God's image, was essentially separate from and "above" the
rest of creation, evolutionary theory repositioned man in nature, fundamentally a product of its history. One of the most influential aspects of this
repositioning, argues Cynthia Eagle Russett, was the notion that ontogeny

recapitulated phylogeny, or the development of the individual recapitulated that of the species. Both developments proceeded hierarchically toward an apex of adult Anglo-Saxon maleness. Lower down, and more preserving of primate and infantile characteristics, white women were equated with savage racial Others. Following the logic of recapitulation, the Anglo-Saxon male had to overcome traits not only embodied in woman but also, by implication, inscribed in his own organism, in order to attain his rightful place atop the phyletic ladder (50–55). This made conquest of woman—and the nature and savagery with which she was conflated—a more literal and immediate as well as metaphoric necessity for male self-actualization.

Moreover, the conqueror could proceed in this quest with the related assumptions that women, like savages, were more tolerant of pain than he and that they were less distinctive as individuals (Russett 56, 74). Evolutionary theory reserved the greatest degrees of human sensibility and variability for Anglo-Saxon males, who differentiated in contradistinction to the more generic and physically insensate female. Being less variable, woman was also deemed inherently "conservative," that is, conserving of the ontogenetic and phylogenetic traits acquired through evolution. The female provided the "perpetuating factor," as opposed to the male's "originating factor," of evolution's "unresting progression" (92–100). While demeaning to white women, the concept of female "conservatism" also contributed to her deification as a generic vessel or repository of the attainments of her race. As the leading American evolutionary psychologist G. Stanley Hall put it, woman was "a magnificent organ of heredity" (qtd. in Russett 61).

The cultural saliency of these notions intensified as various social and demographic forces raised the stakes for Anglo-Saxon male self-actualization and nation formation. Awareness of limits to westward expansion increased markedly after mid-century, along with the prospect of the disappearance of available "free" land for continued escape and remasculization. The nation's urbanized Anglo-Saxon middle and upper classes grew more alarmed at the mass immigration of Irish, Italians, and Jews, the migration of freed blacks into Northern cities, and mounting lower-class unrest. Additionally, the advance of the women's rights movement into the Darwinian age threatened to overturn the ontogenetic and phylogenetic hierarchy invoked to buttress the patriarchal social order. Dominant cultural responses to these pressures involved transposing the discourse of frontier conquest onto urban realities and fashioning imagery of generic, "conservative" femininity to mark Anglo-Saxon male evolutionary superiority. Major New York papers, including the *Times, Tribune, Herald,* and *World,* used frontier battles—most notably "Custer's Last Stand"—as allegories for class and racial anxieties in the industrialized East (Slotkin 435–59). In a related rhetorical move political and military leaders, such as Roscoe Conkling, Chester Arthur, and Daniel Sickles, issued verbal paeans to "our pure and progressive," "world conquering and enlightened womanhood" (Beer 11–12). Commercial artists such as Charles Dana Gibson and Howard Chandler Christy, who became prominent in the 1880s and 1890s, visually codified the national WASP feminine ideal as the American Girl (Banta xxxi–xxxiii).

These larger race, class, and gender discourses converged with dominant cultural attitudes toward the theater to impact the development of Augustin Daly's career. According to Joseph Daly, it was "much to the distress of our dear mother," who had raised the boys as a single parent after the death of their father, that Augustin determined to wage his "battle of life" in the theater (13–14). Joseph aligns Mrs. Daly's opinions with moral tracts that diametrically opposed the theater to the home, construing the latter as a space of settlement and right upbringing and the former as a space of temptation, itinerancy, and degeneracy. At the crux of these antitheatrical prejudices lay the fear of uncontained female sexuality that the spectacle of "public" women evoked. If a respectable wife and mother was the pure, stabilizing center of home and family, the professional female performer was the primary source of instability and decadence in the theater (Johnson 3–35). Flagrantly defying canons of feminine purity, piety, dependency, and modesty, actresses made vivid the metaphoric and scientific correlations between women's bodies and savage nature. The linkages were especially acute in the case of actresses like Julia Dean, Charlotte Cushman, and Matilda Heron, whom young Daly admired in spite of his mother's warnings and whose emotionally and physically extreme performances critics attributed to a direct channeling of natural forces. That actresses could gain professional independence and socioeconomic power as stars made their savage connotations and the theaters they inhabited still more threatening for many bourgeois moralists.

Thus situated beyond the pale of respectable civilization, the theater constituted a frontier onto which the seductive and potentially devouring forces of both wilderness and cityscape could be projected. As such, the theater provided the male adventurer with an escape from domestic tyranny and opportunity, through conquest of savagery embodied in actresses, to shed the skin of his European heritage and become an American man. As a self-described theatrical pioneer, Daly was drawn to this frontier like Boone to Kentucky with "a haunting desire to become familiar with management." His early models for the managerial mode of theatrical conquest were William E. Burton and James W. Wallack, who both also acted with their companies. Daly's civilizing efforts surpassed even theirs, Joseph implies, because "he was absolutely without ambition to act" (13). The stage remained for him an Othered territory over which he would assert a more absolute dominance and from whose savage actresses he would attain a more complete onto- and phylogenetic differentiation.

The gendered power dynamics of Daly's struggle became apparent during the first decade of his career, when he negotiated a variety of non-acting positions until he could marshal the resources to open his own theater. He "worked upon" theatrical savagery as a drama critic, tour manager, publicist, and, most formatively, a playwright. Although he wrote vehicles for some male as well as female stars, his scripts for women proved the most consequential, garnering him his most devastating rejection, from Laura Keene in 1858, but also his biggest successes—*Leah, the Forsaken* with Kate Bateman in 1862 and *Under the Gaslight* with Rose Eytinge in 1867, both of which featured high levels of female emotional and physical pyrotechnics (Felheim, *Theatre* 3–7). While providing Daly with an invaluable apprenticeship, most of these ventures obliged him to engage with the actresses who attracted him primarily on their terms, subject to their acceptance, rejection, or solicitation of his services.

Over the next thirty years, beginning with the opening of his first theater in 1869, Daly strove to reverse these power dynamics. He assumed greater authority than Burton and Wallack by styling his establishment on the model of militaristic paternalism validated during the Civil War. For many Northern U.S. business and political leaders of Daly's generation, the war experience had served as a management "school" whose lessons were emblematized in the election of General Ulysses S. Grant to the presidency in 1868 (Slotkin 282–95). Hailed by the *New York Times* as the leader of "that great national conquest" ("New Administration"), Grant himself, in his inaugural address, projected militaristic rhetoric onto a range of political, economic, and cultural forces, including those of frontier savagery, that might impede the expansion of Northern industrial interests: "I will favor any course toward [the Indians] which tends to their civilization, Christianization, and ultimate citizenship," proclaimed the new president ("Inauguration"). In the business world, the mantle of conqueror went to the industrial capitalist, in whom the ethos of militaristic paternalism vested the combined authority of father, husband, owner, and commander-in-chief. Identifying as a business manager as well as a theater manager, Daly seized this power. When actor Richard Mansfield questioned him about why he disallowed opinions other than his own, the manager replied: "I cannot afford to be less than Commander in Chief of all my forces from the highest officer under me to the humblest. Only in this way can I lead you on to victory—the victory which we both would desire" (qtd. in J. Daly 548). Near the end of Daly's career, George Parson Lathrop, writing in *Century Magazine,* asserted, "This manager is a general; his ability is nothing less than that of a great commander, when you reflect that he is managing and directing every day some two hundred people" (273–74).

Daly's regime marked the ascendancy of an increasingly powerful, male-dominated order of theater managers that countered threats posed by so-called petticoat governments regnant in many acting companies as well as female domestic tyrants and women's rights advocates in the larger society. The most successful nineteenth-century female manager, Laura Keene, had run her theater from 1855 to 1863 with a level of discipline in many ways comparable to that of her male contemporaries. But, whereas the discourses of conquest and bourgeois morality legitimated authoritarian male manage-ments, they undermined hers because she was a woman and an actress. Commenting on the sexist hostility she faced, Keene herself stated in a curtain speech: "unless I can meet the attack as a man, I had best own myself conquered" (Dudden 123–32). Ultimately, she could not overcome the biases pervading the media, banks, and courts that cast the actress as the savage in the gendered metadrama of American civilization and conferred the conquering role exclusively on men.

In addition to entitling men to managerial positions, discourses of conquest gave male managers greater proprietary claims and greater license to exert more stringent authority over the female than the male members of their companies. Numerous accounts by associates and memoirs of members of Daly's company attest to the pervasiveness of his supervision and his extraordinary catalogue of rules governing personal as well as professional conduct. While these rules ostensibly applied to all company members, several anecdotes indicate that male actors, whom Daly viewed as potential "conservative and prosperous capitalists," sometimes committed serious vio-lations with impunity, like improvising their own business and acknowledg-ing the audience without permission (Eytinge 116–17; Hall 188–91). But actresses, whom he viewed as "the stage's active ornaments," primary matter to be worked upon and displayed, were severely reprimanded and/or sum-marily dismissed for similar infractions (Ranous 53–54, 156–57). About one such episode May Irwin, who had acted under several managements before coming to Daly's, commented to biographer Lewis Strang: "I had never been spoken to like that in my life. And before all the company! . . . I broke down and blubbered. [He was] inexorable" (180–83). He subjected actresses to more rigorous scrutiny and to more extreme humiliation than actors in rehearsals, and he used his authority to take sexual liberties with the women that he apparently did not with the men (Skinner 82; Duncan 41). The gender dynamics of the conquest myth worked to justify these exploitations of managerial power and the double standard of sexual morality.

In forging his private empire, Daly's most self-transformational encounters with frontier savagery occurred through his direction of emotionalistic leading ladies. Rather than quell actresses' exciting displays of fervid emotionalism, he endeavored initially to manipulate and deploy such displays as his own creations in order to impress more respectable audiences with his mastery of feminine nature in all its savage beauty. Being in cahoots with Augustin on his upwardly mobile quest, Joseph wrote him while he was on tour with his company in Cincinnati in the fall of 1873: "I suppose the ladies of the company were the objects of much attention and observation at the Hotel. Did Fanny [Morant] crush 'em with her queenly presence? Did [Clara] Morris spring on their susceptibility with a 'panther-like spring'?" (Daly and Daly, 4 September 1873). Two days later, Augustin replied in the affirmative, adding "the audiences grow in quality also" (Daly and Daly, 6 September 1873). When these performers exceeded the limits of his direction and/or received what he considered too much popular or critical acclaim in their own right, he would demote them to a subordinate role in the next production and pointedly elevate another actress to the position of leading lady (Morris 319). In this context, Daly's much vaunted eschewal of the star system proved as much a power play as an aesthetic principle; he strove to ensure that his leading ladies' luminosity reflected most on him and his evolving American manhood.

The Darwinian frontier ideology informing Daly's enterprise made it especially difficult for actresses to resist his manipulations. Along with the constant threat of dismissal or salary forfeiture, an actress's challenges to managerial authority often only contributed to the savagery already projected onto her, further ripening her for taming and ennobling Daly when he prevailed. The final recourse for many actresses, after garnering the professional stature obtainable through Daly's productions, was to leave the company of their own accord. Daly interpreted these departures as violations not only of his manhood—epecially since actresses usually left to seek a more advantageous situation with a rival male manager—but of his rights of ownership and husbandry. He analogized actresses' previously "unsuspected talent" to available "free land," which he believed he had cultivated and was therefore his as of right; no one else, including the performer herself, should "reap the whole harvest" of the seeds he had sown (J. Daly 153–54).

Correspondence between the Daly brothers reveals that they attributed some of the most embarrassing defections from the company—those of

Agnes Ethel (1872), Clara Morris (1873), and Ada Dyas (1874)—to "wild passions" inspired by emotionalistic acting in popular melodramatic and tragic works. To keep such disruptive expressions of frontier savagery under tighter rein, Joseph proposed emphasizing comedy instead (Daly and Daly, 12–15 September 1874). Accordingly, when Daly opened his new theater at Broadway and 30th Street in 1879, he instituted comedy as the primary genre of theatrical conquest and assembled his most famous ensemble to play the repertoire—the Big Four comprised of character actors James Lewis and Mrs. [Ann Hartley] Gilbert, leading man John Drew, and, most luminous of all, leading lady Ada Rehan (Felheim, *Theatre* 23–26).

Daly's relationship with Rehan was distinguished from those with previous leading ladies by its longevity—she remained with him for the next twenty years until his death—and intensity. W. Graham Robertson, costume designer for Daly's Theatre, viewed their relationship as a "real-life Trilby-Svengali drama" (Felheim, *Theatre* 42). Cornelia Otis Skinner, daughter of actor Otis Skinner—who was a member of Daly's company—agrees with Robertson's assessment and explicitly divulges that the two were lovers, though Daly was a strict Catholic and remained married to his wife. "Ada Rehan, besides being leading lady," writes Skinner, "enjoyed the off-stage role of *grande-maitresse*—although *enjoyed* is a debatable word" (80–81). Deeming this leading lady a "Lioness" where others were merely "Cats," Daly endowed her with even more potent connotations of beautiful, savage nature (Felheim, *Theatre* 40–44). According to contemporaries, she was a striking figure—tall in stature, with classical facial features, long, thick reddish hair, and possessed of extraordinary wit, vitality, and athletic and vocal ability. The fact that she was also Irish-born and Catholic may have exacerbated Daly's compulsion to tame her; through her he could repress and overcome the most denigrated aspects of himself in order to ascend the phyletic ladder. He worked upon her savagery in "Old English" (Restoration and eighteenth century) and contemporary drawing-room comedies with titles such as *Needles and Pins* (1880), *Love on Crutches* (1884), and *Love in Harness* (1886). Being himself a tireless workaholic, Daly could drive Rehan to even greater exertion on the evolutionary assumption that as a woman she could endure more stress. He severely taxed her energies and health with an unrelenting year-round performance schedule. Although he allegedly adored her, he could also be devastatingly cruel during rehearsals, by reducing her to "a tear besoaked pulp" with personal insults, as the New York *Graphic* reported in 1885, or by pointedly favoring another actress in her presence (Hendricks-Wenck 128–30). Cornelia Otis Skinner assessed his intentions: "To hold the whip handle by keeping a woman of her beauty and prominence in the compromising position an extra-marital liaison involved in those cautious times was a sop to his will to power. It gave him a feeling of prestige" (80–83). Over time Rehan's position as indispensable leading lady and *grand-maitresse* became more entrenched, but the pattern of Daly temporarily pursuing other actresses to assert his sexual and managerial mastery continued into the 1890s (Duncan 38–41).

For her part, Rehan seems to have supported and complemented Daly's agenda with her own desires and ambitions, though her testimony may have been muted by the illicit nature of their personal relationship and the autocrat's edict prohibiting company members to talk to outsiders about the mechanics of his operation. After Daly died, she confided some of her feelings in a letter to longtime supporter William Winter:

> I was fully alive to all he ever did for me & he knew my devotion to him & his ambitions. It was all so well understood between us that we had really grown into being One. we [*sic*] both worked with heart & soul—for one end. My loss. No one can ever understand. (7 August 1899, Folger Shakespeare Library; qtd. in Hendricks-Wenck 320–21)

As many aspiring performers had before her, Rehan came to Daly seeking professional training and advancement, but, to an extent matched by none of her predecessors, she had fallen in love with and devoted herself to him and thus may have been more tolerant of practices that drove others away. Like Daly, she was marked by her own social stigmas, including being Irish-Catholic, an actress, and a married man's mistress, and harbored her own assimilationist ambitions, which Daly's tranformational agenda could help her fulfill. Whatever the reasons for her complicity, she attained an unprecedented level of social and professional prestige for an American actress by playing her part in the gendered metadrama of frontier conquest.

Enacting the tropes of imperial self-formation with Rehan, Daly forged an eminently civilized, expensively appointed theater. His leading lady became a dominant cultural icon of desirable femininity lauded in the popular media: "The whole woman is essentially womanly, blending much of gentle bright tenderness with visible energy and elan," gushed the New York *Sun*. As Daly's audiences grew more respectable, they were increasingly dominated by white middle- and upper-class women who, in the 1880s, specifically sought to emulate Rehan. Ladies of fashion hired couturiers to copy her costumes, and Delsarte girls imitated her stage bearing and movement. Daly catered to this market with Wednesday and Saturday matinees enabling female shoppers to consume his mises-en-scène like the goods they purchased before and after the performances (Hendricks-Wenck 121–33, 147).

While a testament to the height of respectability Daly's Theatre had achieved and a force for the expansion of American economic and cultural empire, female consumerism also raised the specter of emasculating over-civilization and domestic tyranny. For Daly personally, consuming women threatened to destabilize his autocracy by appropriating Rehan's image as their own and enacting it outside the representational frame he controlled. Their efforts also invested Rehan with enormous star power, which he had spent his career repressing. For the larger patriarchy to which Daly sought admittance, wives and daughters trying to emulate the feminine ideal Rehan embodied challenged male authority by driving markets and depleting household coffers.

Given his polite, urbane repertoire and female-dominated audiences, Daly's adaptation of *Taming of the Shrew,* which opened on 18 January 1887 with Rehan as the eponymous Katharine, may be read as a regenerative project, one fueling American economic and cultural expansion but reasserting male control of the territory. As such, the play partook of the widespread fascination with physical force T. J. Jackson Lears finds expressed in other literary forms of the period as "a return to pre-modern tales of adventure . . . when 'men sang a manlier way' " (103–4). Through manipulation of dramatic and theatrical elements Daly made this step backward in mythic time a potent thrust forward for his own and Anglo-Saxon patriarchy's imperial ambitions.

Although he cut close to one-third of Shakespeare's words, including most all of the linguistic bawdry, Daly billed his *Shrew* as the first staging of the complete play in America (Haring-Smith 54). Unlike earlier versions, his included the Induction, featuring Sly the Tinker, who, after being kicked out of a tavern by the tyrannical Hostess, falls asleep and frames the play within a dream. In an American cultural context, this device invoked the popular Rip Van Winkle story, thereby setting up Daly's adaptation as a flight from feminized overcivilization. Stylistically, Sly and the servant characters carried most all of the play's farcical elements, while the major characters were played more naturalistically in the vein of romantic comedy (Haring-Smith 60–61). Rather than suppressing the play's brutality, however, these manipulations of language, plot, and playing style allowed the play's archaic justice to be integrated into modern bourgeois consciousness (Boose 181–82).

Most potently, Daly visually superimposed the mythos of American imperialism onto Shakespeare's text by consolidating scenes transpiring in the same locale to facilitate changes of lavishly realistic sets and rearranging key events to create iconic tableaux. The production's signal iconic moment was Katharine's first entrance which was forestalled until the opening of the second act to maximize anticipation (fig. 3). Daly directed Rehan to incarnate all the primordial femininity he had her so assiduously repress in the drawing-room comedies to create a spectacle that awed fashionable audiences from New York to London to Paris. Clad in a flaming crimson gown, she made Katharine "a magnificent animal. Her rage was devastating, like some great convulsion of nature," wrote A. B. Walkley, of the *Times* (qtd. in Haring-Smith 71). Playing the savage off stage as well as on heightened the "volcanic" energy of her performance. Before the high-stakes London premiere Daly enraged Rehan by flirting with another actress in her presence. In retribution, she refused to perform. The Governor had to implore her on bended knee, whereupon, according to a witness, she took his hand to her mouth, bit his flesh "to the bone," and, with the taste of his blood still fresh on her lips, commanded the play to begin (Skinner 91–92). Graham Robertson described her ensuing entrance:

> Not a whit of her shrewishness did she spare us; her storms of passion found vent in snarls, growls, and even inarticulate screams of fury; she paced hither and thither like a caged wild beast, but her rages were magnificent like an angry sea or a sky of tempest, she blazed a fiery comet through the play, baleful but beautiful. (216)

After demonstrating the magnitude of Katharine's ferocity, Daly collapsed Shakespeare's several taming scenes into a single episode set at Petruchio's residence in the country, where the husband insisted upon taking his wife immediately after the nuptial ceremony. Thus, in Daly's version, most of the taming process coincided with the occasion of marital consummation in a place distinctly beyond city borders. As he readied himself for this conquest, Petruchio declared:

> I will be master of what is mine own:
> She is my goods, my chattels; she is my house,
> My house-stuff, my field, my barn,
> My horse, my ox, my ass, my anything.
>
> (A. Daly 50)

Arriving at the country outpost ahead of the newlyweds, Grumio recounted to Curtis, as in the original Shakespeare, Petruchio and Katharine's struggles to make the trip across rugged terrain on horseback. For U.S. audiences in the late nineteenth century, this narrative further invoked Western frontier mythology. The hero ventured away from civilization to prove his manhood in a rustic setting whose naturalness his ferocious new bride embodied.

FIG. 3. Ada Rehan as Katharine in *Taming of the Shrew.*
(Courtesy of the Art Collection of the Folger Shakespeare
Library.)

In Daly's iconic scheme, these rough circumstances mandated Petruchio's brutish behavior. With his sword holstered conspicuously over his
groin, the debonair Drew managed to play the brute convincingly by crack-
ing a whip and angrily hurling food, dishes, and blustery verbal jousts to
impress his might on Katharine (fig. 4). If, as a few commentators argued,
Katharine's conversion came too rapidly and defied the logic of human
character development, it fulfilled the logic of ennobling atavistic struggle in
the Wild West. Invoking the image of a regal lioness, Rehan described her
character as "a grand creature, a very noble nature, of high breeding . . .
high-strung and nervous, though, at the same time, strong and thoroughly

FIG. 4. John Drew as Petruchio in *Taming of the Shrew*.
(Courtesy of the Museum of the City of New York. Gift of
Mrs. John S. Garrity.)

healthy." In her estimation, the very qualities of extraordinary nobility and
power by which the lioness had heretofore defied domination enabled her
to realize when

> she had, at last, met her master. No one knew this better than she. She
> braced herself for her last grand fight, and fought it with vigor. Being

defeated, like a true soldier, her submission was absolute, and she acknowledged her conqueror as frankly as she had defied him. ("Ada Rehan's View of Katharine")

Through this encounter, Daly's Petruchio transformed himself, conquering his own bestial nature and acceding to a fuller, nobler manhood.

In celebration, Petruchio returned with his trophy to her father's house for the final banquet scene, literally and symbolically a lush spread of the fruits of conquest. For the spectacle, Daly had his scene painters and carpenters copy the Paolo Veronese painting *Marriage Feast at Cana* and filled the palatial structure with an anachronistic melange of authentic Italian, French, and English antiques and Oriental rugs (Felheim, "Career" 378). When the curtain opened on this imperial splendor (fig. 5), audiences were so dazzled they called Daly himself out for a triumphant bow, acknowledging him above Petruchio as the play's ultimate conqueror (Haring-Smith 66).

Daly's personal quest further superseded that of his Shakespearian analogue in the ensuing wager scene, in which the three new husbands—Petruchio, Lucentio, and Hortensio—bet their manhood along with their money on the obedience of their wives. When they dispatched messengers to see whose wife would obey her husband's summons, only Katharine passed the test. Her sister Bianca, seemingly the more gentle and obedient before marriage, and the Widow conspired "by the parlor fire" to defy their husbands (A. Daly 73). The capitalist who had ventured farthest and engaged with the greatest savagery won the truer wife and, in so doing, became the truer man. Following this theme, Daly's own victory was greatest of all; he had conquered the depraved theatrical frontier and made a true woman out of an actress, one truer, by implication, than the seemingly more respectable women in the audience. In the play's last moments, his Katharine bowed before the banquet table, a submissive lioness deferring to the lion king enshrined within the palatial architecture. Repeating, open-ended classical archways receded into the mist toward an indeterminate vanishing point, a scenographic realization of the mythos of infinitely expanding empire and untrammeled masculinity. This theatrical conquest promised continued triumph over both feminine savagery and overcivilization; Sly never woke up to close the frame, keeping Daly's American dream a reality.

In its initial run, *Taming of the Shrew* played 121 performances, a remarkable record for a Shakespeare play during the period, and remained a regenerative force in Daly's career through frequent revivals for the next thirteen years (Felheim, "Career" 384–85). According to Rehan, "Mr. Daly watched and directed most every performance." With each one, he reasserted his prowess

FIG. 5. Banquet scene from *Taming of the Shrew*. (Courtesy of the Art
Collection of the Folger Shakespeare Library.)

as man and maker of iconic femininity, inducing consumers to continue
copying his leading lady while reminding them of his possession of her. This
message became particularly apparent on the occasion of *Shrew's* one hun-
dredth performance, when Daly distributed to all the ladies in the audience
specially bound volumes fronted with side-by-side photographs of himself
and Rehan and containing both the verbal and iconic texts of his adaptation of
the play (Shattuck 67). After this performance he hosted a banquet on the set
with the Big Four (Rehan, Drew, Gilbert, and Lewis). The fifty-member
guest list included many important literary, theatrical, media, and business
figures, such as Horace Howard Furness, Mark Twain, Laurence Hutton,
William Winter, Bronson Howard, Lester Wallack, and Wilson Barrett,
whose admiration and respect Daly had earned over the years. With his
longtime friend General William Tecumseh Sherman as toastmaster, the
event confirmed Daly's place among the prominent ranks of American patriarchy (Haring-Smith 67).

Yet perhaps the greatest tribute to Daly's imperial capitalist self- and
nation-forming enterprise came many performances later, when officials
selected his leading lady as the model for an allegorical statue of Justice to be
Montana's exhibit at the 1893 World Columbia Exposition in Chicago, the
era's most elaborate display of American imperial power (fig. 6). According

FIG. 6. Montana Silver Statue, Miss Ada Rehan as "Justice."
(Courtesy of the Museum of the City of New York.)

to the exhibit directors, Rehan was chosen because under Daly's management she had achieved fame as "one of the finest types extant of American physical womanhood" (Ada Rehan Scrapbook). The classical form of the statue conflated the actress's apotheosis with that of the epitome of generic, conservative femininity, the American Girl, a singularly Anglo-Saxon deity, whose features were inscribed in the fair's central icon, Daniel Chester French's monumental Republic towering over the Grand Basin (Banta xxviii). Fellow American Girl iconographer Howard Chandler Christy deemed her "the culmination of mankind's long struggle upward from barbarism to civilization," feminine perfection "won from the tight fist of nature's grudging hand" (69–70). Eight feet tall and molded from unprecedented quantities of precious ore mined from the Montana wilderness, Justice, even more thoroughly than the only superficially gilded Republic, embodied the westward settlement Frederick Jackson Turner argued had defined America.

Thus emblematizing the civilization of feminine savagery, Rehan's solid silver form reiterated on the World's Fair stage the mode of imperial nation formation Daly's theater also reproduced. In his leading lady's likeness, the manager's own evolutionary progress was conserved along with that of Anglo-Saxon nationhood, which made the statue the ultimate realization of his assimilationist ambitions. Poised walking atop the world on the back of a winged eagle, scale in one hand, sword in the other, Justice proclaimed the moral righteousness of both an expanding public empire and an expanding private theatrical autocracy. Rehan's taming and Daly's heroic self-transformation informed this shining trophy, signifying continued conquest of savage nature and shrewish Others on an ever-receding American frontier line.

REFERENCES

Ada Rehan Scrapbook. Robinson-Locke Collection of Theatre Scrapbooks. No. 497. Vol. 1. Billy Rose Theater Collection, New York Public Library at Lincoln Center, New York City.

"Ada Rehan's View of Katharine." Unmarked clipping reprinting preface to *The Taming of the Shrew*, adapted by Augustin Daly, 1901 ed. Ada Rehan Personality File, Theatre Collection, Museum of the City of New York.

Banta, Martha. *Imaging American Women: Idea and Ideals in Cultural History, 1876–1918.* New York: Columbia UP, 1987.

Beer, Thomas. *The Mauve Decade: American Life at the End of the Nineteenth Century.* Intro. Frank Freidel. New York: Vintage, 1960.

Boose, Lynda E. "Scolding Brides and Bridling Scolds: Taming the Woman's Unruly Member." *Shakespeare Quarterly* 42 (Summer 1991): 179–213.

Christy, Howard Chandler. *The American Girl as Seen and Portrayed by Howard Chandler Christy.* 1906. Reprint. New York: Da Capo, 1976.

Daly, Augustin. *Taming of the Shrew, A Comedy by William Shakespeare, as Arranged by Augustin Daly.* Intro. William Winter. Privately printed for Daly. New York, 1887.

Daly, Augustin, and Joseph Daly. Correspondence, 1858–1899. 10 vols. Billy Rose Theater Collection, New York Public Library at Lincoln Center, New York City.

Daly, Joseph Francis. *The Life of Augustin Daly.* New York: Macmillan, 1917.

Dudden, Faye. *Women in the American Theatre: Actresses and Audiences, 1790–1870.* New Haven: Yale UP, 1994.

Duncan, Isadora. *My Life.* New York: Boni and Liveright, 1927.

Eytinge, Rose. *Memories of Rose Eytinge.* New York: Stokes, 1905.

Felheim, Marvin L. "The Career of Augustin Daly." Diss. Harvard U, 1948.

———. *The Theatre of Augustin Daly: An Account of the Late Nineteenth Century American Stage.* 1956. New York: Greenwood, 1969.

Hall, Margaret. "Personal Recollections of Augustin Daly, Part III." *Theatre* (August 1905): 188–91.

Haring-Smith, Tori. *From Farce to Metadrama: A Stage History of* Taming of the Shrew, *1594–1983.* Westport, CT: Greenwood, 1985.

Hendricks-Wenck, Aileen A. "Ada Rehan: American Actress (1857–1916)." Diss. Louisiana State U, 1988.

"Inauguration." *New York Times* 5 March 1869: 3.

Jennings, Francis. *The Invasion of America: Indians, Colonialism, and the Cant of Conquest.* Chapel Hill: U of North Carolina P, 1975.

Johnson, Claudia D. *American Actress: Perspective on the Nineteenth Century.* Chicago: Nelson Hall, 1984.

Kolodny, Annette. *The Lay of the Land: Metaphor as Experience and History in American Life and Letters.* Chapel Hill: U of North Carolina P, 1975.

Lathrop, George Parson. "An American School of Dramatic Art: The Inside Working of the Theatre." *Century Magazine* ns 56.34 (June 1898): 265–75.

Lears, T. J. Jackson. *No Place of Grace: Antimodernism and the Transformation of American Culture, 1880–1920.* New York: Pantheon, 1981.

McConachie, Bruce A. *Melodramatic Formations: American Theatre and Society, 1820–1870.* Iowa City: U of Iowa P, 1993.

Morris, Clara. *Life on the Stage.* New York: McClure, Phillips, 1901.

Muccigrosso, Robert. *Celebrating the New World: Chicago's Columbia Exposition of 1893.* Chicago: Ivan R. Dee, 1993.

"The New Administration." *New York Times* 5 March 1869: 6.

Norton, Anne. *Alternative Americas: A Reading of Antebellum Political Culture.* Chicago and London: U of Chicago P, 1986.

Pugh, David. *Sons of Liberty: The Masculine Mind in Nineteenth Century America.* Westport, CT, and London: Greenwood, 1983.

Ranous, Dora Knowlton. *Diary of a Daly Debutante, Being Passages from the Journal of a Member of Augustin Daly's Famous Company of Players.* New York: Duffield, 1910.

Robertson, W. Graham. *Life Was Worth Living.* New York: Harper, 1931.

Russett, Cynthia Eagle. *Sexual Science: The Victorian Construction of Womanhood*. Cambridge: Harvard UP, 1989.

Shattuck, Charles H. *Shakespeare on the American Stage*. 2 vols. Vol. 2: *From Booth and Barrett to Sothern and Marlowe*. Washington, DC: Folger Shakespeare Library, 1976–87.

Skinner, Cornelia Otis. *Family Circle*. Boston: Houghton Mifflin, 1948.

Slotkin, Richard. *Fatal Environment: The Myth of the Frontier in the Age of Industrialization, 1800–1890*. Middletown, CT: Wesleyan UP, 1986.

Smith, Henry Nash. *Virgin Land: The American West as Symbol and Myth*. Cambridge: Harvard UP, 1950.

Strang, Lewis. *Famous Actresses of the Day in America*. Boston: L. C. Page, 1899.

Sun 21 February 1886. Untitled clipping in vol. 16 of Daly's Theatre Scrapbooks, 1863–99. 43 vols. Billy Rose Theater Collection, New York Public Library at Lincoln Center, New York City.

Trachtenberg, Alan. *The Incorporation of America: Culture and Society in the Gilded Age*. New York: Hill and Wang, 1982.

Turner, Frederick Jackson. "The Significance of the Frontier in American History." *The Turner Thesis: Concerning the Role of the Frontier in American History*. Ed. and intro. George Rogers Taylor. 3d ed. Lexington, MA, Toronto, and London: D. C. Heath, 1972.

Van Alstyne, Richard W. *The Rising American Empire*. New York and London: Norton, 1974.

Wilmeth, Don B., and Rosemary Cullen, eds. and intro. *Plays by Augustin Daly*. Cambridge and New York: Cambridge UP, 1984.

Leigh Woods

American Vaudeville, American Empire

If we look at the facts, we find that culture is an index of activity, not of ancestral tradition and opinion. . . . [It is] the result of more satisfying combinations of consumption.
—Simon Patten, "The Reconstruction of Economic Theory"

[Americans] never recognized themselves as an empire, never felt bound by the responsibility (or the moral corruption) that comes with the exercise of so much power. Unlike the Spanish, the French, and the English, they did not create permanent institutions with a set of rules, regulations, and doctrines to deal with their possessions, and, because it was more a question of the marketplace than an occupation of territory, did not feel the need to do so.
—Ariel Dorfman, *The Empire's Old Clothes*

Vaudeville became America's preeminent popular entertainment a century ago in close conjunction with the end of the Indian wars and with a military adventurism marked most conspicuously by the Spanish-American War. In this light, references to empire might seem to have fallen merely circumstantially in a form that probably could not have avoided reflecting an expansionist ethos in any case.[1] Over the past century, however, American influence has not derived foremost from martial exploits, any more than it has proven *only* coercive or figured exclusively in those parts of the world formerly colonized by Europe.

In the last one hundred years, popular entertainment has figured centrally in promoting American influence in surprisingly varied forms and in many parts of the world. If, as Julie Stone Peters has contended, culture belongs to no one (204), popular entertainment has shown itself particularly adaptive in reconfiguring elements of foreign culture to aggrandize Americans' wishful sense of their nation's mission as cultural emissary around the globe and as successor to Europe in this regard. Seamus Deane has written of an "American empire combin[ing] the discourses of moral and material improvement" (359). Vaudeville, by serving up morality only in very light doses and by rendering it playful and materialized, predicted the direction of

73

cultural imperialism American style. Vaudeville signaled the growing capacity of American popular entertainments to create compelling images of both an audience and a nationhood defined in steady opposition to existing European models.

I shall consider vaudeville's part in defining American identity in three ways: first, in its project to recruit theatrical stars from Europe; second, in its appropriation of these stars by removing or adulterating their European trappings and substituting American ones in their place; and, finally, by its standing as a prototype for subsequent American popular entertainments that have reflected nationalistic values. I hope to show how vaudeville's producers and its audiences deferred to European culture in the very act of subsuming it and how, in subsuming it, they developed an ideology to challenge Europe's cultural sway. Images will emerge from this account suggesting not so much that foreign stage stars "performed" America in vaudeville as that vaudeville surrounded these stars with fare and fanfare implying their obsolescence. In this sense, vaudeville promoted performances of America by harnessing and relegating the signifying power of the European stage actors it recruited and by treating these stars as embodiments of the sort of European culture growing numbers of Americans believed to be in a state of eclipse.

Through their efforts, vaudeville's producers and its consumers played a role in transforming America, within twenty years, from a postcolonial nation essentially servile in its deference to European culture into one capable of asserting its own values in cultural spheres that resonated with the overtones of power. The synthesizing vigor of American popular culture beginning, perhaps, with vaudeville helped underwrite an ideology that has the American nation mediating between its former colonial masters and those nations like itself, but newer and poorer, that seek to free themselves from positions of cultural subservience.

Borrowing International Stage Stars

American popular entertainments have recommended themselves for consumption abroad in part by reconfiguring elements of other nations' cultures. Vaudeville pioneered a particularly vital kind of reconfiguration through its distinctively polyglot bills. "Refined" vaudeville staked its commercial identity by recruiting performers from cultural spheres previously too highfalutin for a form tracing its genesis from barroom entertainments. Upon first entering vaudeville in the 1890s, groups of "refined" performers brought their fame with them variously from grand opera, from Lyceums and Chautauquas, from ballet and what would become modern dance, and most glamorously, perhaps, from the legitimate stages of Europe.

These categories of performers never constituted anything more than a conspicuous minority among vaudeville's staple acts in song-and-dance, monologue and patter, animal acts, blackface and other forms of ethnic humor, and feats of skill and daring. In consequence, performers from the more exclusive venues worked by their mere presence to set up cultural hierarchies on each of the bills they helped constitute. Vaudeville's modular acts and its lack of narrative or structural continuity—the bill did not include even a master of ceremonies—promoted exchanges between different realms of culture.

From 1897 until the end of World War I, a succession of foreign stage stars appeared in vaudeville, including, in order of their first appearances there, Maurice Barrymore, Fanny Janauschek, Charles Hawtrey, Jessie Millward, Lillie Langtry, Mrs. Patrick Campbell, Sarah Bernhardt, Olga Nethersole, and Alla Nazimova. The British stage was most frequently represented among this group, in a sampling that typifies America's cultural fealty to its former colonizer.[2] If the recruitment of these stars commenced in a spirit of deference, however, it came quickly to betoken the absorbent qualities of American culture in general and of American popular entertainment in particular.

These actors were drawn into vaudeville by weekly salaries far in excess of what they could have earned on the legitimate stage. Maurice Barrymore first capitalized on vaudeville's demand for ready-made refined attractions when he received three times his usual fee. His appearances in vaudeville over the last four years of his career initiated a pattern shared among many of the major stage stars to enter vaudeville, who also made their entry in the waning years of their careers. Nevertheless, Barrymore and the stars who followed him became instant "headliners" in vaudeville, and they almost always performed in the most elegant and expensive theaters among the hundreds that made up the far-flung vaudeville chains. Generally, foreign stars favored the circuits east of Chicago, and they often concentrated their efforts in vaudeville's showcase theaters in and around New York City, where they could remain within range of more glamorous engagements in the legitimate theater and the engines of journalism that perpetuated their fame by setting it into fullest transatlantic context.

The title of Barrymore's staple play in vaudeville was *A Man of the World,* suggesting the contradictions inherent in the self-consciously egalitarian brand of cosmopolitanism vaudeville cultivated when it featured noted

European actors. The foreign stars who followed Barrymore into vaudeville qualified as persons of the world, even as he had, through their dress, their accents, and their combination of novelty within vaudeville and their fame drawn from outside it. The commercial appeal of such stars was often reinforced by press coverage of their arrivals by steamship, their pronouncements on the United States, and their encomia of vaudeville and its passion for efficiency. Once inside vaudeville theaters foreign stars' association with their countries of origin was often underscored in other ways, as when, for instance, house orchestras played "The Marseillaise" to herald Bernhardt's entrances or Rachmaninoff at the conclusion of Nazimova's act ("Nazimova"; and "Bernhardt" 66).

Furthermore, European stage stars often appeared in vaudeville theaters decorated in tribute to European art and architecture. Lillie Langtry was hired to open B. F. Keith and F. F. Proctor's Fifth Avenue Theatre in New York in October 1906, and her presence on this occasion was central to the producers' mission of transforming their theater from a well-known legitimate house into one that featured refined vaudeville in a theater fairly festooned with visual quotations from the European past.[3] Langtry and Mrs. Patrick Campbell were also noted for the regularity with which they showcased the latest French fashions in their vaudeville engagements. Thus were high fashion and high art attached to eminent British actresses and exposed to a much broader audience than had witnessed such attractions previously, in their variously glamorous combinations, on legitimate stages across North America.

Edward F. Albee, who decorated many of vaudeville's most refined theaters, believed in an egalitarian and yet patronizing way that such lavishness served "the education of the people" (Copley 47). Albee had, in fact, pioneered the deployment of European elegance in vaudeville while designing his partner Keith's New Theater in Boston in the early 1890s, complete with its "marble pillars, pilasters, gargoyles, and ornamental ironwork, as well as stained glass" (Allen 184–85). Still later, as vaudeville grew in prestige and pretentiousness, Albee became known for acquiring paintings of the European masters to decorate his various theaters, and those paintings together with his decidedly Eurocentric tastes in architecture helped him collapse centuries of European art into a veritable postmodern collage within the walls of his theaters. Albee and vaudeville's other magnates committed themselves to a species of spectacular ostentation in line with the spirit of architect Stanford White's buccaneering dictum that America had the right "to obtain art wherever she could" (Cashman 390). "Art" was defined as that which came from Europe (fig. 7), and this notion was

"Their agents search every capital of Europe"

FIG. 7. "Their agents search every capital of Europe."
European attractions came to be prized as highly in vaudeville
as they had been on the legitimate stage and in opera. The
growing commodification of such performers in vaudeville
followed as a logical extension of their endowments in
European high culture, mimicked in the dress of the agent,
and of vaudeville producers' attempts to elevate the prestige, as
well as the ticket prices, of their only recently "refined" form.
(Courtesy of the University of Michigan Library.)

reiterated and buttressed, on the stage as well as around it, when European stars appeared in the glittering and derivative settings vaudeville's foremost producers favored.

Vaudeville producers were not being merely deferential, however, when they allowed stage stars—like all other performers on their bills—to direct and produce their own acts. By encouraging such autonomy, the producers reduced their overhead and so gained competitive advantage over the more centrally produced and capital-intensive legitimate theater. Through such cost-cutting measures, vaudeville producers were able to pay stars much more than the legitimate theater could and so promote themselves as the ultimate purchasers of refined European attractions.

Vaudeville managers also encouraged their entertainers to perform in presentational ways. As a distinct class within vaudeville, stage stars' tendency to face their audiences frequently and unabashedly derived partly from the relatively poor quality of vaudeville's stock scenery and standardized lighting plots and partly from the carryover effects of vaudeville's many solo performers who needed to pitch their efforts directly at an audience known for its restlessness, impatience, and distractability. More direct and unmediated ways of addressing their vaudeville audiences also suited refugees from the legitimate stage well at a time when their long-standing centrality in production had been eroded by the first generation of modern stage directors. Exhibiting and proclaiming themselves directly to the audience was a way for refugees from the legitimate stage to flaunt the stigma that supposedly attended a less prestigious form, to reassert their dominion over theatrical production, and to elicit responses to their efforts in a manner consistent with Albee's notion of educating the people in environments that evoked the height and the essence of European civilization.

Appropriation as Cultural Imperialism

Vaudeville helped perpetuate a style of virtuosic, heroic, and baldly presentational performing that had come to seem old-fashioned on legitimate stages, and it prolonged the stage careers of stars accustomed to star turns and the sort of presentational performing its audiences embraced. In this connection, vaudeville enlisted foreign stage stars in a spirit that was, on its surface at least, memorial and deferential. Yet, even while refined vaudeville was commemorating European stage stars, it was also in the business of setting such figures into more popular, modern, and decidedly American contexts.

Vaudeville producers achieved much of their institutional control over foreign stage stars by inserting their generally serious fare into bills with seven or eight other "acts," in vaudeville's atomizing parlance. Most or all of these acts would have been light, and such billings worked not only to set the stars' dramatic offerings against a backdrop of pratfalls, stunts, and topical or local references, but also to put stage actors of note into close proximity with ethnic stereotypes of much rougher derivation than the stars themselves embodied.

All the while, the stars understood that they had to conform to many of the same specifications applied to even the lowliest acts that surrounded them on the bills. The most important and universal condition was that of brevity, including an absolute limit on the length of time any act, including headlined ones, could take up. Headlined performers were further expected to make the earliest appearance possible within their own acts and to achieve the same successive and growing climaxes demanded of less prestigious performers. Such climaxes took place much more frequently in vaudeville than on the legitimate stage. Indeed, headliners' eventual appearances near the ends of their bills represented the last and the largest climax within the structure of the vaudeville show and so put added pressure on stage stars to conform to the rhythm and pacing of the preceding elements on their bills.

Such pressures in vaudeville left little time for the kind of lengthy exposition used in full-length plays to prime the stars' grand entrances. Nor did it leave time for reappearances in a succession of new costumes that Lillie Langtry and Mrs. Patrick Campbell, in particular, had employed as models for the latest European fashions, the former in her fondness for Parisian designer houses and the latter in her uses of couture in the name of emancipation (Kaplan and Stowell 80). Vaudeville's passion for "efficiency," in these instances, fell squarely in line with Progressives' affinity for Taylorism (named after the father of the assembly line) as the credo of industry.

In this sense, stars saw themselves recruited onto the figurative assembly line that had been constituted in the vaudeville producers' modular manner of producing and packaging their acts. Jessie Millward and Mrs. Patrick Campbell commented, favorably while touring and damningly later, on vaudeville's mania for efficiency and the ways they had been made to feel mechanized and objectified as headliners.[4] Mrs. Campbell, in particular, identified the relationship between vaudeville's own brand of Taylorism and its demand for mounting climaxes and serial performances, when she complained: "I had to kill a man twice a day and shriek—and it had to be done from the heart—the Americans see through 'bluff' " (241).

More tellingly and subtly, perhaps, vaudeville converted foreign luminaries from stars into its trademark headliners. This transformation had the effect of integrating international celebrities into the accelerated rhythms, incongruous juxtapositions, and cultural leveling characteristic of vaudeville. "Stars" were seen to have derived from the natural world, as connoted by the word that categorized them in legitimate venues. As headliners, however, these same figures saw themselves defined less by the qualities of their acting and more by vaudeville's mechanical way of constructing and publicizing its varied fare. In vaudeville, foreign stage stars also found themselves constructed more than ever before by commercial journalism. Their names were used to promise an initial sensation, headline fashion; the stars delivered that sensation, though briefly, on the bills and then were moved along vaudeville chains by the week in reconstituted bills, where their headlined act had continually to find a new point of balance with the fare around them.

Even when stars appeared in foreign plays in vaudeville, or spoke their own language there, as Bernhardt did, they did so in a setting that put high culture into a conspicuous but often subordinate, or at least tightly bounded, position (fig. 8). Foreign stars were invariably sandwiched on bills between typical vaudeville fare, and the "chasers" that closed bills following most headliners (who usually came next-to-last) were often nonspeaking acts, constituting the least prestigious stratum among vaudeville entertainments. Vaudeville introduced stage stars not by means of the cohesive narrative exposition typical of full-length plays, but rather through a series of at least a half-dozen acts of various descriptions, none of them linked by theme or content to the one-acts or the cuttings from full-length plays in which the stars appeared. Furthermore, there are instances of other more lowly performers on the bills burlesquing either the stars themselves or the pieces they performed that must have seemed lofty and pretentious in conjunction with vaudeville's standard offerings.

Generally, however, a more reverential attitude prevailed when foreign stars played in vaudeville, and this was certainly the case in May 1913, when Keith and Albee used Bernhardt not merely to open, but rather to consecrate their recently acquired Palace Theatre near the heart of New York's Times Square. Bernhardt's iconic function in her first Palace engagement resembled Langtry's in transforming the Fifth Avenue from a legitimate house into a vaudeville theater well furnished in European gloss. Bernhardt's presence also legitimated a new price scale that extended upward, for the first time in vaudeville, to two dollars for orchestra seating at the Palace.

By the time of World War I, producers were positioning vaudeville as a guardian of European culture at precisely the time when that culture was seen to be in danger of destroying itself. Bernhardt then appeared in

FIG. 8. Sarah Bernhardt at the Palace Theatre. This image of a Bernhardt slightly more youthful than the actual one graced the program on the Palace Theatre, New York, for her first appearances there in May 1913. On the one hand, her image largely fills the inset and is surrounded with imperial icons in the form of crown and fleurs de lis. On the other hand, such trappings have been appropriated and bracketed by the Palace Theatre, whose name takes pride of place. (Courtesy of the Museum of the City of New York.)

patriotic vehicles, first as Joan of Arc and later in a topical work called *From the Theatre to the Field of Honor,* written expressly for her to use during her last vaudeville tour. The wartime re-recruitment of actresses who signified as broadly as Bernhardt and Lillie Langtry, who also toured again, suggested a brand of entertainment capable of revitalizing tradition or of replacing it entirely (fig. 9).

Even before the war, however, vaudeville's leading producers had seen a connection between the domestic monopoly they had cultivated and an international monopoly that would have extended their influence—together with American free enterprise—to Europe. Such visions held Europe riper for colonizing (though its cultural materials were hardly "raw" in the common estimate) than were less familiar, less "refined," and more far-flung places. In this connection, vaudeville worked to challenge the fealty to Europe that had long characterized the American cultural scene, and, although vaudeville never succeeded in exporting itself in any significant way, the American films that flourished first under its sponsorship would do so after the war.

The activities of Martin Beck exemplify the efforts of vaudeville producers to extend their reach internationally. The year before he recruited Bernhardt, Beck had found himself desperate to strengthen his position at the helm of the western Orpheum circuit against the ascendance of Keith and Albee at the head of vaudeville's vast booking system and its chains of theaters in the eastern states. Accordingly, Beck concluded an agreement with British producer Alfred Butt to form an international circuit that would "ultimately encircle the globe" (Grau 279). This circuit would have joined Beck's chain of Orpheum theaters to the London Palace, which Butt controlled, to prestigious music halls in Paris, Berlin, Glasgow, Aberdeen, Liverpool, Birmingham, Manchester, Bristol, and to seventeen other halls in smaller cities around Great Britain. At odds with Keith after a recent lawsuit, F. F. Proctor may have been party to this agreement, or he may have concluded separate agreements with Butt and the American agent William Morris that would have booked his acts and Beck's into the London Palace in exchange for taking performers from that theater into their own vaudeville houses (Marston 108).

Beck's grand design fell victim to Keith and Albee's final success, by 1912, in bringing refined vaudeville together with its putative showcase, the Palace in New York City, under their exclusive control. In this way, they removed what would have become Beck's showcase theater—and Beck, too, as a rival seeking international visibility in order to contest their domestic monopoly over refined vaudeville. In a way that signified the growing

ADIEU

FIG. 9. The Palace Theatre presents Sarah Bernhardt in
Vaudeville. Besides documenting one of the more grandiose
phases of a career nearing its end, this photograph marks the
passing of a larger cultural and imperial order in which
Bernhardt was contained and, in some ways, herself had come
to signify. (Courtesy of the Theatre Collection, Special
Collections Library, University of Michigan.)

reach of popular culture in the United States, however—and of American commercial monopolies over the world economy—"playing the Palace" became a standard American idiom for reaching the pinnacle of success in any endeavor at the same time that it trivialized palaces as a generic category.

Bills that included international stars embraced the world in figurative terms that recapitulated vaudeville producers' most grandiose designs and America's as well. In January 1918, during the last year she toured in vaudeville, Bernhardt played Joan of Arc with, among other acts, Haruka Onoki, billed as "the Japanese prima donna," at the Palace. For her next engagement at the Brooklyn Orpheum, Bernhardt performed in a French patriotic play in a breeches role as a "youthful standard bearer, a former actor and poet, mortally wounded yet determined to save his battallion's flag from enemy hands" (Skinner 324). In this piece she shared billing with "The Children of Confucius" and with the "Flatlows," billed as "sammy" (i.e., blackfaced) singers ("Bernhardt" 68). America's was a friendly embrace, at least as it was oriented to refer to its wartime allies, but it was a controlling one, too, with its constant reminders of the permeability of American culture and the volatility of American tastes.[5]

Prewar bills had also evoked American empire, though in less ostentatious ways. In 1898, Fanny Janauschek, like Maurice Barrymore, appeared opposite the "War Graph," involving filmed footage (and re-creations) of the Spanish-American War. The presence of Josephine Gassman and her Pickaninnies on the same bill, together with Bert Williams and George Walker, billed as "the Best of all 'Coon' Comedians" in this instance (Janauschek playbill) but occasionally as "The Tobasco Senegambians,"[6] conjured up the image of a single, inclusive American family. The blackface humor in which Williams and Walker specialized was also better integrated in the proceedings than the heavyset and magisterial Janauschek and her own associations with a German empire noted for its only relatively recent and still-growing role in the "scramble for Africa" that had followed the Berlin Conference of 1885 (Deane 355). In this instance, a crude prefiguration of multiculturalism served for purposes of display, subjecting Janauschek to the synthesizing capacities of vaudeville in ways that reconfigured and to some extent trivialized her.

In November 1913, the English actress Olga Nethersole appeared on a bill with motion pictures showing the passage of the first ship through the Panama Canal.[7] The canal's promotion in vaudeville must have seemed quite wholesome, however, when joined with the cutting from Nethersole's torrid *Sappho,* a play William Winter included among a group of works about fallen women he termed "shockingly pernicious in their influence, and not less so because tagged with the sickening putridity of 'moral lessons' " (337). Many would have been happy to see Nethersole's "moral lessons," set in France and associated with Continental abandon, qualified and made the more wholesome in association with an American-made, American-controlled body of water built in the name of international partnership and trade. Images of empire building framed in these terms would have been made to seem especially innocent in conjunction with those spectacles of the feminine (though itself heavily commodified) erotic that the foreign stars so often brought with them into vaudeville.[8]

All of the European stars I have mentioned were headliners. In vaudeville, however, these figures' residual status was subject to the responses of audiences that did not necessarily receive them as headliners as warmly as they did "lesser" elements on the bills, including blackfaced entertainers, film footage of canals, or wartime propaganda, for that matter. In this sense, vaudeville bills represented tentative hierarchies, composed and initiated in a European key in the previous examples but subject to the capricious nature of individual response and to growing measures of American chauvinism.

Such hierarchies were made more tentative, and more volatile, too, by the prominence of actresses among them. Foreign actresses served refined vaudeville as a legitimating matrix. On the one hand, advertising and promotion portrayed actors such as Bernhardt, Nazimova, and Langtry in such a way that they would personify their countries of origin: France, Russia, and Great Britain, respectively. On the other hand, associations between these noted actresses' countries of origin and the subordination of European high culture to American popular culture were strengthened by wartime tours and underscored, in Bernhardt's and Nazimova's cases, by the actresses' appearances in playlets linking the nations of their birth with hypothetical outcomes driven by American military might.

Bernhardt appeared in two such vehicles during her 1917–18 tour of vaudeville, as the last appearances she made in the United States. The first of these pieces, in which she acted a "youthful standard bearer," was the aforementioned *From the Theatre to the Field of Honor,* whose action explicitly weds the world of entertainment to the world of combat. Bernhardt's second patriotic piece was even more direct in its deference to American sympathies and American power. It was called *Arrière les huns* ("Stopping the Germans"), and in it she played "a French Countess who refused to leave her chateau during the German invasion and gave shelter to French and American soldiers" (Bernhardt obituary).

As the final one among the great international actresses to enter the form, Russian expatriate Alla Nazimova caught vaudeville's appropriative

FIG. 10. Alla Nazimova in *War Brides*. Alla Nazimova is second from the right, and her husband, Charles Bryant, third from the left. The setting and dress suggest a sort of generic image of middle Europe. This image is consistent, on the one hand, with the actress's interest in creating a universal drama before a mass audience and, on the other, with the scant scenic resources typical of vaudeville and with the form's tendency to mix and elide national referents. (Courtesy of the University of Michigan Library.)

project at its crest in 1915, two years before America's entry into World War I. Her play was Marion Craig Wentworth's *War Brides*. This piece set out the consequences of empires contested in traditional ways by forcing its female characters (including Nazimova's) to marry men in order to replenish anticipated losses in an unnamed warring country (fig. 10). The "war brides" were then left alone to absorb the deaths-in-battle of their young husbands. Events in the play had been inspired by Kaiser Wilhelm II's directive at the beginning of World War I that all German recruits marry before departing for the front, with a view to procreation as antidote to the possibility of a long war.

In September 1914, four months before beginning what would prove to be her first vaudeville tour among several, Nazimova recalled her youthful dream of acting in plays that would be "characteristic of each country, in each of the great countries. I wanted to play in English in England—in France in French—in the German Empire in German and in Russia in Russian" ("Nazimova"). She then used her vaudeville engagement as a stepping stone into films, with her cinematic version of *War Brides* making her a new kind of star at Metro Studios by the end of the war. Silent films only advanced Nazimova's dream of overcoming language barriers country by country, and the actress showed herself more than willing to exploit an emerging branch of popular entertainment that favored images over words.

Nazimova's yearning after international expression was nurtured by film as the popular entertainment that, before the advent of television, lent itself best to export. By virtue of her visionary sense of the possibilities of popular entertainment, which brought her into vaudeville before she made her first film, Nazimova can be said to have "performed" America more consciously and dutifully than any of her noted predecessors from the legitimate stage. Indeed, she may have embraced this brand of performance consistent with her own notions of acculturation and assimilation. In contrast, the group of European actors who preceded Nazimova in vaudeville had seen their signifying capacities merely subverted in accordance with the ascendance of nativist and, later, xenophobic values. In this respect, noted foreign actors before Nazimova might be said to have performed America in vaudeville only in negative and, probably, in largely unwitting ways. Nevertheless, these stars' recruitment and their reconfiguration by vaudeville testify to the subtle and often indirect political ramifications of popular entertainments.

Vaudeville's Imperial Legacy

Nazimova's vaudeville piece and the film that sprang from it were preachy in a way that demonstrated many Americans' burgeoning feelings of moral superiority over Europe and Europeans. Such superiority came from a new capacity to distinguish American influence, derived from culture and capital, from the territorial acquisition and escalating militarism that had precipitated World War I. The films that succeeded vaudeville as America's foremost popular entertainment in the war's aftermath would prove influential in creating little outposts of American culture in darkened rooms across the globe, their spinning reels borrowing from vaudeville's mechanical, segmented, and serial manner of presenting its entertainment.

The discontinuous and fleeting images typical of vaudeville, and rendered up in the motion pictures that first found popularity on its own bills, grew until they began to contest the ability to speak particular languages in particular countries. Zygmunt Bauman has written that the "reproduction of the capitalist system is . . . achieved through individual freedom (in the form of consumer freedom, to be precise), and not through its suppression" (51). A virtual treasury of highly attractive and readily consumable images, minted by an entertainment industry that has continued to proliferate and mutate until the present day, has conferred on America its own and, perhaps, its most distinctive successes as an imperial force.

The nation has tried in various ways to captivate the world. If it has not succeeded, it has surely inspired widespread imitation of its fixation with images suggestive of its own inclusiveness and the correlative richness of its material resources. The current vogues for cyberspace and virtual reality descend from the easy accessibility of vaudeville's decontextualized images, later disembodied and shrouded in silence for projection on screens and, still later, disseminated in ever-growing numbers and multiplying venues all over the world.

Technology, like culture, according to Julie Stone Peters, may belong to no one. If this is so, America's technological offspring, like vaudeville's in films, may yet recoil on the nation as films did in usurping their originating matrix. Or the community of nations may yet synthesize itself into a composite identity through the wonders of microchips, telecommunications, and screens as substitutes or synecdoches for lived experience. Such an outcome might reformat America in various versions abroad or lead it to another of its own reconstitutions, in turn—or both. Should any of these possibilities come to pass, however, it would stand as America's contribution to the history of empires. I hope to have shown how such contribution has come in part from the energy of American popular culture and from the synthetic capacity that vaudeville, in particular, demonstrated in offering up a still largely Eurocentric version of multiculturalism that also anticipated some of the salient features of what has come to be known as postmodernism.

NOTES

1. The Caribbean, in particular, became an imperial arena of great importance once the Spanish-American War yielded up the former Spanish possessions of Cuba and Puerto Rico. The first island came under U.S. influence, and the latter became a U.S. possession closer to the European model. These developments, in turn, fed the United States's meddling in the internal affairs of the Dominican Republic and Haiti and strengthened its proprietary attitude toward the Western Hemisphere as a whole, leading

to the building of the Panama Canal. Venezuela also fell within the sphere of U.S. influence once the Rockefellers and Standard Oil began to tap petroleum reserves there. American presence in the Pacific increased due to acquisition of the Philippines (also spoils of the war with Spain) and of Hawaii, Samoa, and the Aleutian Islands as well as military interventions in China during the 1890s and the first decade of the new century.

2. Janauschek traced her reputation to the newly imperialistic Germany and Nazimova to the more established imperial Russia. Bernhardt, of course, enjoyed a kind of celebrity that in some ways transcended her own clear associations with France, although her far-flung international tours were tribute in themselves to her nation's reach as a diplomatic and imperial power in its own right.

3. The color scheme alone for the remodeled Fifth Avenue included references to "Parisian gray, chartreuse green . . . deep Chambertin red . . . Burgundy red . . . [and] absinthe green," according to one newspaper account of the grand opening. Large painted panels, done in the style of noted European expatriate and Renaissance imitator Domenico Tojetti, were also prominently featured ("Langtry").

4. Millward later complained, "When the first week of [her vaudeville tour] was over, I caught myself jumping out of bed in the middle of nights and rushing to the door mechanically as if I were going to take another car to somewhere or other" ("Millward"). The play her countryman Charles Hawtrey brought with him into vaudeville, and played in parallel with Millward's first tour, was called *Time Is Money.*

5. One sign of Bernhardt's concession to America's commercial and military power lay in her willingness during wartime—which she had not shown during her 1912–13 vaudeville tour—to appear with blackface performers. Her compromise suggests one of the more sinister sides to America's visions of democracy as these extended and promoted themselves abroad.

6. This was the billing they enjoyed when featured with Maurice Barrymore in *A Man of the World* at Keith's Union Square, in April 1897 (*New York Clipper*).

7. These films, like those of the Spanish-American War, must have been staged in some measure, too, since the Canal did not open formally until August 1914.

8. No fewer than four of the other foreign stars among the women—namely Langtry, Mrs. Patrick Campbell, Bernhardt, and Nazimova—also appeared in vaudeville in plays involving some degree of "fallenness" in their characters.

REFERENCES

Allen, Robert. C. *Horrible Prettiness: Burlesque and American Culture.* Chapel Hill: U of North Carolina P, 1991.

Bauman, Zygmunt. *Intimations of Postmodernity.* London: Routledge, 1992.

Bernhardt obituary. Clipping without source or date. Firestone Library, Princeton U.

"Bernhardt, Sarah." Robinson Locke Collection, vols. 66 and 68. Billy Rose Theater Collection, New York Public Library at Lincoln Center, New York City.

Campbell, Mrs. Patrick. *My Life and Some Letters.* London: Hutchinson, 1922.

Cashman, Sean Dennis. *America in the Age of the Titans: The Progressive Era and World War I.* New York: New York UP, 1988.

Copley, Frank B. "The Story of a Great Vaudeville Manager." *American Magazine* 94 (December 1922): 46–47, 152–55.

Deane, Seamus. "Imperialism/Nationalism." *Critical Terms for Literary Study*. 2nd ed. Ed. Frank Lentricchia and Thomas McLaughlin. Chicago: U of Chicago P, 1995. 354–68.

Dorfman, Ariel. *The Empire's Old Clothes: What the Lone Ranger, Babar, and Other Innocent Heroes Do to Our Minds*. New York: Pantheon, 1983.

Grau, Robert. *The Business Man in the Amusement World*. New York: Broadway Publishing, 1910.

Janauschek playbill. MWEZ + n.c. 13,387. Billy Rose Theater Collection, New York Public Library at Lincoln Center, New York City.

Kaplan, Joel H., and Sheila Stowell. *Theatre and Fashion: Oscar Wilde to the Suffragettes*. Cambridge: Cambridge UP, 1994.

"Langtry, Lillie." Robinson Locke Collection, vol. 310. Billy Rose Theater Collection, New York Public Library at Lincoln Center, New York City.

Marston, William Moulton, and John Henry Feller. *F. F. Proctor, Vaudeville Pioneer*. New York: Richard R. Smith, 1943.

"Millward, Jessie." Robinson Locke Collection, envelope 1478. Billy Rose Theater Collection, New York Public Library at Lincoln Center, New York City.

"Nazimova, Alla." Robinson Locke Collection, vol. 357. Billy Rose Theater Collection, New York Public Library at Lincoln Center, New York City.

New York Clipper 10 April 1897: 92.

Patten, Simon. "The Reconstruction of Economic Theory." 1912. *Essays in Economic Theory*. New York: Alfred A. Knopf, 1924. 273–340.

Peters, Julie Stone. "Intercultural Performance, Theatre Anthropology, and the Imperialist Critique." *Imperialism and Theatre: Essays on World Theatre, Drama and Performance*. Ed. J. Ellen Gainor. London: Routledge, 1995. 199–213.

Skinner, Cornelia Otis. *Madame Sarah*. Boston: Houghton Mifflin, 1967.

Winter, William. *The Wallet of Time*. 2 vols. New York: Moffat, Yard, 1913.

Charlotte Canning

"The Most American Thing in America": Producing National Identities in Chautauqua, 1904–1932

Teddy Roosevelt's exuberant pronouncement about Chautauqua, as quoted in the title of this essay, was eagerly taken up by everyone involved, from founders to spectators, as a particularly appropriate description. Seen as definitively of the "United States," the term *Chautauqua* came to mean entertainment and education, open debate and the inculcation of values, and commonality and difference. Thriving in rural areas, once a year it brought live music, singers, lecturers, comic performers, eminent public figures, and inspirational speakers to isolated communities. Unlike other popular touring forms—vaudeville, medicine shows, circuses, or additional suspect entertainments—Chautauqua was considered respectable and safe as well as desirable. Communities throughout the West and Midwest welcomed the Chautauqua and encouraged family attendance. The sight of the characteristic brown tent "meant Chautauqua and nothing but" (Horner 185). The circuits lasted from 1904 to 1932 and left an indelible mark on the millions who witnessed them. Everyone who wrote or commented on this forum celebrated its "Americanness," constructing it as the clearest expression of what was best about the nation and what it meant to be a citizen of the United States.

The circuit Chautauquas were mass entertainment before the technology of mass entertainment. People in areas as scattered as the Dakotas, Ohio, Georgia, and Utah all might see the same quartets, orchestras, impersonators, and speakers, and all knew that other towns and counties, too, were hosting the same events. The repetition of content and of form was a crucial aspect of Chautauqua's identity as purely "American." Loren Kruger, writing on the Federal Theatre Project that began in 1935, asserts that the argument for a national theater in the United States was not for an institution located in the capital but "for *federated* theaters whose national standing might no longer exclusively depend on the mass presence of the national audience in one place, but which might include a national federation of local audiences" (5). Before the Federal Theatre Project, the circuit Chautauquas created one version of the "federated" theater that both positioned itself and was positioned by the country as national. Chautauqua helped mold and was molded by the dominant shape of national identity.

I

> "I do not think any country . . . but America could produce such gatherings as Chautauquas."
> —Jesse L. Hurlbut, *The Story of Chautauqua*

Chautauqua's first and most enduring incarnation was (and is) in upstate New York. Originally, it provided summer training for Methodist Sunday School teachers, but by 1876, two years into its existence, it was a source of nondenominational (but still heavily Protestant) general education for anyone interested. Founded by John Heyl Vincent, later a Methodist bishop, and Lewis Miller, an inventor and businessman, the Chautauqua Institution expanded to include the first correspondence degree program in the United States, the Chautauqua Literary and Scientific Circle. This combination of correspondence and on-site programming identified Chautauqua as a place for self-improvement and informed discussion.

The Chautauqua Institution, or Assembly, as it was first called, was the first version of Chautauqua to be identified as "American." This is nowhere clearer than in the preface to Jesse Hurlbut's 1921 history of the institution. It consists primarily of quotations from eminent people who all stress the link between Chautauqua and the United States, usually by conflating the two. A chaplain of the United States Senate wrote, "If you have not spent a week at Chautauqua, you do not know your own country" (qtd. in Hurlbut xvi). This unified view of the U.S.A. and Chautauqua would continue to be a part of the discourse of Chautauqua as it expanded. Being created equal, in Chautauqua terms, meant being the same. Chautauqua was thus the highest expression of democracy; as one commentator said: "It is the glory of America that it believes that all that anybody knows everybody should know" (qtd. in Hurlbut xvii). Given this overwhelming sentiment, it is not surprising that Chautauqua did not remain confined to New York.

Quickly other towns and counties began to set up Chautauquas of their own. By the end of the nineteenth century the movement had stretched as far west as Kansas and as far south as Missouri.

> The Chautauqua idea was much too good to remain uncopied. Within two years a group in Ohio . . . set up a similar assembly . . . with . . . the

identical overlay of respectability. . . . [T]he race was on, until by 1900 fully two hundred pavilions had been set up . . . each following as faithfully as they could the pattern set by Vincent. (Case and Case 17–18)

Mimicking the original, these independent assemblies, as they were called to distinguish them from the "Mother" Chautauqua, followed the Chautauqua ideal, defined as "education for everybody, everywhere in every department, inspired by a Christian faith" (Hurlbut 27). The ideal, no matter how sincerely adhered to and believed in by those of the independent assemblies, was becoming formulaic, and it was only a short jump from there to commercializing the "ideal."

"Culture" and "uplift" were the intentions of the circuit Chautauquas, and "propriety, decorum, restraint, and reason" were the watchwords for what appeared in the tents (Kent 34). Streamlined and commercial, they survived by adhering to the most conservative interpretations of these words. Ultimately, there were around one hundred different circuits with five companies dominating the field (Horner 28). In 1924, considered by many to be the peak year of the circuit Chautauqua, attendance was almost thirty million, with performances in over twelve thousand small towns and villages (Case and Case v).

By the late 1920s the Chautauqua was clearly in decline. Radio and movies were providing local challenges, and the circuit managers were no longer sending out first-rate attractions. This combination made towns reluctant to spend the money needed to guarantee the event (Horner 187–89). Concomitantly, in the mid-1920s the real estate market had begun to collapse, and the farm economy was also troubled. Chautauqua depended on audiences whose income was largely agriculturally based: without that income there could be no circuits. The men who ran the largest circuits began to sell their interests, and under less visionary and successful management the circuits limped along until 1932.

II

"Tent Chautauquas were American to their roots."
—Harry Harrison, *Culture under Canvas*

The United States that Chautauqua presented to its audiences was one predicated on homogeneity of process, product, and spectators. Keith Vawter, according to Harry Harrison, "believed that people were pretty much alike. If given free choice, audiences at all the assemblies scattered through the middle west would be interested in the same fare" (51). All the parts of a Chautauqua were interchangeable; the lecturer booked for Iowa was assumed to be equally effective in North Dakota or Alabama, and the advertising campaign designed for Iowa would work in Texas. The implication of these assumptions is that Americans themselves were interchangeable. Culture, in Chautauqua, was produced on an assembly line—itself an American invention. Chautauqua was living out a cultural version of Henry Ford's 1903 dictum about the economically effective manufacture of cars: "The way to make automobiles is to make one automobile like another automobile, to make them all alike" (Lacey 84). Similarity and repetition were cost-effective, and the link between the two systems was not lost on many observers. Victoria Case and Robert Ormond Case state the matter bluntly: "The circuit had been laid out with the care of an assembly line" (139). Marian Scott noted about her first year: "Everybody on the circuit had his job and worked very hard at it. The result was a large, swiftly turning, highly efficient organization that moved with near machine-like precision for three months of the season" (Scott 36–37). The 1916 Chautauqua system that Scott admired, however, did not spring to life full-blown in 1904.

In the beginning, from about 1904 to 1908, as the Lyceum and independent Chautauqua managers moved in to supply the needs of the independent assemblies, they were at the mercy of the locations of the assemblies, uneven travel distances, and railroad schedules. Equipment and crews backtracked and crisscrossed one another as did the performers and speakers creating huge financial deficits for the managers. In 1910 a new system was put into effect that, if the accounts by performers are accurate, did little to alleviate travel hardship but clearly made Chautauqua not just financially viable but very profitable.

The new system owed a lot to the assembly line idea. Each circuit would have one or two more "outfits" (tent, crew, and supervisor) than were performing at any given time. On Horner's first circuit, for example, there were always seven in operation with two in transit, each outfit needing two days to strike, travel, and set up. The length of the Chautauqua could be anywhere from three to seven days, and towns were guaranteed a different program every day (Horner 62–69). All outfits shared the same performers and speakers. "First-day talent remained first-day all season, second-day remained second-day, and so on for the seven days. Thus all groups traveled the same routes for the first time and railroading and programming became simplified" (Harrison 81).

While the new system made success with Chautauqua possible, the contract with the local communities made it a foregone conclusion. The managers of the Chautauqua circuits took few financial risks, despite their claims, because the "committee" of local businessmen and community leaders deposited a non-negotiable guarantee of two to three thousand dollars against the managers' loss, to be recouped in the sale of season tickets (adults for two or three dollars and children for one dollar). The contract was only a page long, yet it spelled out a stiff financial arrangement. The managers got the first $2,500 of the gross and 50 percent after that, and all proceeds from single ticket sales, which could be in the thousands for a popular attraction like William Jennings Bryan, went to the management (Orchard 120). The management promised only a Chautauqua—they would determine the dates and the slate of performers at their convenience. In the negotiations nothing was stated this baldly. "They would sell the 'Chautauqua idea' to the community as a duty, a privilege, a consecration of local spirit. They would not talk about profits or financial values to the town but hold fast to uplift, inspiration, and culture" (Case and Case 30). The managers mystified the commercial nature of the Chautauqua, preferring instead that the towns see them as partners in achieving the ideal rather than business people selling it. Charles Horner could have been speaking for Vawter, Ellison, and the rest when he wrote that the managers worked

> more to avoid loss than to gain wealth. That feeling was inherent in the business because if we had not shared in the application of the ideals we were trying to impart and awaken, we would not have made much progress in gaining public approval. (68)

Case and Case, in one of the few books on Chautauqua not written as a reminiscence by a manager or performer, wrote what could stand as a rebuttal: "Chautauqua had become big business, with the take running in the hundred millions" (32). It was important that this "American" event be seen as an expression of civic pride and a means of personal/community uplift and not as an enterprise run to maximize profit, since part of the image of the United States they were trying to promote was one with its eyes fixed on the finer things in life, not the profit margin.

Ultimately, what was important to the community was not the stiff terms of the contract or sales techniques of the managers but the people who appeared on the Chautauqua platform, the "Talent" (Horner 41). The term covered everyone from William Jennings Bryan to the Military Girls singing group. When the spectators walked up to the characteristic brown tent, they expected to hear great music, edifying lectures, and challenging ideas. Lectures like "Pie, People, and Politics" or "How to Master One's Self" were standard fare (Harrison 138–43). Referred to by the cynical as "Mother, Home, and Heaven," these lectures were a familiar part of Chautauqua, but the devotees felt differently. Gay MacLaren, herself a popular Chautauqua performer, remembers when Chautauqua came to the area in South Dakota where she lived as a child. "For weeks nothing was talked of but Chautauqua and it seemed as if everyone was planning to go" (MacLaren 8). Women saved money from their household budgets and saw Chautauqua as a way to better their children's lives. The speakers were understood to be an important part of that mission. As Sue Humphrey stresses, whatever the nature of the "talent's" presentation, spectators valued the Chautauqua experience.

> The town [Havensville, Kansas] never was the same after Chautauqua started coming [in about 1910]. The Chautauqua brought a new touch of culture which we immediately applied to our lives: new ways of speech, dress, ways of entertainment. . . . It broadened our lives in many ways. (Qtd. in Tapia 45)

Humphrey's observations foreground the pleasure and importance of Chautauqua—it entertained, educated, and expanded people's lives.

Important public figures were also a vital part of Chautauqua. William Jennings Bryan, who, in the days before the Scopes trial, was known as the "Great Commoner," was the most popular speaker. Famous Progressives such as Robert La Follette, reformers such as Ida Tarbell (who wrote an expose of Standard Oil), as well as numerous politicians were also standard fare. Central as well were interpreters or readers, who would read or recite an entire play or characters from a play, and impersonators, who would perform a variety of characters. Gradually, plays performed by actors made their way into the repertory and by 1913 appeared routinely on the circuit, soon becoming the most popular aspect of the Chautauqua, despite the prevalent moral and religious suspicion of theater.

> Bringing in the theater has a great influence on the Chautauqua. It was not altogether an unmixed asset. . . . The play gave a tint of commercialism, without a doubt, and yet many thousands of customers had their first opportunity to enjoy the thing. (Horner 187)

People certainly did come to "enjoy" the theater; having been prepared by the elocutionists and play readers, they were able to make the leap to fully mounted productions, and, having seen them, the audience wanted more. "Plays were so popular and drew so well, that when we had begun to offer them there was no way to stop" (185). Music also had a prominent place with opera singers, a wide variety of musical groups from classical to humorous in content and appearance, bell ringers, yodelers, and other "novelty" acts making up just around half of the offerings.

Working on the circuit was extremely difficult. "They faced six to fifteen or more weeks of solid booking, or as much as 120 consecutive daily appearances" (Case and Case 136). Stories about the difficulties of travel and sleep were ubiquitous in Chautauqua reminiscences. In her nostalgic 1939 memoir, Marian Scott wrote: "I learned to sleep anywhere. . . . The custom . . . of indulging in small, unimportant acts that you believed essential to your happiness and well-being. You got rid of those" (33). But audiences appreciated their effort. For their part they endured terrible heat, the temperatures in the tents often rising to well over a hundred degrees Fahrenheit, in order to be part of the Chautauqua experience. Performers who lost sight of the meaning of Chautauqua for their audiences were reminded in no uncertain terms that Chautauqua was worth the sacrifice and discomfort. One manager recalled:

> Marge [a performer] was on her way to the tent . . . one hot, disagreeable windy dusty day. She was joined by a local lady who said she was also going to the Chautauqua. Marge remarked "If it were not my job, I would certainly not be going on a day like this." The reply came back, "If you lived in this part of the country where the Chautauqua is your only chance from one year to the next to see and hear programs like these, you would not miss it for anything." (Qtd. in Tapia 49)

Chautauqua was also a party. Gay MacLaren remembered her first Chautauqua as a great celebration:

> The streets were crowded with people all dressed up as if it were the Fourth of July, and there were flags and banners everywhere. The banners had the word "Chautauqua" printed across them in colored letters. Farmers' wagons piled high with bedding, cooking utensils, and children rattled along the dusty roads to the Chautauqua grounds. (12)

Chautauqua was not confined to what happened on the platform; it was also a matter of socializing with rarely seen friends and neighbors, of escaping from intense agricultural labor, and of glimpsing the larger world usually available through weeks-old newspapers and gossip from passing strangers. Often the Talent would be housed in private homes, and it was a time to get to know the people who appeared on the platform. One woman was said to have told the Talent who were staying at her home:

Do you know what this means to us? What the Chautauqua means to thousands of intellectually and musically starved country people? It is our oasis—our life belt. The music we hear during assembly week is the music we sing and play all through the year. The lectures we discuss for months. My husband remembers all the jokes and the politics and I try to remember . . . all the new ideas set forth. . . . Sometimes I think we could not endure the privations and loneliness of this new land if it were not for the Chautauqua. ("The Uplift" 684)

While this praise is effusive, it does make it easier to understand why a town might continue to bring in a Chautauqua year after year and why it was so valued and revered by spectators who returned every year.

III

"Chautauqua has served to reveal the individual American community to itself at its best."
—Charles Horner, *Strike the Tents*

It was not simply the ubiquitous presence of Chautauqua that made people repeatedly define it as American. Certainly, its origins and geography located it within the United States, but geography alone was insufficient to make it seem unique in the eyes of its spectators, participants, and creators. Instead, it was a complex combination of political, religious, and historical circumstances that intersected to produce what Chautauqua constructed as "American." But, as Chautauqua was representing what spectators and participants understood as American, the same discourses that Chautauqua constructed as American were constructing Chautauqua. For Charles Horner, writing in 1954, Chautauqua had been "the essence of an Americanism in days gone by" (11–12). What Chautauqua claimed to present was a true depiction of the United States that was predominately homogeneous, unconflicted, and stable. If this was one possible representation of the nation, it is important to examine how and why it was both possible and credible.

As is clear in the history and workings of the circuit Chautauquas, a nation exists largely in the realm of representation. The U.S.A. that rural, white Chautauqua audiences recognized on the platform was quite different from the U.S.A. experienced by, for example, a recent immigrant working in an industrial city or an African American living in the Deep South. The difference lay not so much in geography as in representation. In his widely cited delineation of "nation," Benedict Anderson states that it is "an imagined political community—and imagined both as inherently limited and sovereign." Imagination is crucial to the existence of the nation for several reasons. Since no one individual who claims citizenship in a nation can ever know all others who make the same claim, "meet them, or even hear of them" and thereby verify the tangible existence of the citizenry, the nation exists largely in the realm of assumption and trust. What distinguishes one community, or nation, from another is not, for Anderson, a question of how well or poorly the representations are realized or if the representations have some natural basis, for he assumes they do not, but "the style in which they are imagined." That style becomes an icon of the nation so that all its constituents can recognize it as such or, as Anderson puts it, "in the mind of each lives the image of their communion" (6). Anderson elaborates his definition through a history of the production of books and the ways in which their content demonstrated ideas of nationality. While his argument has many merits, it is perhaps even more productive to apply his definition to live performance, a form of representation that carries with it a great deal of immediacy and compelling power.

Not all performance operates from the assumption that the audience must identify completely with what they see on stage, but Chautauqua certainly worked to achieve that effect as fully as possible. As one actor on the circuit put it, "a [Chautauqua] play should reflect the emotions and especially the problems of an audience" (Row 227). While he was obviously referring to only one aspect of the Chautauqua program, his observation could stand in for the whole approach, and part of it was that all the audiences had the same emotions and problems.

One way in which Chautauquas assumed and created a homogeneity has already been discussed. Yet homogeneity was not simply a matter of sound economic practices; it was also a way to imagine the United States, a method of representing it to itself. Chautauqua helped those living in the United States "imagine" "the image of their communion" by emphasizing the ways in which Chautauqua was ubiquitous. Charles Horner stressed precisely this feature as one of the strengths and founding assumptions of Chautauqua. "Chautauqua people are not likely to forget that their own community is part of America, and that the whole nation is a great family of neighborhoods" (90). All the citizenry might never know one another and have to assume the rest exist, but Chautauqua gave substance to that assumption by both creating a sub-community ("Chautauqua people") and relating that sub-community to the larger community (the United States) by conflating the two. As spectators looked around the Chautauqua tent, they were encouraged to elide what they saw with the whole of the United States. The tent became an icon for the "imagined" nation.

The use of the word "community" is key because it is another reason why imagination is crucial to the construction of a nation. Community is the way in which the nation is imagined. It implies, in Anderson's terms, a "deep horizontal comradeship," often in complete contradiction to the actual "inequality and exploitation" of relationships among citizens in practice; in theory they are conceived as completely equitable (7). Community is constructed as particularly "horizontal" when the political system of the "imagined political community" is democracy, and Chautauqua aligned itself closely to the democratic system.

People had a duty to participate in Chautauqua, the managers seemed to argue, because it served the greater communal good and provided a vital service to the country. It has already been discussed how the circuits reinterpreted a basic tenet of American democracy, transforming "all men are created equal" into "all men are created the same," but that was not the only maneuver Chautauqua used to align itself with the political system. A commentator wrote that the circuits were "rendering a service to democracy by fostering an interest in things of the mind, by quickening the social spirit, and by helping create the public opinion" (Vincent 19). Similarly, Harrison states that Chautauqua "spelled out the meaning of democracy" (271). Both men shift the focus away from Chautauqua as a commercial enterprise to Chautauqua as central to the survival of the nation. If the United States is a democracy and Chautauqua is crucial to the survival of the democracy, then the boundaries between Chautauqua and the United States are successfully blurred.

Representing Chautauqua as democracy was a powerful way to align the nation and the circuits, but that alone did not provide the most complete expression of national identity. Anderson qualifies his definition of national by noting that nations are "inherently limited and sovereign" (6). He uses the word "limited" in the sense that any nation has boundaries, no matter how flexibly they might be defined. Chautauqua was adroit at defining the limits of the nation. The United States was represented both by what it "was" and by what it "was not." The presence of the clearly "foreign" on the circuit served as a contrast to that which was positioned as American and provided an "Other" against which the U.S.A. could measure itself. Those not of British Protestant descent were clearly the exoticized Other against which Americans should compare themselves.

> Six dark-skinned, black-eyed people got off the train. This would be the magicians' troupe . . . [it included] a girl about twelve years old who, if she lived here in this small town, would probably be in the eighth grade, but she didn't look like any little girl anywhere and couldn't even speak English. (Case and Case 36)

The group becomes an object of curiosity and even trepidation because its members do not fit the popularized model of American. The girl who does not "look like any little girl anywhere" does not look like the townspeople who have cast themselves as the norm. The reactions of suspicion and wariness to the magicians' group foregrounds the way in which Chautauquan America valued its homogeneity. Since it does not fit the model of the United States, the exotic troupe functions as a negative model that clearly demarcates and reinforces the national limits.

Notions of foreign also served another limiting purpose: nostalgia. Popular on the circuits were musical groups like the Swiss Yodelers, Scotch Bluebells, White Hussars, or the Imperial Russian Quartet. Costumes were almost a requirement if a group was to achieve popularity, and often they wore authentic heirlooms.

> Grandmothers, even some of the mothers, dreaming happily of other times, had brought native costumes with them from the old country, stored now tenderly in an attic trunk, and music of the homeland struck a deep note when rendered by singers arrayed in the dress of that beloved homeland. (Harrison 108)

In this instance, foreign represents not the Other but the irretrievable past. Romanticized, the musical groups performed nostalgic memories of other cultures, reminding Americans of what they had left to become assimilated to the (apparently) ethnically neutral American culture. The "limits" of the nation were represented negatively: not this (any more) but this (now). Plays on the circuit emphasized the value of assimilation as well (Kent 50). *The Melting Pot,* a popular offering from 1914 on, stressed the benefits that accrue to a young Russian Jewish immigrant when he assimilates to American culture. By abandoning the old ways, he is able to become a successful American composer unhampered by the restrictions of the country he left behind, thus reassuring audiences that the homogeneity of assimilation was superior to the heterogeneity of distinct cultures. As a brochure advertising *The Melting Pot* emphasized, the play "is offered in all sincerity in the hope and belief that it will make this a better community, and every man and woman better citizens." Circuit managers and publicists were quick to emphasize the values and ideas they believed were popular with Chautauqua audiences.

As *The Melting Pot* demonstrated, homogeneity was certainly the argument of the plays that began appearing with increasing regularity after 1914. For example, three typical plays—*The Mollusc* (written 1914), *The Man from Home* (written 1907), and *The Next-Best Man* (published 1931)—all strenuously dramatize the dangers of deviating from the norms and values of the

Chautauqua audience. Being too lazy to tend to household chores (*The Mollusc*), throwing over a small-town fiancé for a glamorous movie star (*The Next-Best Man*), or abandoning the United States for a potential marriage to a titled Englishman (*The Man from Home*) were all presented as negative and damaging choices on the part of the characters (Kent 64–157). By the end, the prevailing social values and norms of hard work, respect for tradition, and the superiority of the United States are vindicated and reinforced, and are all presented as uniformly applicable to everyone in every situation.

While the mainstream American culture represented in and by Chautauqua was to be seen as unique and unhampered by European influences, it was the product of a specific group of American immigrants who had successfully manipulated their values and norms into the monolithic values and norms of the nation. Clifton Olmstead, in *Religion in America,* noted that "no institution in American history so effectively blended religion and culture and presented them in such a palatable form" (116). But Chautauqua did not simply "blend" religion and culture; it blended a specific religion with culture and blended it in such a way as to present it as monolithic and unchallenged. The United States of the nineteenth and early twentieth centuries was dominated by Protestants of British descent. As Mark A. Noll notes, this period was marked by the belief that they had the power to "translat[e] their moral vision into the law of the land" (299). This "public" Protestantism, highly evangelical in nature, dominated all public spheres from politics to education, from literature to popular culture (243). Despite the circuit Chautauqua's official claim to a multi-denominational platform, a claim they buttressed by the appearance of rabbis and Catholic priests, the Chautauqua platform was one of the most prominent promoters of what Handy calls "the national religion, a religion of civilization" presented simply as universal moral values and the American way of life (115). By the early twentieth century, the dominance of that form of Protestantism was on the wane. "Protestant control . . . gradually receded as the nineteenth century gave way to the twentieth" (Noll 312). This is primarily apparent through hindsight, however, as most scholars agree that the crowning achievement of this dominance was the Eighteenth Amendment to the Constitution in 1919 prohibiting the sale and manufacture of alcohol in the United States. The circuit Chautauquas represented a United States that was ceasing to exist as it trumpeted its strength and longevity.

Perhaps the best example of this seamless melding of Protestantism, Chautauqua, and the United States was in businessman-turned-minister Russell Conwell's "Acres of Diamonds" speech. In forty years, Conwell gave this speech over six thousand times, most of these deliveries occurring on the Chautauqua platform. The speech's message was simple: being poor was sinful, being rich was a sign of inner goodness.

> You have no right to be poor. . . . I know there are some things higher and grander and sublimer than money. . . . Nevertheless, the man of common sense also knows that there is not any one of those things that is not greatly enhanced by the use of money. (Qtd. in Case and Case 253)

There were specific qualifications about how one was to gain this wealth. Money had to be earned and not inherited. "I pity a rich man's son. . . . A rich man's son cannot know the very best things in human life" (255). For Conwell, being given riches was the worst way to become rich, and hard work was the best. The wealth gained at home· was to be spent at home as well.

> He who can give to . . . people better homes, better schools, better churches . . . he that can be a blessing to the community in which he lives . . . will be great anywhere, but he who cannot . . . will never be great . . . on the face of God's earth. (272)

Conwell could have been speaking for the majority of Protestants who, including the clergy, supported the inseparable linking of wealth, Protestantism, and the United States "as though it represented the coming of the kingdom" (Hamilton 40). The United States was a place where poverty indicated personal failing, while hard work and personal initiative were always rewarded.

Similar arguments were made in what was perhaps the most popular Chautauqua play, Roi Cooper Megrue and Walter Hackett's *It Pays to Advertise* (published 1917) in which Rodney's wealthy father and fiancée conspire to get him to take a job so that he will not be, in the father's words, "an idler, a rich man's son" (21). Rodney, who is "underdeveloped by reason of the kind of life he has led under appallingly frictionless conditions," resists because he believes his father has made enough money to last for generations (9). Arthur Row, who played Rodney's friend Ellery Peale, testified to the popularity of the play's message, saying that it "made an immediate appeal. [I]t fascinated advertising men who followed us literally from town to town in order to get precise arguments in favor of advertising" (Row 231). While the spectators in this instance are described as valuing the play for utilitarian reasons ("arguments in favor of advertising") rather than Conwell's more philosophical and religious ones, it seems clear that the play had a strong impact and that it would have been less likely that audiences would have embraced the play had it not promoted values and norms already positioned as central.

The United States foregrounded in Chautauqua was a rural one, partly because of circumstances but also because the United States had long seen itself as a rural nation with a great frontier. The real United States, Chautauqua seemed to say, was outside the cities. Like the role of Protestantism, however, the seemingly placid surface of the Chautauqua representation was mystifying a shift in American demographics out of rural areas and into the cities. In 1900 almost 70 percent of the United States lived in rural areas, but by 1930 that percentage had dropped to 43. Cities, to Chautauqua, were inferior and by implication perhaps not American.

> Naturally the Chautauqua idea grew up in the forests and prairies, not in the cities. It grew up, that is, where the native American runs free and true to type, not where he has been infected by the worldly and effete European notion of going out and having a gauzy and gaseous Good Time utterly unbuttressed by Uplift. (*Everybody's Magazine* 323)

Being rural was part of Chautauqua and hence part of the United States.

The United States that Chautauqua represented and was representative of was a seductive yet problematic portrait of a nation. Kruger observes, "The idea of representing the nation in the theater, of summoning a representative audience that will in turn recognize itself as a nation on stage, offers a compelling if ambiguous image of national unity" (3). Chautauqua performed a "compelling yet ambiguous" United States for millions of people. A reassuring, stable, and moral representation was repeatedly performed year after year, both creating and fulfilling the spectators' views and beliefs about the United States. This United States bore little resemblance to the heterogeneous, unstable, and complex nation that actually existed outside the comfortable confines of Chautauqua, and it was that United States that people wished to be reassured did not exist. Chautauqua relentlessly performed the dominant values of white Protestants of British descent, even as their influences were waning in the face of increasing immigration and religious diversity.

Despite Chautauqua's arguments to the contrary, "nation" is a highly unstable construction, and, as John R. Gillis cautions, "National identities ... are constructed and reconstructed and it is our responsibility to decode them in order to discover the relationships they create and sustain" (4). The "national identities" and "relationships" constructed by and for Chautauqua offer a complex view of the early-twentieth-century United

States with important consequences for the end of the century. The "most American thing in America" was so because of the power of those involved to promote their representation of the nation as natural and true. This examination of the Chautauqua movement makes that power and its effects visible, providing an opening for more questions about how the United States has been and is "imagined."

REFERENCES

Anderson, Benedict. *Imagined Communities*. Rev. ed. London: Verso, 1991.

Brochure for *The Melting Pot*. Redpath-Horner, 1914.

Case, Victoria, and Robert Ormond Case. *We Called It Culture: The Story of Chautauqua*. New York: Doubleday, 1948.

Gillis, John R. "Memory and Identity: The History of A Relationship." *Commemorations: The Politics of National Identity*. Princeton: Princeton UP, 1994. 3–24.

Hamilton, Neill Q. *Recovery of the Protestant Adventure*. New York: Seabury Press, 1981.

Handy, Robert T. *A Christian America: Protestant Hopes and Historical Realities*. New York: Oxford UP, 1971.

Harrison, Harry P., as told to Karl Detzer. *Culture under Canvas: The Story of Tent Chautauqua*. New York: Hastings House, 1958.

Horner, Charles F. *Strike the Tents: The Story of Chautauqua*. Philadelphia: Dorrance, 1954.

Hurlbut, Jesse Lyman. *The Story of Chautauqua*. New York: G. P. Putnam and Sons, 1921.

Kent, Drew Allan. "The Circuit-Chautauqua Produced Play: Reading Historic Plays as Cultural Scripts of Social Interaction." Diss. U of Texas at Austin, 1992.

Kruger, Loren. *The National Stage: Theater and Cultural Legitimation in England, France and America*. Chicago: U of Chicago P, 1992.

Lacey, Robert. *Ford: The Men and the Machine*. Boston: Little, Brown, 1986.

MacLaren, Gay. *Morally We Roll Along*. Boston: Little, Brown, 1938.

Megrue, Roi Cooper, and Walter Hackett. *It Pays to Advertise*. New York: Samuel French, 1917.

Noll, Mark A. *A History of Christianity in the United States and Canada*. Grand Rapids, MI: William B. Eerdmans, 1992.

Olmstead, Clifton E. *Religion in America: Past and Present*. Englewood Cliffs, NJ: Prentice-Hall, 1961.

Orchard, Hugh A. *Fifty Years of Chautauqua: Its Beginnings, Its Development, Its Message and Its Life*. Cedar Rapids, IA: Torch Press, 1923.

Row, Arthur William. "Acting in Tents in Chautauqua." *PoetLore* 36 (Summer 1925): 222–31.

Scott, Marian A. *Chautauqua Caravan*. New York: D. Appleton Century, 1939.

Tapia, John E. *Circuit Chautauqua: From Rural Education to Popular Entertainment in Early Twentieth Century America*. Jefferson, NC: McFarland, 1997.

"The Uplift of Chautauqua Week." *Literary Digest* 18 October 1918: 684–85.

Vincent, George E. "What Is Chautauqua?" *Independent* 6 July 1914: 17–19.

David Krasner

"The Pageant Is the Thing": Black Nationalism and *The Star of Ethiopia*

Colonialism is not satisfied merely with holding a people in its grip and emptying the native's brain of all form and content. By a kind of perverted logic, it turns to the past of oppressed people, and distorts, disfigures and destroys it.

—Frantz Fanon, *The Wretched of the Earth*

W. E. B. Du Bois's production of the pageant *The Star of Ethiopia* opened at the Twelfth Regiment Armory in New York on 22 October 1913. It brought with it a measure of controversy, for it raised significant issues concerning the portrayal of African Americans during a period of heightened racism and its antithesis, black nationalism. Subsequent productions of *The Star of Ethiopia* continued to portray African American history in a radically different way than it had been portrayed in what historian Patricia Morton describes as a radically racist era "stretching from the late 1880s to the 1920s" (20). *The Star of Ethiopia* stood in stark contrast to the depiction one finds, for example, in Thomas Dixon's *The Clansman* in 1905 and, later, D. W. Griffith's film based on Dixon's work, *Birth of a Nation,* in 1915. In the film, according to Du Bois, the black man was portrayed as a "fool, a vicious rapist, a venal and unscrupulous politician or a faithful but doddering idiot" ("The Clansman").

The Star of Ethiopia, according to Du Bois biographer David Levering Lewis, was "the most patent, expansive use yet made by Du Bois of an ideology of black supremacy in order to confound one of white supremacy" (461).[1] After surveying some background to *The Star of Ethiopia*, I will examine in this essay the significance of Du Bois's production considered within the historical context of emerging black nationalism. First, I will define Du Bois's multilayered intent in creating the pageant; second, I will consider the pageant in relation to other pageants of its time, paying particularly close attention to the rise of Ethiopianism; third, I will describe the

FIG. 11. *The Star of Ethiopia,* unidentified performer. (Courtesy of the Special Collections and Archives, W. E. B. Du Bois Library, University of Massachusetts Amherst.)

pageant itself in some detail; and, finally, I will propose an analysis of the pageant as a symbolic representation of black nationalism.

I

> So dawned the time of *Strum* and *Drang*.
> —W. E. B. Du Bois, *The Souls of Black Folk*

A pernicious effect of racism is the internalization of negative stereotyping. Du Bois observed in *Black Reconstruction in America* that, in propaganda directed against blacks, African Americans "face one of the most stupendous efforts the world ever saw to discredit human beings, an effort involving universities, history, science, social life and religion" (727). In reaction to racist misrepresentation, Du Bois wrote *The Star of Ethiopia* in order, as he said, to "get people interested in the development of Negro drama and to teach on the one hand the colored people themselves the meaning of their history and their rich emotional life through a new theatre, and on the other, to reveal the Negro to the white world as a human, feeling thing" ("Drama Among Black Folk" 171). As the *Washington Bee* acknowledged, *The Star of Ethiopia* "is a serious effort by our most distinguished scholar to use the drama in a large form to teach the history of our origin, to stimulate the study of the history of the peoples from whom we have sprung, to ennoble our youth and to furnish our people with high ideals, hope and inspiration" ("Star of Ethiopia").

In *The Star of Ethiopia,* Du Bois sought a cultural representation of black diaspora, the collective consciousness among black people centered upon a common history and ancestry.[2] Awash in racist propaganda proclaiming that African Americans lacked culture, Du Bois set out to prove such ideology wrong. His interest in *The Star of Ethiopia* was to show that African Americans have indeed contributed to the rise of civilization and to show, further, that this contribution was as rich and diverse as the Anglo-European. In addition, he wanted to demonstrate that African Americans have what Arnold Rampersad has called a capacity "for cultural regeneration even where they [African Americans] seemed to be in permanent social disarray" (*Art and Imagination* 230). In the pageant, slavery would be viewed as a phenomenon attesting to the resilience of black people. For Du Bois, the invocation of black collective history could be seen in a positive light; it should inspire the black community, in Darwinian terms, to higher stages of development. He believed that historical pageantry provided a means to achieve black solidarity.[3]

The Star of Ethiopia was also an introduction to Du Bois's conception of black aesthetics, setting the stage for his vision of a didactic folk theater. Frederic J. Haskins notes a dual purpose in Du Bois's pageant: first, "to stimulate the pride" of African Americans by portraying the historical process of the black race; and, second, to develop black "dramatic talent" (75). Walter C. Daniel adds to this, remarking that productions of *The Star of Ethiopia* were designed to establish a black national theater "that was written by blacks about blacks and acted by blacks" (418). For Du Bois, theatrical pageantry among African Americans "is not only possible, but in many ways of unsurpassed beauty and can be made a means of uplift and education and the beginning of a folk drama" ("Drama Among Black Folk" 173). *The Star of Ethiopia,* Du Bois hoped, would serve as a powerful stimulus for the creation of a black national theater associated with interests in racial uplift and indigenous black culture. "Art is propaganda," he wrote, "and ever must be, despite the wailing of the purists" ("Criteria" 296).

Ultimately, the aim of the pageant was to bolster an African American moral regeneration that would promote black culture. Each episode was designed to inspire interest in black history by entertaining and calling attention to the historical record. The production engaged dance, music, and historical reenactments of African history, the Middle Passage, slavery, emancipation, and reconstruction that celebrated black uniqueness. Except for two selections from Verdi's *Aida,* all aspects of the production were conceived and produced by African Americans. Despite the difficulties in overcoming financial shortages, notwithstanding scheduling problems (the show involved over a thousand actors), and irrespective of production obstacles, Du Bois proudly proclaimed that the pageant "sweeps on and you hang trembling to its skirts. Nothing can stop it. It is. It will. Wonderfully, irresistibly the dream comes true" ("The Star of Ethiopia" 93). Directed by Charles Burroughs, the pageant's four productions were altered only slightly; an overview therefore need only mention its prologue and five scenes in thirteen episodes: scene 1, The Gift of Iron; scene 2, The Dream of Egypt; scene 3, The Glory of Ethiopia; scene 4, The Valley of Humiliation; and scene 5, The Vision Everlasting. *The Star of Ethiopia,* Du Bois explained,

> begins with the prehistoric black men who gave to the world the gift of welding iron. Ethiopia, Mother of Men, then leads the mystic procession of historic events past the glory of ancient Egypt, the splendid kingdoms of the Sudan and Zymbabwe down to the tragedy of the American slave trade. Up from slavery slowly . . . the black race writhes back to life and hope . . . on which the Star of Ethiopia gleams forever. ("The Star of Ethiopia: A Pageant" 162)

The Star of Ethiopia was, up to that time, the most impressive presentation toward the point of view of pan-African nationalism ever to appear on an American stage. *The New York Outlook* called it "an impressive spectacle" (*Star*). The pageant demonstrates that African Americans, like all Americans other than native indigenous peoples, bring their culture from foreign soil to American life. David W. Blight argues that Du Bois's collective writings reveal that "he was not merely crying foul at racist historians for leaving blacks out of the story of American history. He was trying to restore his people's history, while at the same time, he believed, enriching American history" (46). Anthony Appiah adds to this view, maintaining that Du Bois's revaluation of African Americans sought an "acceptance of difference," with each ethnic and racial group contributing to the whole. Appiah explains that for Du Bois, "the white race and its racial Other are related not as superior to inferior but as complementaries; that the Negro message is, with the white one, part of the message of humankind" (25).

The Star of Ethiopia looked emphatically toward Africa in much the same way that white pageantries of the period looked to Europe. In fact, Du Bois hoped that white America would view the splendor of his pageant as coexistent with white historical pageants. A disappointed Du Bois, however, would write of *The Star of Ethiopia* that it was "given by Negroes for Negroes . . . to audiences aggregating tens of thousands—but the white American world hardly heard of it despite the marvelous color and drama" ("Criteria" 68).

II

> *Semper novi quid ex Africa,* cried the Roman proconsul; and he voiced the verdict of forty centuries. Yet there are those who would write world-history and leave out this most marvelous of continents.
>   —W. E. B. Du Bois, "The African Roots of War"

The significance of Du Bois's *Star of Ethiopia* can be understood best from within the context of the more general pageantry movement, which reached the zenith of its popularity around the 1910s. Broadly speaking, pageants extolled the virtues of American history through historic reenactments of major events and actively participated in a burgeoning spirit of cultural nationalism through their enactment of immigrant identity, often juxtaposed to the assimilationist or melting-pot ideologies of their institutional sponsors. In 1914, William Chauncy Langdon wrote in the *Bulletin of the American Pageant Association* that pageantry is the drama of a community, "showing how the character of that community as a community has developed." Along similar lines, historian Steve Golin recently noted that pageants were being used throughout the United States "to promote patriotism and civic pride" (56). Nonetheless, Du Bois had moved cautiously into the field of pageant drama, having little experience in playwriting.

Du Bois held that historical pageantry could supply the required framework for an African American cultural renewal. In June 1913, he wrote to Ellis P. Oberholtzer, a member of the Board of Directors of the American Pageant Association, that he was "going to have in New York a celebration of Emancipation, and among the things which we have planned is a pageant of Negro history."[4] For Du Bois, historicism—Negro history—was crucial to any understanding of black culture and society. History was not merely evidence on which data rests; for Du Bois it was the way to apprehend the spirit of a community and the way toward the creation of a cultural ideology. According to Frederic Haskins, the purpose of Du Bois's pageant was similar to other historical pageants, "except that it is confined in scope to the interpretation of the highest ideals of Negro life" and, it might be added, was specifically nonassimilationist (75). The advance guard of African American people, Du Bois noted in 1897, must realize "that if they are to take their just place in the van of pan-Negroism, then their destiny is not absorption by the white Americans." Rather, African American destiny is "a stalwart originality which shall unswervingly follow Negro ideals" ("Conservation" 487–88). Pageantry would be instrumental in conveying "Negro ideals."

Du Bois's greatest fear, or so it would appear, was the extinction of Africanisms through apathy and cultural impoverishment. Samuel Hay has observed that in *The Star of Ethiopia* Du Bois wanted not only to stop white racism but also "to stop African Americans from being raceless" (133). The underlying purpose of *The Star of Ethiopia* was to enlighten people of all races. According to Freda Scott, Du Bois used the pageant's themes as weapons in the black "cultural and political propaganda arsenal" (1). Pageantry was a political instrument that could bring together visual spectacle and dramatic performance, amounting to a useful device for creating a sense of community. Art historian Linda Nochlin maintains that a pageant could function "in the realm of participatory *dramatic* action rather in the way Diego Rivera's Mexican murals did in the realm of public, *visual* art." As a result, pageantry would forge what Nochlin calls "a sense of contemporary purpose, self-identity and social cohesion out of a vivid recapitulation of historical fact heightened by symbolism" (67). While Du Bois doubtlessly borrowed certain structural arrangements from white pageants—emphasizing episodic scenes, historical reenactments, music, grand spectacle, and generalized rather than detailed dramas—his pageant would stress black nationalist themes.

Du Bois's black nationalist ideology emphasized not only the advancement of black economic and political independence but inner pride as well. Black nationalism, in general, surfaced from the desire to reverse an intolerable situation; as historian James Turner notes, black nationalism viewed the basis of social life as competition between cultures "for social and economic power" (67). Du Bois desired equality and empowerment for African Americans in the American system. He wrote in *Dusk of Dawn* that the plan of action for black nationalism would encompass "full Negro rights and Negro equality in America; and it would most certainly approve [of] . . . continued agitation, protest and propaganda to that end" (199). Du Bois also stressed aesthetic goals. According to Sandra Adell, Du Bois maintained that "music, poetry, and dance unite a nation's folk heritage" because artistry "is the bulwark of nationalism (23)." For Du Bois, folk nationalism challenged the popular belief that blacks have failed to contribute to American culture.[5]

The roots of Du Bois's nationalism are also closely tied to Hegelianism and the German folklore movement spearheaded by Johann Gottfried von Herder (1744–1804). Du Bois, like Hegel, was strongly positivistic; both viewed history as the spirit that moved through specific world historical peoples. Du Bois argued that each ethnic or racial group raises the collective consciousness of its members by what Joel Williamson calls a pursuit "of its Volksgeist, its spirit, its soul, its genius" ("W. E. B. Du Bois as a Hegelian" 34). Du Bois increasingly viewed racial conflict in America as resolvable through a *Sturm und Drang* struggle: blacks and whites would eventually advance toward a mutual appreciation, ultimately finding the Hegelian *Geist* in a cooperative world spirit. He would follow Herder's advice that only "amid storms can the noble plant flourish: only by opposing struggle against false pretensions can the sweet labor of man be victorious" (qtd. in Kedourie 48). Du Bois, writes Bernard W. Bell, believed that Herder's theory of folk art laid the foundation "for high art and the corollary conception of folksong as a spontaneous, indigenous expression of the collective soul of a people" (21).[6]

Black nationalism for Du Bois developed in recognition of African American racial heritage. In many ways he belonged to a line of thinkers inculcated in the ideology of African American liberation movements that, as August Meier notes, developed from needs felt by African Americans "in their subordinate status in the American social order" (51). Building on initiatives that had their antecedents in the nineteenth century, Du Bois reconstructed African history as proof of Africa's contributions to humanity. His focus on black nationalism led Du Bois not only to stage black history, but also to document it in his short but important work *The Negro*. There he wrote that race "is a dynamic and not a static conception," yielding "a social group distinct in history, appearance, and to some extent in spiritual gift" (9). *The Negro,* like *The Star of Ethiopia,* should be viewed as evidence of Du Bois's continuing intellectual development as a historian and social critic. Around this time he also established the *Crisis,* a pioneering journal whose fundamental aim, says Arnold Rampersad, was "to defend, praise, and instruct black people" in attaining their goal, "black power" (*Art and Imagination* 143).

American pageantry and nationalism were not the only agendas that characterized Du Bois's nationalist commentary. Broadly speaking, he sought a form of black nationalism dubbed "Ethiopianism." In fact, Du Bois originally titled his pageant *The Jewel of Ethiopia: The People of Peoples and Their Gifts to Men.* Ethiopianism began as an independent church movement inspired by black religious secessionists who, according to J. Mutero Chirenje, used the terms *Ethiopianism* and *Ethiopia* in the Greco-Roman and biblical sense, "that Africa was the land of black people (or people with 'burnt faces')" (1). In the Bible Psalm 68:31 reads, "Ethiopia shall soon stretch out her hands to God." F. Nnabuenyi Ugonna maintained that this biblical passage was not only a message of hope; the passage also "echoed and re-echoed in all black nationalist literature" as "a metaphysical black heaven" (xxiv). History, wrote B. F. Lee in 1904, supplies accounts of Ethiopian people who "reached a high state of civilization long before the Christian era" (389). Ethiopia symbolized for many a coming black cultural Renaissance. The fact that, along with Liberia, Ethiopia managed to escape European colonization provided the symbol with a richness of content. In 1896, Ethiopians defeated an invading Italian army at Adowa, and the Italian government subsequently sued for peace. The impact of the Ethiopian victory, writes Edmond Keller, "was profound, sending shock waves throughout Europe." European powers, Keller adds, realized for the first time that Ethiopia was "an African power to be reckoned with" (34).

Ethiopianism was also a late-nineteenth-century movement that sought an independent Africa rooted in African Christianity and, in particular, based on the African Methodist Episcopal Church. According to African historian Clarence Contee, Ethiopianism provided "the major portion of the ingredients of the foundation for early African nationalism" (50). Its purpose was threefold: to preserve African cultural values, to instill racial pride, and to promote a mystical belief that Africa's redemption would be accompanied by a decline of the West. Ethiopianism was espoused by black nationalists such as Martin Delany (1812–85), Henry Highland Garnet (1812–82), and Alexander Crummell (1818–98). Joining them were poets such as Frances Ellen Watkins Harper (1824–1911) and Paul Laurence Dunbar (1872–1906). Meta Warrick Fuller's sculpture *The Awakening of Ethiopia* (ca. 1914) depicts a proud African woman dressed, as art historian Richard Powell observes, "in the classical headgear and apparel of an ancient Egyptian pharaoh" (36). In 1848, Garnet wrote that Ethiopia is one of the few countries "whose destiny is spoken of in prophecy" (qtd. in Bracey 119). In 1879, Delany remarked that "there is little doubt as to the Ethiopians having been the first people in propagating an advanced civilization in morals, religion, arts, science and literature" (72). For the most part, Ethiopianism represented to black Americans what Europe meant to white Americans, Asia to Asian Americans, and South/Central America to Latin Americans—a cultural link to the past that served to nurture pride and identity.

By the late nineteenth century many African American publications used Ethiopia as symbolic both of the unity and the diversity of the black cultural experience in the United States. In an *Indianapolis Freeman* essay entitled "Ethiopia Shall Stretch," Chas. Alexander wrote in 1898 that "the Negro of today is up to every new art, every strange device, every new invention, every important discovery in the scientific world, every new religious thought, every social and economic movement—every important public question is of question to him, and he is working his way into every position of honor and worth to which the white man aspires." Du Bois presented in his pageant a diversity of African Americans from all walks of life: "Enter 20 [African American] women in modern dress: doctor, nurse, teacher, musician, actress, hairdresser, book-keeper, stenographer, merchant, reporter, cook, artist, photographer, dressmaker, milliner and 5 women of fashion" (*Star*). The pageant would bring together ideas of nationalism and Ethiopianism in a broad display of African American cultural plurality.

III

> *The Pageant is the Thing: That is what the people want and long for.*
> —W. E. B. Du Bois, "The Star of Ethiopia"

The first production in New York was staged in six scenes using three hundred and fifty actors, with a reported total audience of some thirty thousand. In *Dusk of Dawn,* Du Bois wrote:

Encouraged by this response I undertook in 1915 to reproduce this in Washington. We used the great ball field of the American League, a massive background of an Egyptian temple painted by young Richard Brown, and a thousand actors. A committee of the most distinguished colored citizens of Washington co-operated with me. Audiences aggregating fourteen thousand saw the pageant. (272–73)

While productions in New York (1913), Washington, DC (1915), Philadelphia (1916), and Los Angeles (1925) enjoyed high attendance, they were not financially successful. The venture was costly in the extreme: the 1915 Washington pageant alone cost over five thousand dollars. The 1916 Philadelphia pageant cost a "mere" forty-one hundred dollars. The economic burden on Du Bois as well as the Hudson Guild, an organization run by Du Bois to sponsor the production, was enormous. Du Bois promoted the Philadelphia pageant by offering prizes to those selling the largest number of tickets (Hay 262). Despite the cost, the pageants were, according to advertisements, "a great human festival and may be of singular beauty and lasting impression" (Star).

In the opening moments of The Star of Ethiopia, the prelude sets the stage with four banners declaring the four gifts Africans and African Americans present to the world: iron, the Nile, faith in righteousness, and humility. The Herald proclaims at the opening prologue the "Glory of Ethiopia" (Star). Each succeeding episode portrays different periods of black history. The first episode, "The Gift of Iron: 50,000 Years B.C.," depicts Africans "fleeing from beast and storm, pray[ing] to Shango, and receiv[ing] from his daughter, Ethiopia, the Star of the Fire of Freedom" ("The Star of Ethiopia: A Pageant" 206). Ethiopia, portrayed in the form of the Veiled Women, appears "commanding in stature and splendid in garment, her dark face faintly visible, and in her right hand Fire, and Iron in her left" (Du Bois, "National Emancipation" 339). Africans, as the pageant suggests, invent the welding of iron. For Du Bois this episode establishes Africa as the regional source of iron smelting, illustrating one of the continent's many contributions to civilization.[7]

The second episode, "The Gift of the Nile: 5,000 B.C. and Later," depicts Egypt coming from Central Africa to worship the Black Sphinx. One reviewer wrote that "priests and worshippers file out of the temple. They are in the midst of their worship when the Kushites, having conquered all of their neighbors, rush in, but are appeased by the friendliness of the Egyptians and perhaps dazed by the splendor of the civilization and culture before their eyes. The two peoples fraternize and finally blend"

(*Star*). This episode illustrates human cooperation and establishes Africa as an early center of art and commerce.

The third episode, the "Gift of Faith: 1,000 B.C. and Later," portrays the Queen of Sheba, who "visits Solomon and shows him how Ethiopia has triumphed" ("The Star of Ethiopia: A Pageant" 206). The episode also depicts the rise of Muhammadanism through its battles with the Songhay. Gradually, war depletes Africa's strength, providing white slave traders with their opportunity. In the end, "Christians and Muhammadans chain and enslave all the people." The slave traders proceed to "set fire to the Black Rock. Ethiopia burns lifting the Cross to God and the Rock becomes her tomb" (*Star*). This episode depicts the evolution of human conflict, with Africans struggling against both external and internal strife.

Diaspora and slavery are the themes of the fourth episode, "The Valley of Humiliation: 1,500 A.D. and Later." Ethiopia appears "on the West Coast in an African Village" ("The Star of Ethiopia: A Pageant" 206). Blacks are subsequently enslaved. The abolitionist John Brown then appears, Toussaint L'Ouverture leads the Haitians, and Nat Turner inspires a slave revolt. The fourth episode portrays black humility and fortitude in their heroic resistance to oppression.

The final scene emphasizes "Freedom and the Vision Everlasting." African Americans are seen in various professional roles. One reviewer wrote:

> When all these different groups are quietly enjoying their freedom . . . they are continually and most viciously attacked by the "furies" of race prejudice, envy, gambling, idleness, intemperance and the ku klux. . . . At first some of the groups give way, but others stand their ground. . . . The freedmen appeal to "Ethiopia" with the sorrow song, "Nobody Knows the Trouble I See."

The episode ends optimistically with victory for Ethiopia over greed, indolence, and intolerance. Ethiopia, who has taken position in the throne chair, "extends her hands in benediction" (*Star*).

In *Dusk of Dawn*, Du Bois observed that the pageant was forced to close owing to a lack of funds and the advent of motion pictures (274). While neither a financial success nor recognized by white critics, *The Star of Ethiopia* served Du Bois's immediate purpose: to draw black people into the theaters and raise interest in a national black folk drama.

IV

> We believe that the Negro people, as a race, have a contribution to make
> to civilization and humanity, which no other race can make.
> —W. E. B. Du Bois, "Conservation of Race"

In *The Star of Ethiopia,* writes Sterling Stuckey, Du Bois "attempted to use
the past, in Négritude style, to erase self-hatred among his people, to inspire
in the present and ennoble in the future" (*Slave Culture* 276). Stuckey calls
Du Bois's form of Négritude a celebration of blackness that attempts to
transmute "negative attributes into positive ones" (*Going through the Storm*
134). If one assumes that Stuckey is correct, it may then be argued that, in
applying Négritudist taxonomies (i.e., turning negative attributes into positive identities), Du Bois may have oversimplified black nationalism, thereby
compromising, in some respects, the very goals he sought. Stuckey's identification of *The Star of Ethiopia* with Négritudism, however, is flawed.

Négritude, wrote Léopold Senghor in *Négritude et humanisme* (1964),
"is the whole of the values of [black] civilization" that characterizes black
people as "essentially *instinctive reason*" (qtd. in Finn 58). Négritude defined
the essence of blackness by deploying a dialectical response to whiteness: it
indicates black intuition, what Senghor calls *l'homme de la nature,* in opposition to white rationalism. For Senghor and the Martinican poet and fellow
Négritudist Aimé Césaire, the restoration of the primacy of intuition over
reason was, as Sandra Adell observes, "essential to their struggle to recover
their ethnic and cultural identity" (33). Frantz Fanon argues, however, that
the poets of Négritude, while opposing "the idea of an old Europe" in favor
of "a young Africa, tiresome reasoning to lyricism, oppressive logic to high-
stepping nature," created a bipolar universe: "one side stiffness, ceremony,
etiquette, and scepticism, while on the other frankness, liveliness, liberty,
and . . . luxuriance: but also irresponsibility" (213). Consequently, the
Négritudists trapped themselves into what Wole Soyinka calls "the defen-
sive role, even though [Négritude] accents were strident, its syntax hyper-
bolic and its strategy aggressive." Négritudism found itself defending the
idea that blacks were instinctual rather than intellectual. In doing so, it failed
to incorporate a multifaceted system of values: it stereotypes black people,
even if the stereotype reflects positive attributes. Négritude, as Soyinka
reminds us, adopted the European Manichaean tradition, borrowing "from
the very components of its racist syllogism" (127).

Du Bois's project avoided Négritudism by promoting a plurality of black contributions to civilization through commerce, science, and the arts. By presenting black cultural diversity in *The Star of Ethiopia,* Du Bois created a polyphony of black voices. In doing so, he would eschew any call for a monolithic black culture. No doubt Du Bois constructed the pageant as a response to white nationalism, depicting black evolution from irrationality to rationality. Arnold Rampersad is most certainly correct when he asserts that Du Bois affirmed Lukács's nineteenth-century positivist vision of art as "the product of social development" ("W. E. B. Du Bois" 62). Early African American aesthetics *had little choice* but to borrow from the dominant culture; as Edward Said reminds us, one of the first tasks of cultural resistance is "to reclaim, rename, and reinhabit" the space reserved initially by and for the dominant society (226). Moreover, Du Bois's notions of a racialized Africanism moved toward essentialism through identity politics. In concentrating on Africa as the nexus of his aesthetic plan, however, Du Bois's pageantry acknowledged the significance of a shared, communal experience. Rather than inverting racial logic in Négritude fashion (suggesting that black intuition counters white rationalism), Du Bois intended a more subtle attack on racist presumptions, paying homage to black cultural diversity. The pageant, Du Bois remarked, is a folk play "based on the history, real and legendary of the negro race" ("Negro Art" 27). *The Star of Ethiopia* was the source of a new, reflexive black consciousness, one that looked toward an African past that was synonymous with the black diaspora while simultaneously affirming the plethora of black contemporary contributions.

Anthropologically, colonialism has, as part of its intent, to homogenize the world, to shape other cultures according to its images. Du Bois resisted hegemony by facilitating a new Afrocentricity from the hybridization of African and African American aesthetics. To be sure, Du Bois's pageant reflected Eurocentric patterns and forms, projecting them onto African American theater. Yet Du Bois critiqued traditions that stereotyped all nonwhite cultures as creatively unsophisticated. He hoped to endow Africa symbolically, through pageantry. Cary Wintz has noted that for Du Bois, as well as other New Negro advocates, "Africa's heritage should be a source of pride and the basis of racial solidarity" (45). By representing Africa in the pageant as the matrix of cultural reunion, Du Bois set in motion a healing process for African Americans who had been denied their cultural roots.

Moreover, Du Bois's views on drama sounded the challenge of a black national theater; the true potential black drama, Du Bois argued, would not be realized by African Americans until it turned toward nationalism. He maintained that "plays of a real Negro theatre" must be *"About us, By us, For us,* and *Near us"* ("Criteria" 134). Throughout Africa, Du Bois observed, "pageantry and dramatic recital [are] closely mingled with religious rites and in America the 'Shout' of the church revival is in its essence pure drama" ("Drama Among Black Folk" 169). Du Bois recognized early on that the call-and-response pattern found in black churches was central to African American dramatic art. The pageant, he surmised, "is not a tableau or playlet or float. It is a great historical folk festival, staged and conducted by experts with all the devices of modern theatrical presentation and with the added touch of reality given by numbers, space and fidelity to historical truth" ("African Roots" 230).

In performing black pageantry, Du Bois challenged the master narrative of U.S. history. He realized that early-twentieth-century pageantry was contributing to an American mythology that would establish the providential view of the United States as an omniscient and economically thriving society. Conscious of this emerging American identity, Du Bois sought to include African Americans in the creed of jingoism and expansionist ideology. David Blight notes that the "endless dialectic between the beauty and the pain" that lies at the root of American history "is just what Du Bois sought to capture by bringing the black experience to the center of the story" (50). Despite the odds, *The Star of Ethiopia* projected the diversity of the black experience onto the fabric of American life.

NOTES

1. *The Star of Ethiopia* was presented at New York's Emancipation Exposition, 22–31 October 1913; Washington, DC's American League Baseball Park, 11, 13, and 15 October 1915; Philadelphia's Convention Hall for the General Conference of African Methodist Episcopal Church, 16, 18, and 20 May 1916; and Los Angeles's Hollywood Bowl, 15 and 18 June 1925. See "Negro Exposition Opens"; and Du Bois, "The Star of Ethiopia: A Pageant" (161); and "The Pageant of the Angels."

2. In using the term *diaspora,* I draw on Paul Gilroy's notion that the "diaspora idea," which grew from the "temporality and historicity, memory and narrativity that are the articulating principles of the black political countercultures," emerged "inside modernity in a distinctive relationship of antagonistic indebtedness" (191).

3. My use of the term *nationalism* avoids categories of black nationalism that have been coined in our time—cultural nationalism, revolutionary nationalism, Afrocentrism, or other ideologies gaining currency during the Garveyite period and the Harlem Renaissance and continuing through the 1960s. Du Bois's nationalism grew out of Alexander Crummell's nineteenth-century conservative values that were more authoritative than equalitarian. Du Bois was an agitator for racial equality who opposed the assimilation of African Americans and African American culture. Although an essentialist, he was not a radical separatist along the lines of Garvey and Malcolm X. For studies of pan-Africanism and black nationalism, see Bracey, Cruse, Esedebe, Meier, Moses, and Stuckey.

4. My thanks to Linda Stanley, Manuscripts and Archives, Historical Society of Philadelphia, for providing me with a copy of the Oberholtzer letter.

5. Du Bois was not a back-to-Africa emigrationist, as were Bishop Turner and Edward W. Blyden and, later, Marcus Garvey (see Redkey). During the time of the pageant Du Bois was essentially optimistic about prospects for black advancement, despite racist propaganda, Jim Crowism, and lynching. For a study of Du Bois's African nationalism, see Contee.

6. For discussions of Hegelian influences on Du Bois, see Lewis 139–40; and Williamson, "W. E. B. Du Bois"; and *The Crucible of Race,* 402–13; for German influences, see Broderick.

7. For a discussion of Africa's contribution to iron smelting and Du Bois's take on the historical evidence, see Stuckey, *Going Through the Storm,* 130.

REFERENCES

Adell, Sandra. *Double-Consciousness/Double Bind: Theoretical Issues in Twentieth-Century Black Literature.* Urbana: U of Illinois P, 1994.

Alexander, Chas. "Ethiopia Shall Stretch." *Indianapolis Freeman* 2 April 1898: 1.

Appiah, Anthony. "The Uncompleted Argument: Du Bois and the Illusion of Race." *Critical Inquiry* 12 (Autumn 1985): 21–37.

Bell, Bernard W. *The Folk Roots of Contemporary Afro-American Poetry.* Detroit: Broadside, 1974.

Blight, David W. "W. E. B. Du Bois and the Struggle for American Historical Memory." *History and Memory in African-American Culture.* Ed. Geneviève Fabre and Robert O'Meally. New York: Oxford UP, 1994. 45–71.

Bracey, John H., Jr., August Meier, and Elliot Rudwick, eds. *Black Nationalism in America.* Indianapolis: Bobbs-Merrill, 1970.

Broderick, Francis L. "German Influence on the Scholarship of W. E. B. Du Bois." *Phylon Quarterly* 19 (Winter 1958): 367–71.

Chirenje, J. Mutero. *Ethiopianism and Afro-Americans in Southern Africa, 1883–1916.* Baton Rouge: Louisiana State UP, 1987.

Contee, Clarence G. "The Emergence of Du Bois as an African Nationalist." *Journal of Negro History* 54 (1969): 48–63.

Cruse, Harold. "Revolutionary Nationalism and the Afro-American." *Black Fire.* Ed. Leroi Jones and Larry Neal. New York: William Morrow, 1968. 39–63.

Daniel, Walter C. "W. E. B. Du Bois' First Efforts as a Playwright." *College Language Association Journal* 33 (1990): 415–27.

Delany, Martin R. *Principia of Ethnology: The Origins of Race and Color.* Philadelphia: Harper, 1879.

Du Bois, W. E. B. "The African Roots of War." *Atlantic Monthly* (May 1915): 707–14.

———. *Black Reconstruction in America, 1860–1880.* 1935. New York. Atheneum, 1992.

———. "The Clansman." *Crisis* 10 (May 1915): 33.

———. "The Conservation of Races: Speech to the American Negro Academy." 1897. *African-American Social and Political Thought, 1850–1920.* Ed. Howard Brotz. New Brunswick: Transaction, 1993. 483–92.

———. "Criteria of Negro Art." *Crisis* 32 (October 1926): 290–97.

———. "The Drama Among Black Folk." *Crisis* 12 (August 1916): 169–73.

———. *Dusk of Dawn.* New Brunswick, NJ: Transaction, 1983.

———. Letter to Ellis P. Oberholtzer. 20 June 1913. Historical Society of Philadelphia.

———. "The National Emancipation Exposition." *Crisis* 6 (November 1913): 339–41.

———. *The Negro.* 1915. London: Oxford UP, 1970.

———. "A Negro Art Renaissance." *Los Angeles Times* 14 June 1925: 26–27.

———. "The Pageant of the Angels." *Crisis* 30 (September 1925): 217–18.

———. *The Star of Ethiopia.* Du Bois Papers, Special Collection and Archives, University of Massachusetts, Amherst, reel 87.

———. "The Star of Ethiopia." *Crisis* 11 (December 1915): 90–94.

———. "The Star of Ethiopia: A Pageant." 1915. *Pamphlets and Leaflets by W. E. B. Du Bois.* Ed. Herbert Aptheker. White Plains, NY: Kraus-Thomson, 1983. 161–65, 206–9.

Esedebe, P. Olisanwuche. *Pan-Africanism: The Idea and Movement, 1776–1963.* Washington, DC: Howard UP, 1982.

Fanon, Frantz. *The Wretched of the Earth.* Trans. Constance Farrington. New York: Grove, 1968.

Finn, Julio. *Voices of Négritude.* London: Quartet, 1988.

Gilroy, Paul. *The Black Atlantic: Modernity and Double Consciousness.* Cambridge: Harvard UP, 1993.

Golin, Steve. "The Paterson Pageant: Success or Failure." *Socialist Review* 13 (1983): 45–78.

Haskins, Frederic J. "The Gift of Ethiopia." *Crisis* 11 (December 1915): 75–76.

Hay, Samuel A. *African American Theatre: An Historical and Critical Analysis.* Cambridge: Cambridge UP, 1994.

Kedourie, Elie. *Nationalism.* Oxford: Blackwell, 1993.

Keller, Edmond J. *Revolutionary Ethiopia: From Empire to People's Republic.* Bloomington: Indiana UP, 1991.

Langdon, William Chauncy. "The Pageant—Grounds and Their Technical Requirements." *Bulletin of the American Pageant Association* 11 (1 December 1914): 1.

Lee, B. F. "Selection, Environment and the Negro's Future." *A.M.E. Church Review* 20 (1904): 388–90.

Lewis, David Levering. *W. E. B. Du Bois: A Biography of a Race.* New York: Henry Holt, 1993.

Meier, August. *Negro Thought in America.* Ann Arbor: U of Michigan P, 1966.

Morton, Patricia. *Disfigured Images: The Historical Assault on Afro-American Women.* New York: Praeger, 1991.

Moses, William Jeremiah. "The Evolution of Black National-Socialist Thought: A Study of W. E. B. Du Bois." *Topics in Afro-American Studies.* Ed. Henry J. Edwards. Buffalo: Black Academic Press, 1971. 77–99.

———. *The Golden Age of Black Nationalism, 1850–1925.* New York: Oxford UP, 1978.

"Negro Exposition Opens." *New York Times* 23 October 1913: 5.

Nochlin, Linda. "The Paterson Strike Pageant of 1913." *Art in America* 52 (May–June 1974): 65–68.

Powell, Richard J. *Black Art and Culture in the Twentieth Century.* London: Thames and Hudson, 1997.

Rampersad, Arnold. *The Art and Imagination of W. E. B. Du Bois.* New York: Schocken, 1976.

———. "W. E. B. Du Bois as a Man of Literature." *Critical Essays on W. E. B. Du Bois.* Ed. William Andrews. Boston: G. K. Hall, 1985. 57–72.

Redkey, Edwin S. *Black Exodus: Black Nationalist and Back-to-Africa Movements, 1890–1910.* New Haven: Yale UP, 1969.

Said, Edward W. *Culture and Imperialism.* New York: Alfred A. Knopf, 1994.

Scott, Freda. "The Star of Ethiopia." MS. Hatch-Billops Collection, New York.

Soyinka, Wole. *Myth, Literature and the African World.* Cambridge: Cambridge UP, 1976.

"The Star of Ethiopia." *Washington Bee* 23 October 1915: 1.

Stuckey, Sterling. *Going Through the Storm: The Influence of African American Art in History.* New York: Oxford UP, 1994.

———. *The Ideological Origins of Black Nationalism.* Boston: Beacon, 1972.

———. *Slave Culture: Nationalist Theory and The Foundations of Black America.* New York: Oxford UP, 1987.

Turner, James. "Black Nationalism." *Topics in Afro-American Studies.* Ed. Henry J. Edwards. Buffalo: Black Academic Press, 1971. 59–76.

Ugonna, F. Nnabuenyi. "Introduction." *Ethiopia Unbound: Studies in Race Emancipation.* Ed. J. E. Casely Hayford. London: F. Case, 1969. v–xxxvi.

Williamson, Joel. *The Crucible of Race: Black-White Relations in the American South since Emancipation.* New York: Oxford UP, 1984.

———. "W. E. B. Du Bois as a Hegelian." *What Was Freedom's Price?* Ed. David G. Sansing. Jackson: U of Mississippi P, 1978. 21–49.

Wintz, Cary D. *Black Culture and the Harlem Renaissance.* Houston: Rice UP, 1988.

Ann Larabee

"The Drama of Transformation": Settlement House Idealism and the Neighborhood Playhouse

Community theater, by its very name, announces itself as the representation of community. It articulates and enacts community identity, usually posing as a model of resistance against hegemonic cultural forces. But even communities with the best political intentions suppress difference through the privileging of unity and mutual identification (Young 300). In the very nature of collaboration, community theater presents a social ideal that may subsume resistance in the dream of shared language and common ground. Mark Weinberg describes "people's theater" as "creating a bond with a specific community as defined by geography, occupation, class, sex, sexual preference, ethnicity, age, or race" (18). In that high-minded creation—in the very act of identifying a community's specificity—the theater also defines, selects, eliminates, and interprets. Historically, American community theater has been closely aligned with social work and has interpreted group identities within such a frame. It attempts to harmonize these identities within an ideal of oneness, wholeness, and unity. But as a model of a community whose ontological complexity can never fully be represented, community theater is self-referential, articulating only itself within its historical moment. The persons that community theater claims to represent always remain elusive, offstage.

In the United States, the community theater, or little theater, movement began in the second decade of the twentieth century with the establishment of several such theaters in major cities—Boston, Chicago, and New York. It developed in tandem with a broader social reform movement that advocated civic participation and assimilation of community differences. Its practitioners set themselves against what they perceived as the commercialization and banality of mainstream American theater and the corrupting influences of vaudeville and cinema on immigrants and workers. The most vocal theorist of the movement, Percy MacKaye, believed that theater was the most effective solution to the "problem of leisure," the "most baneful habit of mature human beings—the habit of 'killing time' " (29). MacKaye saw self-directed leisure activities, including all forms of play, as "disorganized, chaotic," and in need of public reform and institutional management (31). Sheldon Cheney, editor of *Theater Arts,* also called for the creation of "public standards of amusement" through theatrical education (222). Such standards would ward off some perceived natural tendency toward passivity especially among workers and students, giving them "opportunity for self-activity and creative work so that the ever-increasing inertia in the recreation of our coming generation might be somewhat counter-acted" (Dean 50).

This social theory that all aspects of people's lives needed channeling into constructive activity was accompanied by a romanticizing of native creativity. As Constance D'Arcy Mackay wrote: "Little Theatres are not imposed on the community. They are the natural out-growth of its art-life—free, spontaneous, resilient" (21). Community theater supporters, generally middle-class community organizers and wealthy philanthropists, often claimed to fulfill a "latent impulse" to be found primarily among working people with no arts education. This mysticized, essential impulse was variously defined as a "spirit" in need of expression (Cheney 227), an "instinct" in need of shaping (Dean 56), and, more amorphously, needs, wants, and desires. A community theater might channel this impulse into social and artistic constructions.

By claiming to know the needs of the people, however, community theater exponents actually constructed "needs" as a rhetorical device to sell their view of theater and community. "Latent art impulses" took a particularly Americanized form (Gard and Burly 10), presented as the foundation for a "spiritual unity" and an "ideal of intimacy" (Cheney 85, 99), that would transcend barriers of race, class, and gender. Thomas Dickinson, a proponent of the "insurgent theater," claimed that various ethnic groups with "transplanted instincts" could be "welded into a mass" (qtd. in Gard and Burly 11). Play production would furnish "disclosure of a community's latent talent" in "general democratic meetings in a wholesome environment," drawing "members of the community closely together," and community productions would remedy the breakdown of "neighborhood life" and "national patriotism" caused by materialism and various national and global migrations (Dean 52, 55). The little theater movement helped promote a utopian vision of civic America, unified in pluralism, run by benevolent institutions, and driven by public spirit rather than crass commercialism. Thus, the theater had a public task of mediating differences and erecting an

edifice in which "petty feuds and ill feelings are overlooked and consequently forgotten under pleasant social activity" (51). The local familiar
activity of artistic collaboration would ideally widen to encompass the nation. "Community" was thus given its shape and meaning in "theater" with
its overt ideological mission of erasing people's differences, complexities,
conflicts, shifting aggregations, and fluid identities.

Nowhere was this vision more apparent than in the settlement house
theaters, especially at Jane Addams's Hull House in Chicago and Lillian
Wald's Henry Street Settlement in New York, where the sociological purpose of integrating immigrants into American life was explicit. The Neighborhood Playhouse at Henry Street achieved most renown as a little theater
with high artistic standards as well as an assimilative social function. The
Playhouse, which emerged in 1915 from the club activities of the settlement, located on Manhattan's Lower East Side, had an overt project of
defining an immigrant community within the Progressive era, a project that
revealed the constraints and ambiguities of theater with a social work mission. The Playhouse shared the aims of the settlement house, to both represent its clientele and to reconstruct them into active, American citizens who
would "participate more widely than they do in the affairs of the going
world" and thus be inspired to a greater "faith in democracy" (Wald, *Windows* 11). In return, the nation would benefit from the influx of different
cultures, orchestrated into loving community by social workers. Thus, the
settlement house ideal was based on the liberal democratic view that models
of citizenship can be imposed through education and that the student will
rationally choose to conform to a higher political Self. The *citizen* is a
performative identity, constructed and deployed in social institutions that
only grant agency to this type of actor. Hence, theater can serve to enact the
appropriate citizen identity for an audience that is then expected to reconstruct itself according to these conventions. In the case of the Neighborhood
Playhouse, participants and observers, by their very presence in the milieu of
cross-cultural theatricals, performed new identities as citizens in the pluralistic pageant of the American civic utopia.

Community theaters with a social agenda, such as the Neighborhood
Playhouse, claim to speak both *for* and *from* their members, a contradictory
project caught between what Michel Foucault called "technologies of
power, which determine the conduct of individuals and submit them to
certain ends or domination," and "technologies of the self, which permit
individuals to effect by their own means or with the help of others a certain
number of operations on their own bodies and souls, thoughts, conduct, and
way of being" (18). While their avowed aim might be to provide a medium

for expressive self-representation, the community theater announces itself as a subculture, an alternative territory that is always defined by a larger geography. Its artifacts and practices, used in performing identity, derive their meaning from mapping, and thus erasing, the fractal complexity of the Other. The map serves as a convenient fiction but is more reflective of the map maker's situated knowledge than of the terrain she claims to represent.

In the very act of allowing self-representation, the community theater defined those selves within a particular geography of ideas and practices. Antonio Gramsci's theory of cultural hegemony is useful in explaining this assimilative process, for he describes how the powerful must create symbols that not only legitimize their power but also gain consent from their subordinates. Cultural hegemony is established and maintained through discursive practices that universalize specific class interests and erase contradictions and conflicts (Giddens 193–97). As a cultural practice, theatrical production, as Bruce A. McConachie argues, insists on the audience's identification with a complex of "visual and auditory signs," and this emotive identification and "orientation" may "create and sustain social institutions such as families, governments, and economic systems, each with its own roles, hierarchies, and persuasions" (47).

The founders of the Neighborhood Playhouse, Alice and Irene Lewisohn, carried out a hegemonic practice of "orientation," operating from within their own situated knowledge. As daughters of a wealthy philanthropist, the Lewisohns came to the Henry Street Settlement as volunteers and club organizers, bringing expertise in dance and drama that eventually resulted in the building of a playhouse. They constructed immigrant culture as a reservoir of essential, collective human experience—amorphous artistic impulses—that would heal local divisions in their city and nation. Artistic expression of universal patterns, they felt, would both preserve ethnic heritages and incorporate them into the newly hegemonic Progressive utopian myth of American cultural pluralism.

The pastiche of folk art, dance, and drama that made up the Playhouse's productions was, according to settlement leader Lillian Wald, a way to "interpret anew the rich inheritance of our neighbors" while having an "educational effect" (*House* 184). The use of traditional cultural symbols would attract identification with the goals of the settlement to raise people from poverty and oppression. As Wald remembered, after one of the settlement's early pageants, taken from the Old Testament, a woman "who had suffered bitterly in her Russian home" thanked the organizers for respecting her religion (185). Club leaders at the settlement were expected to encourage "altruistic impulses inherent in normal human kind" and to show how "traditions among the people" might affirm a shared vision (182). This vision was the orientation of "rudderless" strangers to the land where "human interest and passion for human progress break down barriers centuries old" (286, 310).

The reconstruction of leisure, with its fearful aspect of rudderless, time-wasting activities proscribed as immoral or delinquent, could be done through encouragement of "dramatic instinct" (Wald, *House* 182). The identification of "instinct" naturalized the construction of immigrants as childlike subordinates in need of paternal care. Identifying the Neighborhood Playhouse as one of the two most important theaters in the country, Thomas Dickinson described its work as the "nurturing and care" of immigrants' "natural impulses of play," found in their "folk life" (162–63). Thus, the Playhouse shared in a nationwide dramatic movement that promoted the use of festivals and pageants to identify and subsume folk customs under an overall vision of fellowship that rendered its participants harmless.

The ideology of the community theater fit very well with the overall goals of the settlement house. Founded in 1893, Wald's settlement was part of a broad philanthropic impulse to bring middle-class values and mores to the urban poor.[1] Systematizing the economic, medical, and social needs of its surrounding inhabitants, the settlement house served as both a laboratory for the study of public health and labor issues and a service organization, providing medical care, citizenship and language lessons, arts education and activities, and child care to mostly Eastern European Jewish and Italian immigrants. In its comprehensiveness, the settlement became a metaphor for an idealized nation, one in which rational management of the socius was romanticized as a curative for prejudice and social conflict. The settlement house movement was grounded in nineteenth-century antiutilitarianism and social organicism, the belief that "each individual conceived his or her life and work in relation to the whole" (Carson 7). Victorian Christian reformers believed in the transcendence of class and ethnic differences through an encompassing social vision of human fellowship, opposing the alienation and self-serving divisiveness of the new utilitarian industrial order. As Mina Carson notes, the settlement house movement had intellectual roots in the theories of Thomas Carlyle and John Ruskin, who idealized traditional craftsmanship against factory production (3). Fellowship would find expression through local customs, including traditional arts and crafts, idealized as a spiritual expression of wholeness and unity.

For Wald, as for many of her American colleagues, the arts represented an educational opportunity, a means of assimilating immigrants while reinventing America as a world home, centered on the settlement hearth.

Extolling the civilizing influence of the arts on potentially delinquent children, Wald wrote that "music, drama, handicrafts, gentle manners, cleanliness and order, organized family meal times" were "things of the spirit, making for a broader humanity" (*Windows* 133). But she decried the "stern" and "sad" legacy of the Puritans, wishing to incorporate a more "colorful" folk art into the American fabric (164). Like Jane Addams, who formed a dramatic club at Hull House to keep boys from searching for more stimulating entertainment, Lillian Wald provided space for community-based artistic projects such as the Neighborhood Playhouse that overtly existed to preserve immigrant culture against the contaminating forces of capitalist exploitation and mass consumption. In 1913 she told a *New York Times* reporter, "The east side never will contaminate and harm society; some method must be found by means of which society may be prevented from contamination of the east side" (qtd. in Marshall 6).

The force of Wald's personality and her position as an influential woman solidified the public image of the Henry Street Settlement and its theater as a domestic world, devoted to harmony and sympathy. As feminized spaces, the settlement houses extended the maternal projects of reproduction and preservation to public administration. Considered a powerful matriarch, Wald was surrounded by a cult of personality, adored as the "Leading Lady" of the settlement, the guiding center of all activity. Thus, the Neighborhood Playhouse, formed by her volunteers, the Lewisohns, functioned as Wald's image maker, and all artistic production fertilized her public identity as queen of the settlement kingdom. Many of the formal plays produced by the Playhouse centered on queens and goddesses, including Yeats's *The Player Queen* and Dunsany's *The Queen's Enemies.* Several years after the Playhouse's production of Shaw's *Great Catherine,* Wald wrote to a friend that she felt like the queen, who, she said, "might easily have lived on Henry Street" (qtd. in Daniels 46).

The mythologizing of the Henry Street Settlement as a maternal world extended to its playhouse. Playwright John Galsworthy praised the Neighborhood as "a House where magic has come to stay" (Crowley 53), New York critics repeatedly mentioned the proliferation of prams that crowded its entrance, and community theater historian Kenneth Macgowan called it "our one thoroughly feminist theater," noting the paucity of male actors (48). The Lewisohns envisioned their theater as a Roman hearth, from which workshops, classrooms, offices, and dressing rooms radiated. But the gender roles of highly educated female settlement house workers, who came from privileged backgrounds, were in the throes of change.

Under Wald's direction, the Lewisohns and their colleagues were steeped in the language of domesticity, but they were also representative of the New Woman, independent, unmarried, and devoted to a profession. From their own ambivalent position, the Lewisohns promoted the liberation of women from domestic servitude while extending the settlement house's maternal ideology, stemming from its care of children and the elderly. As Alice Lewisohn explained, the sisters' "personal values did not conform with the traditional world of family or of producing a family," and yet they felt a "collective demand" to help immigrant children, and later their parents, discover a liberating dramatic world of "play" (Crowley 9). Thus, the traditionally feminine work of establishing a home and rearing children was taken from the domestic arena and given an institutional structure. The Lewisohns hoped that immigrant women would follow them, orienting themselves in institutional activities in which tradition still had its place but was transcended in a broader liberatory vision.

Yet the performance of gender was problematic, since the old-world traditions of Italy and Eastern Europe were preindustrial and patriarchal. In her study of Lower East Side immigrant women, Elizabeth Ewen explains that young women, finding work in factories and eager to embrace urban mass culture, "were torn between traditional affections and the promise of modernity. Daily life became a theater of conflict" (266). These identity conflicts militated against the preservation of a pure folk tradition, embedded in a historically stable community. Preservation implied the maintenance of patriarchal religious and familial codes. Indeed, the Lewisohns ironically hoped to provide a theatrical art that would liberate mothers and children from such constraints while somehow honoring those constraints. Decrying the "law of the father" in orthodox Jewish homes, where children were "forced into a mechanized system" that disallowed play and fantasy, the Lewisohns imagined providing an escape for reticent immigrant girls and their mothers (Crowley 19). Yet they wished to incorporate folk dances, costumes, songs, and rituals into their drama classes.

This paradox reflected a broader problem with the settlement houses' call for cultural preservation. Social reformers' attempts to instill cultural pride in ethnic arts, including ethnic drama, "demanded an ultimately untenable equilibrium between cultural autonomy and social assimilation" (Carson 109).[2] As the most recognizable cultural activity of the Henry Street Settlement, the Neighborhood Playhouse served to represent Wald and her mission to potential uptown contributors while providing the surrounding community with opportunities for artistic education and expression, grounded in ethnic traditions. But the very act of staging the immigrant stood against any claims to pure expression streaming from a

traditional center. In the archival photographs of the Neighborhood Playhouse's festal productions, actors in traditional dress pose in the conventions of silent film, faces painted like Lillian Gish or the Gibson girl from
the new advertising ethos. The Playhouse also offered movies, featuring
Douglas Fairbanks, Mary Pickford, and Charlie Chaplin. Movies, the cheap-
est of popular entertainments, had begun to attract a huge, unprecedented
audience, rich and poor. Despite these democratizing qualities, even the
Playhouse stood against the "blood-and-thunder display" and the "cheap,
standardized type of picture" (Crowley 49). Constance D'arcy Mackay,
who promoted the community theater movement as a "potent and democratic" force (1), described the Neighborhood Playhouse's movies as "of a
high order, an antidote to the blood-and-thunder cinemas that flaunt their
luridly melodramatic posters the length and breadth of the East Side" (57).
By presenting movies at the settlement, the Lewisohns hoped to replace
the "dark, smelly, ramshackle nickelodeon" with "fresh paint, brighter
electric lights, and more hygienic allurements" (Crowley 49). Furthermore,
the Playhouse presented motion pictures as part of a larger festival program
that included interludes of live performances of skits and dances. The
theater could adopt the new powerfully alluring look of cinema and its stars
while promoting their less glossy performances in the interludes. Immigrants eager for the new cinema were expected to respond to these interludes by "unconsciously bringing their share of consideration in the way of
more courtesy, less aggressiveness" (48).

   The inclusive surface of the Playhouse's experimental festal productions
evoked an urban mass culture that allowed broad participation of all social
classes in leisure activities such as cabarets, amusement parks, and nickelode-
ons. These entertainments allowed the "elite to meet the street," belying
growing economic and geographic divisions. Thus, the press extolled popular style and image as a social leveler; a New York reporter wrote in 1898
that because the East Side sweatshop worker could make a copy of a high
society gown for herself, "Fifth Avenue and Grand Street walk hand in
hand" ("Keeping in Style"). The Neighborhood Playhouse had an ambivalent relationship to high society, soliciting contributions and inviting famous
actors but then burlesquing Broadway in its annual *Grand Street Follies*. The
Playhouse supported the work of Albert Carroll, a female impersonator who
mimicked famous theatrical artists and dancers. The amalgam of popular
forms introduced the aesthetics of upper-class urban culture while maintaining injunctions against it.

   To justify the theatrical collage of modernity and old-world tradition,
the Lewisohns promoted a metaphysical view of performance, a secularized,

essentialist theory of ritual that could absorb all other cultural signifiers. Their first informal productions were seasonal celebrations, supposedly common to all cultures, through which they hoped to tap a universal theme of a healing cyclical order, inherent in a romanticized nature. Children gave "impressions" of various world myths through skits, songs, and dances. Explaining the need for these rituals, Alice Lewisohn wrote, "Although the children of the neighborhood had inherited an old culture from their ancestors, in the city practically no contact remained with its source—nature" (Crowley 16). "Nature" was also revealed through movement and gesture that would transcend cultural differences—such as language—in an increasingly diverse urban milieu.

Thus, the Lewisohns favored pageantry, song, and dance over dramatic text, extolling the liberatory potential of the body in movement. As Alice Lewisohn (later, Alice Lewisohn Crowley) wrote:

> At the mother's meetings when we all laughed at the oldest and staidest who had to dance with a broomstick in lieu of a partner, she would suddenly become nimble-footed, and forthwith emerged steps and gestures of the folk dances of her youth in the old country. So we began to see, behind the ungainly appearance of the women, the unkempt helpless aspect of the men, a yearning for the values of the spirit and gratefulness for any gesture of understanding. (Crowley 13)

Through the Lewisohns' liberation of spirit through the theatrical arts, the "unkempt" immigrant body might evoke sentiment and sympathy, erasing the markers of poverty and ethnic difference.

The Lewisohns established an aura of unity that reflected only the Playhouse's identity, not the multiplicities of social identities and networks around it. This leveling of difference was apparent in their choice of production. In 1917, soon after the publication of Ezra Pound and Ernest Fenellosa's study of Japanese classical theater, the Playhouse presented the Noh play *Tamura*, which was originally performed as a ceremonial play for the temple of Kwannon, the Goddess of Mercy. A priest, traveling to Kioto, comes across the temple, where he is "struck by the spiritual beauty" of a boy, the temple servant. The boy relates the story of the temple's founding: a priest, Kenshin, saw Kwannon's golden light on the river and was approached by a manifestation of the goddess, who instructed him to find a patron to build a temple. Kenshin agreed and found his patron, Tamura Maro. After telling his story, the boy leaves, and the priest waits all night under the cherry trees. The boy reappears as Tamura Maro. Tamura tells tales of his exploits in driving out the evil spirits from the landscape. The play ends with a prayer to Kwannon, who kills the evil spirits with her arrows of wisdom, flung from her thousand hands.

Clearly, the plot elements conveniently promoted the Henry Street Settlement, which had its own version of the protective, wise, and merciful Kwannon, who blesses boys and raises them to higher economic levels. Furthermore, it extolled the virtues of institution building and patronage, though the patron is kept humble. Under the guise of presenting ethnic drama, the Playhouse could inscribe its own self-interest in a structure both exotically foreign and arty. The Playhouse production of *Tamura* had one Japanese actor, Michio Ito, who originally objected to the revival of feudal drama. The rest of the cast was composed of the Lewisohns and Ian Maclaren, thus demonstrating that uptown persons could embody themselves in a romanticized ethnic experience, guided by settlement work. The universalization of cultural forms allowed for this inscription.

The call for universal ritual and gesture was a refusal to acknowledge real class divisions and tensions in the "neighborhood," reducing the settlement's clientele to silent subjects within a theory of their natural, essential identity. Inspired by the theories of Carl Jung, the Lewisohns constructed that identity as antimechanistic, ahistorical, and prelinguistic: an essential part of a new "American unconscious . . . not made and standardized, but grown out of the experience of a people" (Lewisohn 3).[3] While other art theaters, such as the Provincetown Players, traded in popular Freudian theories and intimate psychodramas, the Neighborhood Playhouse found Jung's archetypes more amenable to an American cultural pluralism based on easily identifiable types.

Since an essential immigrant identity was not then tied to specific local customs, the Lewisohns traveled widely, collecting dramatic forms from around the world—Tibetan Devil Dances, Burmese festivals, whirling dervishes—and incorporating them in their theatrical productions. Irene Lewisohn studied Noh theater in Japan while traveling with Wald in 1910: Wald, watching her dance, "saw something Grecian in her movements, and caught at a link between two cultures remote in space and time" (Duffus 125). As the Neighborhood Playhouse grew in reputation, the Lewisohns adapted these world forms to their vision of American culture in festal drama, intended to display a new social harmony: a "dance drama from an ancient Celtic legend," a "pantomime" of a Norse fairy tale, an "impression of Burma," an "Arab Fantasia" (Crowley 252–60). Cultural difference was deflected into "impressions," or "moods," like tourist snapshots. For instance, *An Arab Fantasia* included scenes of milling crowds at a bazaar and a pilgrimage to a shrine, complete with a whirling dervish. A traditional dance called a "debke" was incorporated into a scene of Bedouin life in the desert: "the tribesmen vie with one another in feats of skill, yet with the harmony of a dance, their poise in tune with space, silence, stars" (189). While being educated about other cultural practices, participants in the fantasia could enact an identity that transcended crowds and conflict. That immigrants might have agency in constructing their own identities was not a question. Alice Lewisohn wrote that "baffled and confused" immigrants had "lost all sense of identity" in yielding to the demands of "sweated industry" (Crowley 7). Thus, the Playhouse ignored flexible strategies for constructing identities in a dynamic world of mixed social codes. Rather, they imposed a vision of ethnic types balanced and harmonized within theatrical manifestations of the collective unconscious.

This was most obvious in the Playhouse's adaptation of Walt Whitman's *Salut au Monde,* which the Lewisohns and Lillian Wald considered one of the theater's finest achievements, a "vision of unity formed out of diversity" (Crowley 122). The pageant was advertised as a celebration of the U.S. victory in World War I, a victory that Alice Lewisohn thought had provoked a feeling of "at-oneness that swept the land" (121). It was composed of scenes from the so-called dark and light sides of the "cosmic sphere," a procession of the peoples of the earth holding banners, and a series of religious ceremonies—Buddhist, Jewish, Greek, Islamic, Christian, even a Dionysian ritual—all accompanied by Walt Whitman's apostrophes to the inhabitants of the earth. Although a *New York Times* critic thought the "medley of high masses" was "a little too much" (Brock), Wald remembered that the production inspired broad participation from uptown and downtown:

> So exciting was this performance that distinguished people asked for the privilege of having a place in the processional that ended the play: the enthusiasm reached the colored porter, magnificent in form, who asked to march as the representative of his race, with naked thorax. (*Windows* 171)

The *Salut au Monde* was a blend of ethnic folk festival, canonical poetry, and the new "art theater" of the middle class. In the spirit of social harmony, the Neighborhood Playhouse cultivated experimental forms that would appeal both to local inhabitants and high society, increasingly luring an uptown audience—potential patrons of the Henry Street Settlement—that came slumming to experience the exotic. These forms grew out of the pageant, the "drama of democracy," which usually consisted of historical events reproduced in a linear sequence out in some public space. Throughout the 1910s and 1920s, the pageant movement swept across American towns. Organized by civic groups, often women's clubs, the community pageant was composed of skits, dances, and processions, usually dramatizing historical community moments. Pageant directors had a mission to establish collective local and national memories and instigate progressive social reforms.[4] According to one pageant critic, the movement's goal was to "induct immigrants into knowledge of American history" and to give them "an abiding sense of stability of society" (Bates 6). While the Playhouse aimed to transcend history in collectivity, creating a space in which Dionysus could meet Mohammed, its festal drama owed its appeal to the patriotic rhetoric of American pageantry as well as to the finer arts. Such nationalism might have worn the cloak of high culture, but it still constructed an ideal American citizen performing a civic duty.

Thus, the Playhouse successfully promoted a new vision of immigrant participation in the universalizing American pageant, without apparently erasing their traditions. So palatable was this vision of America that it was upheld as a model of social uplift. The *New York Times* made the Lewisohns' first community pageant into a symbol for the right use of educational propaganda for the working classes. This event was composed of skits from Henry Street's history, native songs and dances, and processions of inhabitants. It coincided with Mabel Dodge's Industrial Workers of the World (IWW) pageant in Madison Square Garden, which depicted events from the Paterson silk mill strike and was performed by over a thousand actual workers: men, women, and children. The *New York Times* was quick to compare, saying: "In the Henry Street celebration the motive was to exalt progress, intellectual development, and the triumph of civilization. In the other the motive was to inspire hatred, to induce violence" (editorial). Since the Lower East Side provided a large female work force to New York's garment industry, the comparison was specially pointed. And so the reputation of the dramatic activity of Henry Street as "wholesome and permanent," warding off labor unrest and the "institution of anarchy," was set. In contrast to the Paterson strike performers, the Lewisohns, despite their rhetoric of difference, provided a feminizing influence, upholding the values of industrial culture.

The Neighborhood Playhouse's ideal of community was articulated on lines of Jungian psychology and settlement house progressivism. But these attempts at unification and intersubjective transcendence were easily absorbed in the text of mass consumption and exploitation, the text of the privileged on whom the theater ultimately relied for its livelihood. Inscribed within the Neighborhood Playhouse's productions, Lillian Wald's vision of a Lower East Side as an enclave of the simple folk, preserved against the voracious influences of capitalism, was illusory and even oppressive in itself.

The immigrant subjects of, and participants in, the Playhouse's pageant and plays enacted a sociological vision of folk theater that subsumed the fragmented memories of old-world cultures. There, new-world identities were performed as transhistorical and transgeographical, essential and archetypal. Thus, old-world identities could easily be marketed and exchanged for new. By erasing differences and insisting on the transparency of its members to one another, the Playhouse prepared the immigrant population for full participation in the commodification of identities. From its inception the community theater represented itself as the emergent voice and public embodiment of the silent Other, but, in so doing, it became a kind of social work agency, instructing and positioning its subjects in the dominant culture's symbolic exchange, the hegemonic interests of the powerful. This articulation of community in itself eroded the possibility of cultural negotiation and liberation.

NOTES

1. Middle-class Reformed Jews who had already adapted to American life had a large role in assimilating immigrant European Jews through benevolent societies. Wald was the daughter of a successful optometrist, Max Wald, a German Jew who had emigrated to the United States in 1848, finally settling in Rochester. Wald used her connections to the wealthy Jewish community to attract patrons. These patrons were motivated by an ambivalent desire to end poverty through economic assimilation while preserving religious heritage. For a discussion of Wald's relationships to both communities, see Daniels 32–45.

2. For other discussions of these tensions in the broader work of settlements, see Ewen 76–91; and Trolander 7–21.

3. Alice Lewisohn was psychoanalyzed by Carl Jung and eventually ended up at the Zurich institute. Under her influence the Neighborhood Playhouse's costume designer, Aline Bernstein, also underwent Jungian analysis.

4. For recent discussions of the pageant movement's sociopolitical aims, see Glassberg and Prevots.

REFERENCES

Bates, Esther Willard. *Pageants and Pageantry*. New York: Ginn, 1912.
Brock, H. I. "East Side, Too, Has 'Synthetic Theater.'" *New York Times* 31 January 1926: V13.

Carson, Mina. *Settlement Folk: Social Thought and the American Settlement Movement, 1885–1930.* Chicago: U of Chicago P, 1990.

Cheney, Sheldon. *The Art Theater.* New York: Knopf, 1925.

Crowley, Alice Lewisohn. *The Neighborhood Playhouse.* New York: Theater Arts, 1959.

Daniels, Doris. *Always a Sister: The Feminism of Lillian D. Wald.* New York: The Feminist Press, 1989.

Dean, Alexander. *Little Theater Organization and Management.* New York: Appleton, 1926.

Dickinson, Thomas. *The Insurgent Theater.* New York: Benjamin Blom, 1917, 1972.

Duffus, R. L. *Lillian Wald: Neighbor and Crusader.* New York: Macmillan, 1938.

Editorial. *New York Times* 9 June 1913: 8.

Ewen, Elizabeth. *Immigrant Women in the Land of Dollars: Life and Culture on the Lower East Side, 1890–1925.* New York: Monthly Review, 1985.

Foucault, Michel. "Technologies of the Self." *Technologies of the Self: A Seminar with Michel Foucault.* Ed. Luther H. Martin, Huck Gutman, and Patrick H. Hutton. Amherst: U of Massachusetts P, 1988.

Gard, Robert E., and Gertrude S. Burly. *Community Theater: Idea and Achievement.* New York: Duell, Sloan, and Pearce, 1959.

Giddens, Anthony. *Central Problems in Social Theory: Action, Structure, and Contradiction in Social Analysis.* Berkeley: U of California P, 1989.

Glassberg, David. *American Historical Pageantry: The Uses of Tradition in the Early Twentieth Century.* Chapel Hill: U of North Carolina P, 1990.

Gramsci, Antonio. *Selections from the Prison Notebooks.* Ed. and trans. Quentin Hoare and Geoffrey Nowell Smith. New York: International, 1971.

"Keeping in Style." *New York Tribune* 3 July 1898. Qtd. in Ewen 26.

Lewisohn, Alice. "Welcoming the Habima to Grand Street." *New York Times* 30 October 1927, sec. 9:4.

Macgowan, Kenneth. *Footlights across America: Towards a National Theater.* New York: Harcourt, Brace, 1929.

Mackay, Constance D'Arcy. *The Little Theater in the United States.* New York: Henry Holt, 1917.

MacKaye, Percy. *The Civic Theater.* New York: Mitchell Kennerley, 1912.

Marshall, Edward. "Good Metal in Our Melting Pot, Says Miss Wald." *New York Times* 16 November 1913, sec. 5:6.

McConachie, Bruce A. "Using the Concept of Cultural Hegemony to Write Theater History." *Interpreting the Theatrical Past.* Ed. Thomas Postlewait and Bruce A. McConachie. Iowa City: U of Iowa P, 1989.

Prevots, Naima. *American Pageantry: A Movement for Art and Democracy.* Ann Arbor, MI: UMI Research Press, 1990.

Trolander, Judith Ann. *Professionalism and Social Change: From the Settlement House Movement to the Neighborhood Centers, 1886 to the Present.* New York: Columbia UP, 1987.

Wald, Lillian. *The House on Henry Street.* New York: Holt, 1915.

———. *Windows on Henry Street.* Boston: Little, Brown, 1934.

Weinberg, Mark S. *Challenging the Hierarchy: Collective Theater in the United States.* Westport, CT: Greenwood, 1992.

Young, Iris Marion. "The Ideal of Community and the Politics of Difference." *Feminism/Postmodernism.* Ed. Linda J. Nicholson. New York: Routledge, 1988.

PART TWO. NATION NOW

Josephine Lee

"Speaking a Language That We Both Understand": Reconciling Feminism and Cultural Nationalism in Asian American Theater

As Asian Americans gain more prominence in various areas of public discourse, there must be a corresponding pressure to acknowledge the complexity of the designation "Asian American." The challenges of self-representation for Asian Americans and other peoples of color are compounded in this age of multicultural initiatives: one must negotiate not just the search for visibility but also the managing of such "hyphenated" identities as they become increasingly visible. In particular, one must be aware of how these identities might be constructed in ways that elide or exclude some of the very individuals or groups that they mean to represent.

I myself experienced such a concern while working on my recent book, *Performing Asian America: Race and Ethnicity on the Contemporary Stage.* There I tried to suggest how certain dramatic works written and produced by Asian Americans have helped to re-form racial identity in the wake of the Asian American movement. Yet I became well aware that the book represented a rather limited population. It focused mainly on plays by second- or third-generation, Chinese and Japanese American, college-educated, and English-speaking playwrights. In a separate article, "Between Immigration and Hyphenation: The Problem of Theorizing Asian American Theater," I suggested that theater work by more recent immigrants from Asia might challenge the canon of "Asian American drama" suggested by analyses such as my own *Performing Asian America,* as much as this theater work might challenge more conventional notions of the "American" canon. My book and essay both acknowledged the many progressive aspects of Asian American activism and the consciousness-raising efforts that grew out of these civil rights movements. These political projects, and many of the theater works that participated in them, aimed to combat the notion of American as monolithically white, in part by insisting that Asian Americans, through their long-term presence and historic contributions to the building of the United States, qualified fully as "American." Yet, as the article more fully explored, by rooting Asian American identities in ideals of historical owner-ship through habitation and work ("my family has been here for genera-tions"; "we worked this land"; "we built this railroad"), one perpetuates the problem of excluding more recent immigrants. Aspiring to the status of the "fully American" does not allow us to problematize American identity, both inside and outside the borders of the United States.

My conclusion upon completing both studies is that plays by Asian Americans do not so much "represent" a stable existing national, cultural, or social identity as they "perform" certain tensions and contradictions that have to do with staking out such positions. This is perhaps true of many genres of Asian American cultural production, such as novels or films; it is particularly evident in the theater. Asian Americans playwrights not only address the long-standing racism inherent within cultural representation in the United States; their works are also subject to the tensions between the desire for a pan-ethnic, politically unified Asian American social "body" and the fissures within that construction. These fissures occur most noticeably in terms of gender and sexuality as well as immigration and citizenship status, ethnicity, generation, and class.

Here I want to follow this line of inquiry by establishing in more detail how the discussion of theater's expression of so-called "Asian American" cultural paradigms must focus more fully on their gendered nature. Certainly there is a strong historical connection that compels us to do so. The recent American theatrical practices that one might associate with either "Asian American" or "feminist" activist politics have similar objectives as well as concurrent histories. Both are rooted in the activist movements of the 1960s and after, which sought to reform sexist and racist cultural representation as well as inequalities in economic and social hierarchy, law, and government policy. Both changed how historically oppressed bodies might be viewed on and off the stage. Yet their relationship is far from straightforward.

Scholars in Asian American studies have long remarked how potential divisions, marked along the lines of gender and sexuality, might belie a "strategically constructed unitary identity" as "Asian American" (Kim xii). William Wei, for instance, documents how the "Asian American women's movement" directly challenged "the Asian American patriarchy mani-fested in the [Asian American] Movement," pointing out how some male activists excluded women from leadership positions or treated them as inferior beings or sexual objects (75). Recent criticism has pointed out the apparent schism between "womanist" politics and the masculinist propensities of "minority" cultural nationalism movements in the United States and the manifestation of this schism in artistic production. For instance, *The Norton Anthology of African American Literature* remarks on "the clear misogyny and ugly homophobia" and the "inescapable, paramilitary, social-realist bravado of male leaders" in the Black Arts movement (Gates 1805). In her study of the activist Chicano theater group El Teatro Campesino, Yolanda Broyles-González suggests that praise for their stagings of labor issues, history, and Chicano culture must be qualified by an awareness of the sexism present in the company's structure and implicit in its early presentations (Broyles-González).

Asian American cultural criticism also has begun to examine the tensions and contradictions within what is presumably "Asian American" or feminist in literature, film, and other arts. Yet, in extending this commentary to look more specifically at recent plays by Asian Americans, we need to ask how to avoid framing these tensions as evidence of some automatic division between "feminist" and "masculinist" cultural movements or as demonstration of Asian American feminism as simply another "colored" version of "white" American feminism's struggle for self-empowerment. Works written for the theater can be crucial in exploring the question of how consciousnesses and bodies are not "gendered" or "racialized" in any simple way. I would like to explore these issues with respect to a number of contemporary works written for the theater by Asian Americans, most notably Diana Son's 1993 play *R.A.W. ('Cause I'm a Woman)*.

I will begin by considering two of the potentially divisive ways in which gender is performed in relation to Asian American cultural nationalism and identity: the first, how Asian American cultural nationalism struggles to recuperate Asian American masculinity; the second, how feminist liberation might imagine itself in rebellion against an imagined Asian patriarchy. Both impulses must be framed within the context of particular events and circumstances of Asian American history and cultural studies.

A distinctive history of gender and racial codes established the conditions by which Asians first came to and lived within the United States. The nineteenth-century influx of Chinese immigrants, for the most part male laborers, followed by the immigration of Japanese, Filipino, and Asian Indian men later in the twentieth century, was regarded with suspicion, fear, and violence. As scholars have suggested, these Asian male immigrants embodied the threat of Asian masculinity to the white, heterosexual ideology that governed "America" as a nation-state.[1] The racialized tensions that ensued led not only to the marking of Asian men as lifelong aliens (with laws that prevented immigration, land ownership, education, and citizenship) but also to the barring of many Asian women from immigration. Laws that increasingly restricted immigration (such as the 1882 Chinese Exclusion Act, which was not repealed until 1943) were compounded by various anti-miscegenation laws, leading to the isolation of significant numbers of Chinese and Filipino men in bachelor communities. Despite substantive changes in law and policy, demographics, and political and cultural visibility of Asian Americans, the continued effects of such a history are still felt. Throughout the last century Asian American men could well be said to have suffered the effects of literal and figurative emasculation that took place on a number of levels: as a result of racist laws preventing immigration, naturalization, marriage, education, and voting; the lack of political power and visibility; and the pervasive racial stereotyping that has continued from early variations on the coolie, the "heathen chinee," or the "yellow peril" to more recent incarnations of Fu Manchu and Charlie Chan, the "model minority," or the "geek."

Countering the ideology disseminated through these stereotypes seems a necessary corollary to other anti-racist strategies. Thus, it comes as no surprise how Asian American playwrights as well as other artists have promoted the necessary but difficult reconstruction of masculinity for the Asian American male. Such an impulse seems to motivate Frank Chin's *The Chickencoop Chinaman* (1972), a play that perhaps most clearly articulates some of these concerns. Although some of the characterization and dialogue of this play might seem somewhat dated, its concerns about gender remains very much in force.

Chin's play follows its Chinese American protagonist, Tam Lum, as he seeks to complete his documentary film on Ovaltine the Dancer, an African American boxing champion. En route, Tam enacts his own anxieties about thwarted or inadequate paternity as he reminisces with his old friend Kenji, spars verbally with the various other characters, and tries to sort out his own failed marriage. Chin not only makes anxieties about masculine adequacy central to the language, action, and characterization of the play; he also links Tam's worries to the larger context of Asian American history. Tam's problems are intimately connected to the emasculation of Asian American males through exclusion laws and racism; as Tam explains to Kenji and Kenji's friend Lee, "The laws didn't let our women in . . . and our women born here lost their citizenship if they married a man from China" (*Chickencoop* 26).

Tam's own attempts to ease his deeply rooted fears that "Chinamens make lousy fathers" are ultimately left unresolved in the play; Tam never successfully interviews Ovaltine's father for his film, nor does he come to terms with his failure to keep his own children, who are in the custody of his ex-wife. But it is the profundity of this tragic emasculation and the terms of his coping with it that distinguish the play and make it so memorable. Through dramatic action and symbol, poetic language, and complex characterization Chin's play lays out many of the theatrical motifs by which other plays, by both male and female Asian Americans, figure Asian American masculinity: a central Asian American male protagonist; a preoccupation with patrilineage and fatherhood; the need for acknowledged Asian American heroes; the construction of Asian American masculine identity through claiming an authorizing history. Many works by both male and female Asian American playwrights seem to follow the preoccupation with literal and symbolic father figures first addressed by Chin. The relationship of Asian American sons and fathers is at the center not only of Chin's two plays *The Chickencoop Chinaman* and *The Year of the Dragon* (1974) but also Momoko Iko's *Gold Watch* (1970), David Henry Hwang's *The Dance and The Railroad* (1981), Laurence Yep's *Pay the Chinaman* (1987), Genny Lim's *Bitter Cane* (1989), and Philip Kan Gotanda's *Fish Head Soup* (1991). Each of these plays tells a very different story. *Gold Watch* describes the impending wartime internment of a Japanese American farming family, *The Dance and the Railroad* examines the relationship of two striking Chinese railroad workers, *Pay the Chinaman* portrays a battle of wits between two con men in the California of 1893, *Bitter Cane* depicts the oppression of plantation workers in Hawaii in the 1880s, and *Fish Head Soup* looks at a contemporary Japanese American family scarred by internalized racism and memories of internment. Yet each also addresses, among its other concerns, the need for the identity of the younger Asian American male character to be affirmed through symbolic bonding with an older Asian American man.

This bonding is also addressed more humorously as well. In *The Chickencoop Chinaman* Tam's need for masculine heroes leads him to a failed attempt to construe the Lone Ranger as a Chinese American hero in disguise, whose mask hides his slanty eyes. Similarly, a preoccupation with finding suitably masculine Asian American role models in popular culture figures prominently in a number of plays such as R. A. Shiomi's 1984 *Yellow Fever* (a detective mystery in which the private eye is Japanese Canadian Sam Shikaze), Lane Nishikawa's 1991 *I'm on a Mission from Buddha* (a series of vignettes, all played by Nishikawa, that depict different Asian American male characterizations), and Eric Michael Zee's 1996 *Exit the Dragon* (the stories of three frustrated Asian American actors). Gotanda's 1988 *Yankee Dawg You Die* gently parodies this tendency when Bradley runs through his audition monologue, a piece from "the first Asian American play I ever saw" (91), for his fellow Hollywood actor Vincent.

> *Bradley:* And I'd drive. Long into the night. Windows down, my girl Bess beside me, the radio blasting away. . . . But it continued to escape me—this thing, place, that belonged to me. . . . And then the D.J. came on the radio, "Here's a new record by a hot new artist, 'Carol' by Neil Sedaka! Neil who? Sedaka? Did you say, "Sedaka"? (*Pronunciation gradually becomes more Japanese.*) Sedaka. Sedaka. Sedaka. *Sedaakaa.* As in my father's cousin's brother-in-law's name, Hiroshi Sedaka? What's that you say—the first Japanese American rock-'n'-roll star? Neil Sedaka! That name. I couldn't believe it. Suddenly everything was all right. I was there. Driving in my car, windows down, girl beside me— with a goddamn Buddhahead singing on the radio. . . . Neil Sedaakaa! I knew. I just knew for once, wherever I drove to that night, the road belonged to me. (*Silence.*)
> *Vincent:* Bradley? Neil Sedaka is not Japanese.
> *Bradley:* Yes, I know.
> *Vincent:* I have met him before. He's Jewish, or was it Lebanese. Very nice fellow. But definitely not Japanese.
> *Bradley:* Yes, yes, I know. It's by Robinson Kan, the Sansei playwright. It shows the need we have for legitimate heroes. And how when you don't have any, just how far you'll go to make them up.
>
> (92)

One might read the playwright's preoccupation with father figures and legitimate heroes as the conscious or unconscious attempt to reproduce a specific version of "normal" or "regular" masculinity: an Asian American masculinity that lays claim to normalized models of family, behavior, and myths thought to be inherently "American"—this is in keeping with an even more subtle manifestation of the problem of restoring an authoritative masculinity to the Asian American male. One might argue that patriarchy is woven even more deeply into the discursive terms of Asian American cultural nationalism, insofar that one of its primary impulses was and still is the construction of a particular kind of validating history. At the end of *The Chickencoop Chinaman,* Tam alludes to such a history in his recollection of the return of his great-grandfather, a Chinese railroad worker; even though Tam's immediate quest for identity remains unfulfilled, the play's search for father figures resolves itself optimistically, glancing toward history to satisfy its urges for an authorizing patrilineage. This ending suggests that the very impulse to validate identity through history might be thought of in terms of such a patrilineage, in which a cultural identity might be claimed through looking for its "roots" in American soil. By emphasizing the long-term presence of Asian immigrants and their descendants in the United States, Asians and those of Asian descent in the United States might argue for their contributions to the building of the country and their identity as Asian Americans rather than sojourners or permanent aliens. Yet it also tends to validate Asian American identity by focusing on Asian American male participation in the building of "America." Genny Lim refers to such a vision in a moment of her 1978 play *Paper Angels,* when the Chinese settler Chin Gung speaks of being "in love with this land."

> I'll tell you one thing though, I know this land, I ache for her sometimes, like she was my woman. When I dig my hands into her flesh and seed her, something grows; when I water and fertilize her, she begins to swell. If you treat her with respect, she responds, just like a woman. A lot of whites don't know this. (40)

Such a speech captures how the very writing of Asian American history—in terms rife with images of land as feminized, ownership and identity as masculinized—might foster a certain paradigmatic gendering of Asian American cultural nationalism. It does so, of course, through reproducing particularly gendered myths of land, ownership, nationalism, and entitlement. Such terms leave unexamined the deeper problematics of these constructions of Asian American history.

As I've suggested, Chin's *The Chickencoop Chinaman* sets up theatrically the terms of the vigorous reconstruction of Asian American male identity, a project in which many have participated. It is not difficult to see within the play the pitfalls of this reconstruction; such a project relies on patriarchal and heterosexual paradigms of masculinity and the disavowal of what is marked as feminine, effeminate, and/or homosexual. As Tam rejects the racist, emasculating stereotypes that have been set up for him, he also dismisses as "feminized," the inferior versions of assimilated Asian American identity epitomized by characters such as Kenji's friend Lee (a Chinese American or Eurasian woman passing for white); Lee's former husband, Tom (who espouses the worth of the Chinese as a "model minority"); and, to some extent, even the now-upper-middle-class Kenji. Homosexuality can be envisioned only as a concession to the psychic emasculation already in progress.

Tam is particularly angered by Tom's view that his only choices lie in selling himself to whites as an self-exoticizing "ornamental Oriental" or as "queer"; to Tam, Tom is "not a man" (*Chickencoop* 59).

Cultural nationalism becomes expressed through fixing race and gender in binary oppositions, in which "true" Asian American identity must be preserved against assimilation or contamination. Of particular concern is exogamy, both literal and figurative. In the symbolic economy of this version of Asian American cultural nationalism, Asian American women embody both the promise of sustaining the Asian American cultural body and the threat of its dissolution. Thus, of particular worry in Chin's *The Chickencoop Chinaman* is the figure of Lee, whose ambiguous racial status and sexual experience with men of many races renders her a potential danger to the already fragile egos of the Asian American male characters and who directly taunts both Tam and Kenji of being "mama's boys and crybabies, not a man in all your males" (24).

Chin also depicts the problem of "marrying out" in his *The Year of the Dragon,* in which the character of Sis, trying to escape her Chinatown roots, has married Ross, the patronizing white Orientophile, self-described as a "sincerely interested student of all things Chinese" (*Dragon* 79). Her brother, Fred, reassures Ross that "it's the rule not the exception for us to marry out white," calling Chinatown "your private preserve for an endangered species" (85). Asian American women have the potential to become race traitors whose bodies and offspring have become assimilated, the most powerful threat to the integrity of a homogeneous Asian American cultural body. Chin and his coeditors of *Aiiieeeee! An Anthology of Asian American Writers* worry about the imminent "extinction" of Asian American communities through marrying out, that "we have become the instruments of our own historical and racial extinction" (Chin and Chan xli):

> The destruction of our history and culture was accomplished in one action that split us culturally, racially, historically, morally, sexually, and generated mutual contempt and less and less love and sex between yellow boys and girls, men and women, as time went by. The moral sexual imperative of the white supremacist stereotype: hate yellow men. The men are responsible for the civilization. The men are the masters. The masters of a perverse civilization are themselves perverts. The women of this perverse civilization are helpless and hapless victims whose entire being and secret soul cry for escape and rescue from this hateful civilization and culture. (xxxix–xl)

A potential splitting along gendered lines seems imminent, given these terms. The masculinist and heteronormative propensities of Asian American cultural nationalism seem incompatible with women's empowerment and self-determination. Aggravating this rift is yet another set of associations linking what is "Asian" with traditional and oppressive patriarchy and what is "American" with feminist liberation.

One set of theatrical examples in which this association seems to be vividly expressed is the playwriting of Asian Americans that in fact predates both the Asian American and the women's movement of the past few decades. It is clearly articulated in a number of early plays by Asian American women writers, whose rediscovery seems consistent with the feminist literary project of resurrecting the works of women writers.[2] A particularly striking example can be found in Li Ling-Ai's *The Submission of Rose Moy* (1927).[3] Rose, a Hawaiian-born Chinese college student, is threatened with a forced marriage to the old and wealthy Kwang Wei. Rose confides in her American teacher, Mr. Donald, who offers her an alternative plan; Rose will live with his sister in Berkeley while she finishes her work. But, just as she makes the decision to run away, her father gives her a letter left for her from her deceased mother. The letter urges her to "bow to the will of your ancestors" and to "remember . . . you are a Chinese" (Li 63). Upon reading this edict from the maternal dead, Rose gives up her dream of education and agrees to marry at her father's request. In the dramatic conclusion, accompanied by the ominous sound of gongs, Rose utters: "I am of the East—I bow. I submit to the will of my ancestors!" and faints before the ancestral tablets, while outside her American teacher waits for her, whistling "Yankee Doodle Dandy." In the stage directions, Ling-Ai adds: "Mr. Donald is still waiting, and he waits in vain!" (64).

The melodramatic tension of this play relies on a gendered and ethnicized opposition between what is "American" (feminist freedom) and what is "Chinese" (patriarchal oppression). Rose's dream is not only personal self-determination but also autonomy for other Chinese women; she declares her wish to finish her graduate education in order to work for suffrage, to help Chinese women "to rise above the shackles of tradition that have bound our women from time immemorial, and have imprisoned their spirits." Such an opposition played out as irreconcilable. The play seems to illustrate, in the most spectacular of ways, what might be called a particular mode of racializing feminist principles: female characters are trapped by an "old-world" Asian patriarchy, with its "dusty and diabolical traditions" (56), or newly liberated by an "American" freedom. Significantly—and perhaps problematically—

feminism involves dispensing with "traditional" Asian or Asian American males and forming an alliance with a "white" masculine America.

The worry that Asian American "womanist" sentiments must be pitted against a masculinist "cultural nationalism" is clearly expressed in the critical reception of artistic works. Critics such as Sau-Ling Wong and Elaine Kim have noted the controversy surrounding the wide acclaim of Maxine Hong Kingston's novel *The Woman Warrior*. The marked commercial success and criticial recognition of this work over other examples of Asian American writing (even Kingston's subsequent novels *China Men* and *Tripmaster Monkey*) seem disturbingly linked to a tendency to read the book as an implication of Chinese and Chinese American male sexism.[4] Despite persuasive refutations, such reductive readings of Kingston as backing feminism against a male chauvinism marked "Asian" persist and are fueled by the anger of critics such as Ben Tong, who perceives Kingston's success as won through creating images of Asian American women in "perpetual torment at the hands of awful yellow men" (5).

Frank Chin's well-known criticisms of Maxine Hong Kingston are also in keeping with such accusations. Chin frames Kingston's success in the mainstream as a kind of betrayal, demonstrating an assimilated and feminized sensibility that ultimately demeans the power and authority of the Asian American male writer.[5] He accuses Kingston in particular of taking liberties with the mythic heroine Fa Mu Lan, turning "her into a champion of Chinese feminism and an inspiration to Chinese American girls to dump the Chinese race and make for white universality" ("Real and the Fake" 27). He also suggests that Kingston has not been alone in her efforts; Chin defines a continuing trend of what he sees as Chinese American "Christian" autobiographies such as Jade Snow Wong's *Fifth Chinese Daughter* (1953), which sustain stereotypes of Chinese American men as "louts" or "so misogynistic they don't deserve to survive" ("Real and the Fake" 25, 9). The relative commercial success of Asian American women writers such as Kingston or Amy Tan can be attributed in part to their perpetuation of these popular stereotypes; "American publishers," Chin insists, "went crazy for Chinese women dumping on Chinese men." Chin implicitly blames a certain kind of feminist enterprise for conspiring to estrange Asian American women from Asian American men, mocking the unwillingness of "Chinese American women . . . to deal with Chinese American men until the men resolve their own conflicts" as "an extreme expression of the identity crisis" that "incapacitates the race" (27).

Must Asian American politics necessarily be split along gendered lines? Can feminist empowerment happen only at the expense of Asian American cultural unity? We might well be cautious about too readily accepting these terms. Scholars such as Lisa Lowe, for instance, have warned us of the propensity to imagine an essentialized Asian American identity that "generalizes Asian American identity as male," thus rendering women "invisible" and fostering "debates where Asian American feminists who challenge Asian American sexism are cast as 'assimilationist, as betraying Asian American nationalism" (30–31). Conversely, Trinh T. Minh-ha has identified the equation of *feminism* with *Westernization* and the apparent incompatibility of "woman" with "ethnic" as the product of a specific brand of Euro-American feminism that assumes a "universal" female condition (106).

It is especially dangerous to leave unexamined the linking of feminism with a racialized "white America." Such an association duplicates the gendering of Orientalist fantasies of imperial rule, in which, as Gayatri Spivak suggests, the prospect of "rescuing" the compliant Oriental female could play a key role in justifying imperialist force and colonial rule: "White men are saving brown women from brown men" (296–97). Thus, an alliance of "America" with Asian American feminism only reiterates another all-too-familiar gendered paradigm of the Asian (American) woman liberated, with the help of "American" values, from her oppressive and barbaric male counterparts. As we shall see, this is remarkably similar to the fantasy that is played out in the numerous versions of the Madame Butterfly story.

I have suggested how some Asian American plays respond to the historic emasculation—both literal and symbolic—of Asian American males by staging aspects of Asian American cultural nationalism framed along masculinist lines. These plays affirm what Cynthia Enloe suggests, that nationalisms have "typically sprung from masculinized memory, masculinized humiliation and masculinized hope" (44). I have noted how others might conceptualize the liberation of Asian American female characters as taking place as a marked repudiation of Asian male privilege. Yet what is even more interesting to me are those instances of refusal to *necessarily* pit feminism against Asian American cultural nationalism. If some of the plays that I have mentioned stage the extremes of a perceived disjunction between the projects of reconstructing Asian American masculinity and feminism, others both reflect upon these tensions and offer us a way out of them.

A range of plays addresses these potential divisions in ways that are even more remarkably self-conscious and careful. To begin with, there is a certain caution in the ways in which plays such as Wakako Yamauchi's *And the Soul Shall Dance* (1977) or Philip Gotanda's *The Wash* (1987) portray the physical and mental abuse of Asian American female characters by Asian American males. In the former, the passionate Emiko is trapped in a loveless marriage with a man who beats her and steals her money; in the latter, the meek Masi still does the laundry for the abusive husband from whom she has separated. Significantly, these more recent plays display a degree of restraint and self-consciousness in their portrayals; markedly different from earlier plays such as *The Submission of Rose Moy;* they counter a direct association of "Asian" and "patriarchy" with more complex sets of characterizations, including other Asian American male characters who are far from abusive or chauvinistic. *And the Soul Shall Dance* contrasts the depiction of Emiko's marriage with the loving relationships of the Muratas, a family on a neighboring farm. In *The Wash,* Masi finds happiness with the gentle and affectionate Sadao, a Japanese American widower. The reconstruction of Asian American history performed in plays such as Lim's *Paper Angels,* Wakako Yamauchi's *12-1-A* (1982) and *The Music Lessons* (1977), Darrell Lum's *Oranges Are Lucky* (1976), and Edward Sakamoto's trilogy *Hawai'i No Ka Oi* clearly gives voice to the experiences of female as well as male characters and examine the roles of both in "building America." Such attempts to reconcile the terms of feminism and Asian American cultural nationalism suggest that the two projects need not be exclusive of one another—or perhaps, at least, that they are conscious of the dangers of their own tendencies to set up binary oppositions and reinforce gendered rivalries.

Perhaps it is in a play such as Diana Son's *R.A.W. ('Cause I'm a Woman)* that we most clearly see the ways in which the supposedly "conflicting" impulses of feminism and Asian American cultural nationalism might work in tandem. Such tensions inform the play's form as well as its content and are at the heart of its staging of Asian American sexual politics. The play can be interpreted on the one level as a debunking of common stereotypes of Asian women as passive, fetishized sex objects. The exploitation inherent in the theatrical display of the Asian American female body, a body that is always already marked as "only sexual" (Cheung 236), is challenged in different ways first by sarcastic one-liners, then by the frank monologues of four Asian American female characters. Both the retorts and the monologues work to create the impression of the "real" and "raunchy" Asian American woman, whose sexuality and emotional life cannot be contained by the limitations of the stereotype.

In the first part of the play musical interludes from Peggy Lee's "I'm a Woman" mark off different sections, each "riff" describing first encounters and personal ads in which these women are typed as "exotic" or "obedient" or "mysterious." The characters ridicule a series of slides in which clichés such as "I love Oriental Women" or "Looking for . . . Sexy Asian Gal" are flashed on a screen (292–93). Son suggests that she chose the use of slides rather than male voices delivering these lines because they afford a kind of neutrality:

> In *R.A.W. ('Cause I'm a Woman)* I wanted the man's lines to be slides because I didn't want lines like "I've never been with an Oriental woman before" to be delivered with exaggeration or mockery. Slides are non-judgmental. I am not trying to condemn men who say lines like this. The words express themselves, no commentary is necessary. (290)

The "non-judgmental" delivery of these words suggests that Son's critique is aimed less at individual men than at a larger discourse permeated by such fetishizing of the Oriental woman. Yet the juxtaposition of slides with actors allows the critique of both to be effective. That she evokes the stereotype through a series of captions, rather than through powerful visual images, allows the characters' live presence to dominate the stage. By presenting these characters in the flesh but keeping the stereotype at the level of the disembodied typeface, Son's "raunchy" Asian American women are made to seem more believable: the "truthful" representation that can easily and humorously debunk the false stereotype. In the second part of the play, as the characters tell moving monologues about their first sexual encounters, problems finding partners, and love affairs, the fake exoticism of the "Oriental" is exchanged for explorations of an even more "authentic" sexuality and vision of self.

Yet interpreting this play as simply responding to popular stereotypes of Oriental geishas or exotica does not go far enough to tell us how such "selves" are constructed. The play does present a refreshing refusal of stock images of Oriental femininity, but it does not stop there. Perhaps even more interesting is how we might understand both the play's challenge to stereotype and its creation of these "real" characters in light of those concerns regarding feminist and Asian American cultural nationalist enterprises and their possible intersection.

It is significant that the stereotype targeted most directly in the play is one that has implications both for Asian American cultural nationalism and feminism. As James Moy suggests, the stereotype of the "butterfly" in the United States, from David Belasco's 1900 stage version of John Luther Long's short story to the Broadway musical *Miss Saigon* in 1988, is connected with Orientalist fantasies and the changing economic and political interests of the United States in Asian countries as well as anxieties about Asian immigrants. The stereotype enforces a paradigm of heterosexual desire between passive Asian female and aggressive white male that ultimately results in tragedy. This stereotype is doubly problematic, for it configures both another means of enforcing the figurative emasculation of Asian American men (by normalizing a paradigm of heterosexual white male sexuality and Oriental female aquiescence) as well as insisting on the passivity (she can only act in alliance with the white male) and victimhood (her action results in a convenient self-erasure) of the Asian female. Doing battle with this particular stereotype, then, is a task in which Asian American cultural nationalism and feminism may be allied. Both have a stake in discrediting this myth of the Oriental female; both must do so in order to address the demonization and erasure of Asian American men as well as the subjugation of Asian American women.

In the case of *R.A.W.* it is clear that these multiple designs are at work. The first part of the play directly targets the butterfly stereotype, addressing its persistence even in a society that is supposedly more sexually "liberated." The butterfly stereotype no longer strictly alludes to an exclusively heterosexual, white-Oriental relationship. It's suggested in the range of "personal ads," including not only "SWM" but also "MBM," "Bi-Curious F" and "Separated HM with kids," that other relationships—even ones that suggest potentially more flexible identity categories and sexual relations—might indeed fall prey to this stereotype of the hyperfeminized Asian women. Yet, significantly, the Asian American male is conspicuously absent from this oppressive model of "masculine" behavior. (Character 3 sarcastically notes that the male "wants to wow me with the size of his non-Asian dick" [Son 292]). The first part of the play makes it clear not only how pervasive and persistent such a stereotype is but also that the problems of the erasure of Asian American male sexuality do not end simply by exposing the hyperfeminized "butterfly" for what it is.

Denying this paradigm of sexuality in favor of a more assertive and more flexible mode of sexual expression for Asian American women means that Asian American men must be also reinscribed, even if they are not allowed an actual presence alongside the Asian American women onstage. In the second part of the play the monologues are notable not only for their articulation of multiple versions of Asian American female desire but also for the ways in which Asian American men might figure in that desire. A subtle but significant aspect of *R.A.W.* is the way in which its monologues allow for the implied presence of Asian American men within the expanded set of relationships advocated for Asian American women.

The first monologue, led by Character 3, describes the relationship of a Korean American teenager with "Paul Rossman." The Asian American female desire for the white male body is clearly figured as a desire to assimilate; the narrator is not only dating what she describes as "six-feet two inches of purebred whiteboy"; she also sees herself as "the only Asian in town . . . a famous preppie" (294). Tropes of cultural purity and assimilation—the sense that white America can or might refuse to absorb these Asian bodies—are reinforced through food metaphors; she is told by her mother not to eat kimchee because "kimchee smells terrible . . . It's not nice for Paul." The narrator consumes more typical American food, including "green jello with little marshmallows," in order that her breath might remain "clean for kissing Paul Rossman."

The narrator and mother's chilling compliance with the tropes of cultural and culinary purity has some interesting dissonances. Through her eating habits, the body of the Asian American girl becomes deracinated in order to be better absorbed into the white American social body. Yet the monologue makes ironic comments on cultural purity as well: Paul has "flaky chapped lips which he marinated in vaseline, kissing him was like licking a carburetor." There is mention of a potentially illicit relationship between Paul and his divorcée mother: "Once I caught them dancing. She was drunk, he was embarrassed. I was glad I came in when I did" (294). Such comments suggest a contamination or degradation of the purely white American social body, which in turn implies a dubious purpose for the interracial relationship: that the Asian American "model minority" might in fact renew the traditionally white society with fresh blood.

Yet, even more significantly, the interracial relationship between Paul and the narrator is offset by another heterosexual relation mentioned in the narrator's story. The lessons learned—of Asian food as "dirty" and "impure"; of white Americans unable to eat the true form of the "other"—are qualified by the girl's question about "daddy's dinner" as it "reeked on the stove":

> But mom ate daddy's food. Mom ate kimchee. "How come you can eat kimchee?" She gave me green jello for dessert. "Because daddy eats it too. You can't smell it if you both eat it." Mom was Asian. Daddy was too. (294)

The presence of her two Asian parents, the implicit knowledge of their relationship as allowing both to partake of the "impure" food, belies the suggestion that her "big love" for the white Paul Rossman is the only sexual relationship available to her.

The second monologue, about a narrator who is rejected by men for being "not beautiful outside," suggests a critique of a specifically racialized version of the beauty myth. That the narrator's problem nonetheless has as much to do with negative as with positive racial stereotyping is emphasized in the highlighting of her features: "They called me plateface when I was a child. Not just to tease me because I was Chinese because I was Japanese because I was KoreanThaiVietnamese all rolled up into no one I know. My face is flat and truly flat when I was a child" (294). Her association of flat faces, "squinty eyes," and "straight flat" hair with ugliness is the very inverse of fetishized, racialized features that make up the butterfly stereotype.

Again, both the positive and negative versions of the racialized beauty myth are shown as no longer exclusively the domain of the white Orientalist. The lonely narrator finds that the many men "of any race" who reply to her personal ad are disappointed by her appearance. These men all generally subscribe to the expectation that Asian women would automatically be beautiful; here even Asian or Asian American men are potentially included in the "bouquet of hopeful suitors" who "wore disappointed faces" and, as the narrator finally concludes, are themselves "not beautiful inside or out" (294). Thus, despite its final gesture toward an ideal of inner beauty divorced from the external body ("This beautiful woman will never beg"), the monologue stops at pointing out how racialized notions of feminine beauty are pervasive, affecting all possible heterosexual relationships. Asian American men are implicitly included in this critique of masculinist behavior and yet in a way that, one might argue, avoids sounding the all-too-familiar charges of abusive "Asian" patriarchy or the "new machismo" by Asian American men.

Just as the second monologue suggests that Asian American men might potentially buy into the myth of Asian women as pretty, so does the third suggest that women, and perhaps Asian American women as well as others, may fall into similarly rigid categories of identity. Character 4, both in her earlier retorts and in her monologue, openly insists on her lesbian desire as a direct counter to the heteronormative values of the butterfly myth:

4: Then he says:
Slide: I love Oriental women.
3: And I want to say.
4: So do I.

(292)

Yet, despite her openness, other women—whose racial identities are again left open—inevitably fail to recognize her as a lesbian. The butterfly stereotype, influencing the perceptions of women as well as men, does not allow for lesbian desire, nor does it permit Character 4 to identify herself in other ways. One of the women she is attracted to is shocked by her disclosure, wondering, "Why would a cute Asian girl have to be queer?" (295).

Character 4's monologue addresses several dimensions of gendered, sexual, and racial stereotypes. As JeeYeun Lee notes, more than one factor influences the perception and enactment of Asian and Asian American lesbian and bisexual identities:

> One of these factors is a particular strain of Orientalist discourse in the U.S. that constructs Asian women of various ethnicities as hyper-feminine, exotic, passive objects of white heterosexual male desire. In an environment where we are constantly confronted by such expectations, our presentations of gender are decidedly not neutral. Another factor is the prevailing image in lesbian communities of what a lesbian looks like, an image that is constructed as white and butch, making invisible lesbian and bisexual women of color and femme women of all races. (117)

In Character 4's dilemma, faced by the apparent rigidity of each of the racial, gender, and sexual categories she inhabits ("I mean am I more cute than Asian? Am I more Asian than queer?") the play also questions stereotypes of lesbians as desperately unattractive or masculinized women. Her monologue resists the compulsory heterosexualization of Asian women as hyperfeminine; at the same time it also specifically targets lesbian butch/femme types, questioning the lengths to which Character 4 must place herself within binary sexual patterns, identifying herself as "butch" by an aggressive physicality, in order to be recognized: "What's a girl gotta do to get some attention from the same *sex* these days, stick my tongue down her throat and say 'and I don't just mean that as friends'?" (295).

The second and third monologues suggest a necessary reformation of the racialized, gendered, and sexualized paradigms that dictate relationships but leave unanswered questions of how such a reform might begin. The final monologue begins to address these questions; it is also, interestingly enough, the one monologue that examines directly the heterosexual relationship of Asian American men and women. The narrator recounts her love affair with a man who is also Korean American. She reads their initial bond as being based on a mutual denial of their "Koreanness"—which is figured as a response not only to certain stereotypes of the polite, passionless relationship of the "classic Korean couple" ("You did not pick me up from my mother's house in Queens in your top of the line Hyundai. I did not kiss

you on the cheek and tell you I had a nice time") but also to the familiar
stereotypes of Asian women:

> I didn't want you to think of me as a Korean woman. Men who have
> been attracted to me for being Korean were interested in who I am
> only on the surface without knowing who I am not in the deepest part
> of my heart. I am not ashamed of the presence of my heritage on my
> face but I mourn shamefully the absence of Korea in my heart. You and
> I had an unspoken pact—I wouldn't be Korean to you if you weren't
> Korean to me.

Yet their passion suddenly gets refigured from being the denial of race to
being raced, in the moment when he tells her in Korean that he loves her and
asks her to return his words. What begins as a love expressed in deracinated
terms ("I grew to love your gentle wildness, your clumsy grace, your spirit,
your spirit. And I had leaned on the hope that there were similar things to love
about me") becomes openly redefined as sexual passion that is re-implicated
in race. Although she sadly cannot fulfill his request, she comes to desire this as
well: "*Sarang hae.* The next time I say it I'll mean it" (295).

   In this monologue is a subtle refiguring of behaviors both masculine
and Asian: the Korean American male lover is the first to share his emotions
and to value her response to them. Through a systematic rejection of the
former heterosexual paradigms—first of the "classic Korean couple" and
then of the oppressive Orientalized stereotypes—a new set of terms, allowing for a new articulation of desire, has the potential to appear. What's
desired is the reconciliation of both ideals of Asian American cultural identity and female sexual desire, in which, as Character 1 suggests, "I will spend
sweaty hours speaking a language that we both understand" (296).

   It is the *specifics* of how *R.A.W. ('Cause I'm a Woman)* challenge the
rigidity of stereotypes of Asian women that are most crucial here. In a
general sense, the play allows us to refuse binary oppositions of both race and
gender. In response to the slide "Where are you from?" the characters reply,
"From a place where I was neither black nor white," "Where I checked the
box marked 'other,' " and "Where I made myself. Where I changed" (292).
Yet its specifics do not simply advocate a certain fluidity or permeability in
identity categories—but, rather, pinpoint quite concretely those tangible
constructions of social identity from which desire and consciousness spring.

   To recognize this, we must recall both the impulse of Asian American
cultural nationalism to restore Asian American masculinity and feminism's
attempt to address sexist representation and to explore possible means of

empowerment for women. These two directives are necessarily at odds only if the former project is thought of *as* restoration, the giving back of masculine authority that is "naturally" or "rightfully" there, for instance, through normative models of family or male primacy; or if the latter project essentializes gender by attributing "natural" or automatically negative qualities to maleness or essentializes other differences even while admitting the constructedness of gender (by, e.g., assuming that *Asian* might be equated with *patriarchal*). *R.A.W. ('Cause I'm a Woman)* reminds us that two projects can come together in terms of reassessing stereotypes, examining patriarchies in their many cultural manifestations, and complicating more thoroughly various gendered and racialized identities.

NOTES

1. See, for instance, chapter 3 of Takaki; and R. Lee, *Orientals*.

2. The repressive nature of patriarchal "Asian" values inflicted on young Asian American female characters is the subject of plays such as Wai Chee Chun's *Marginal Woman* (1936), Bessie (Inouye) Toishigawa's *Nisei* (1947), Mary Akimoto's *Strangers* (1950), and Molly Tani Shell's *Where Dwells the Heart* (1953). Playscripts are housed at the Roberta Uno Asian American Playwrights' Script Collection at the University of Massachusetts and at Sinclair Library at the University of Hawaii, Manoa.

3. (Gladys) Li Ling-Ai's play, *The Submission of Rose Moy*, was produced at the Arthur Andrews Theatre, University of Hawaii, Honolulu, in 1928 and first published in *Hawaii Quill Magazine* in 1927.

4. See, in particular, chapter 6, "Chinatown Cowboys and Warrior Women," in Kim, *Asian American Literature*. See also Cheung and Wong.

5. See Chin's contributions to both *Aiiieeeee!* and *The Big Aiiieeeee!* as well as his essay "This Is Not an Autobiography."

REFERENCES

Berson, Misha, ed. *Between Worlds: Contemporary Asian-American Plays*. New York: Theatre Communications Group, 1990.

Broyles-González, Yolanda. *El Teatro Campesino: Theater in the Chicano Movement*. Austin: U of Texas P, 1994.

Chan, Jeffrey Paul, Frank Chin, Lawson Fusao Inada, and Shawn Wong, eds. *Aiiieeeee! An Anthology of Asian American Writers*. New York: Penguin, 1991, 1974, 1983.

Cheung, King-Kok. "The Woman Warrior versus the Chinaman Pacific: Must a Chinese American Critic Choose between Feminism and Heroism?" *Conflicts in Feminism*. Ed. Marianne Hirsh and Evelyn Fox Keller. New York: Routledge, 1990. 234–51.

Chin, Frank. *The Chickencoop Chinaman and The Year of the Dragon: Two Plays by Frank Chin*. Seattle: U of Washington P, 1981.

———. "Come All Ye Asian American Writers of the Real and the Fake." Chan 1–93.

————. "This Is Not an Autobiography." *Genre* 18 (Summer 1985): 109–30.

Enloe, Cynthia. *Bananas, Beaches, and Bases: Making Feminist Sense of International Politics.* Berkeley: U of California P, 1989.

Gates, Henry Louis, Jr., and Nellie Y. McKay, eds. *The Norton Anthology of African American Literature.* New York: W. W. Norton, 1997.

Gotanda, Philip Kan. *Fish Head Soup and Other Plays.* U of Washington P, 1995.

————. *The Wash* (1987). Berson 29–74.

————. *Yankee Dawg You Die. Fish Head Soup and Other Plays.* 69–130.

Hwang, David Henry. *FOB and Other Plays.* New York: Penguin, 1990.

Iko, Momoko. *Gold Watch.* Uno 105–54.

Kim, Elaine H. *Asian American Literature: An Introduction to the Writings and Their Social Context.* Philadelphia: Temple UP, 1982.

————. Foreword. *Reading the Literatures of Asian America.* Ed. Shirley Geok-lin Lim and Amy Ling. Philadelphia: Temple UP, 1992. xi–xvii.

Lee, JeeYeun. "Why Suzie Wong Is Not a Lesbian: Asian and Asian American Lesbian and Bisexual Women and Femme/Butch/Gender Identities." *Queer Studies: A Lesbian, Gay, Bisexual and Transgender Anthology.* Ed. Brett Beemyn and Mickey Eliason. New York: New York UP, 1996. 115–32.

Lee, Josephine. "Between Immigration and Hyphenation: The Problems of Theorizing Asian American Theater." *Journal of Dramatic Theory and Criticism* 13 (1998): 45–69.

————. *Performing Asian America: Race and Ethnicity on the Contemporary Stage.* Philadelphia: Temple UP, 1997.

Lee, Robert. *Orientals: Asians and the Popular Discourse of Race in America.* Philadelphia: Temple UP, 1998.

Li, Ling-Ai (Gladys). *The Submission of Rose Moy. Paké: Writings by Chinese in Hawaii.* Ed. Eric Chock. Honolulu: Bamboo Ridge, 1989. 50–64.

Lim, Genny. *Bitter Cane. The Politics of Life: Four Plays by Asian American Women.* Ed. Velina Hasu Houston. Philadelphia: Temple UP, 1993. 163–204.

————. *Paper Angels.* Uno 11–52.

Lowe, Lisa. "Heterogeneity, Hybridity, Multiplicity: Marking Asian American Differences." *Diaspora* 1.1 (Spring 1991): 24–44.

Lum, Darrell. *Oranges Are Lucky* (1976). *Kumu Kahua Plays.* Ed. Dennis Carroll. Honolulu: U of Hawaii P, 1983. 63–82.

Moy, James S. *Marginal Sights: Staging the Chinese in America.* Iowa City: U of Iowa P, 1993.

Sakamoto, Edward. *Hawai'i No Ka Oi: The Kamiya Family Trilogy (Manoa Valley* [1981], *The Life of the Land* [1981], *The Taste of Kona Coffee* [1993]). Honolulu: U of Hawaii P, 1995.

Shiomi, R. A. *Yellow Fever.* Toronto: Playwrights Canada, 1984.

Son, Diana. *R.A.W. ('Cause I'm a Woman). Contemporary Plays by Women of Color.* Ed. Kathy A. Perkins and Roberta Uno. London: Routledge, 1996. 291–96.

Spivak, Gayatri Chakravorty. "Can the Subaltern Speak?" *Marxism and the Interpretation of Culture.* Ed. Cary Nelson and Lawrence Grossberg. Urbana: U of Illinois P, 1988. 296–97.

Takaki, Ronald. *Strangers from a Different Shore: A History of Asian Americans.* New York: Penguin, 1989.

Tong, Benjamin R. "On the 'Recovery' of Chinese American Culture." *San Francisco Journal* 30 July 1980: 5–7.

Trinh, Minh-ha T. *Woman, Native, Other: Writing Postmodernity and Feminism*. Bloomington: Indiana UP, 1989.

Uno, Roberta, ed. *Unbroken Thread: An Anthology of Plays by Asian American Women*. Amherst: U of Massachusetts P, 1993.

Wei, William. *The Asian American Movement*. Philadelphia: Temple UP, 1993.

Wong, Sau-Ling Cynthia. "Autobiography as Guided Chinatown Tour: Maxine Hong Kingston's *The Woman Warrior* and the Chinese-American Autobiographical Controversy." *Multicultural Autobiography: American Lives*. Ed. James Robert Payne. Knoxville: U of Tennessee P, 1992. 248–75.

Yamauchi, Wakako. *And the Soul Shall Dance* (1977). Berson 127–74.

———. *The Music Lessons* (1977). Uno 53–104.

———. *12–1-A* (1982). *The Politics of Life: Four Plays by Asian American Women*. Ed. Velina Hasu Houston. Philadelphia: Temple UP, 1993. 45–100.

Yep, Laurence. *Pay the Chinaman* (1987). Berson 175–96.

Tiffany Ana López

Performing Aztlán: The Female Body as Cultural Critique in the *Teatro* of Cherríe Moraga

Cherríe Moraga's writing of the queer body transforms the staging of Chicano community established in early Chicano *teatro*. In the 1960s, cultural nationalism set the scene for the emergence of a fully identifiable Chicano theater. For early Chicano nationalists, most notably Luis Valdez, theater offered a powerful political tool that provided a practical way to bring together large groups of people. Additionally, the presence of physical bodies in performance enabled the translation of nationalist ideology into an immediately accessible vocabulary of community building. Bodies on stage were made to symbolize the various roles one could occupy in the Chicano political movement. In their attempt to forge a discourse of cultural unity, Chicano intellectuals drew upon family as the model of nationalist community building, one exemplified by their references to community members as "carnales," male brothers. In translating nationalism into a visual realm, Valdez staged the brown masculine body of a patriarchal father figure as singularly representative of Chicano community leadership and as the quintessential symbol of Chicano social struggle.

While Moraga situates her work squarely within the tradition of Chicano community-based theater as defined by Valdez, she challenges his vision of Chicano identity, positing the female and, later, the queer body— one able to move among and between myriad related and sometimes oppositional personal and political locations—in an attempt to present a more complex imagining of community. Significantly, the female or queer body does not merely substitute for former patriarchal icons, but rather works to refigure radically the two most problematic terms of community building in early nationalist-oriented Chicano theater: family and nation. Through exploring *Giving Up the Ghost* (1984), I seek to place Moraga's work within a larger political project: the representation of community as more inclusive and diverse, a process Moraga deems crucial to the continuation of a movement-based Chicano activism.

The Role of the Body in Early Chicano *Teatro*

During the 1960s, groups such as Movimiento Estudiantil Chicano de Aztlán (MEChA) drafted statements of action that outlined Chicano civil rights and political goals and emphasized the prerogative of Chicano people to control their own resources, language, and cultural traditions. This formative period promoted nationalism as crucial to the cultural and political survival of Chicanos because it elided differences in favor of organized movement within the public sphere. The foundational document of Chicano nationalism, "El Plan Espiritual de Aztlán," commits all levels of Chicano society to *la Causa,* the Chicano struggle. Springing from a utopian narrative of origins, the notion of Aztlán, a vision of transborder Chicano nation, constructs Chicanos as an essentially coherent group in their sharing a common history of colonization. Aztlán thereby functions as a kind of glue, conveniently connecting Chicanos through a focus on lineage emphasizing biological relations more than socially constructed formations. Emphasizing brotherhood as the foundation of community building, nationalist discourse framed Chicano identity as a coherent category with other potentially fragmenting intracultural differences displaced onto the larger, more slippery notion of gender, read as female difference.

Moraga's writing critiques the language of Chicano nationalism that conflates "family" and "race" as biologically and culturally determined. The target paradigm naturalizes the family as a closed social unit that expands to include all Chicanos on the basis of sharing the same race, language, culture, history, and values. Community then becomes conceptualized as a group of related individuals, and in the performance space individual family members speak not only for themselves but also, implicitly, for members of the national community signified by the archetypal roles of father, mother, sister, or brother.

While Chicano nationalist artists and activists before Moraga readily interrogated structural models of race and class, the patriarchal structure of the family as a model of community building remained largely unquestioned. For example, though the lead character in Valdez's play *The Shrunken Head of Pancho Villa* (1968) has no body by which to account biologically for his gender, Valdez assumes it to be male. In the traditional Chicano family, the father has ultimate authority over all other members.

Drawing on this model, male Chicano nationalists figured themselves as possessing an inherent authority over community members, particularly women. Typically, Chicano men are portrayed as patriarchal fathers struggling to serve and protect their "families," while girlfriends, wives, mothers, and daughters provide them with unconditional emotional and physical support.

While Valdez's portraiture of white males has varied throughout his career, the contests over geographical, physical, cultural, and other ideological borders are consistently and symbolically mapped onto female bodies that hold currency only in relation to the power struggles between white and brown men. In this way, gender differences register as productive, even necessary, to Chicano nation building. Because women have the important function of carrying on the culture through giving birth to the Chicano race, their bodies are represented as highly volatile. When in *Shrunken Head* the father discovers the *pachuco* trying to seduce his daughter, he leaps into protective action as if there were a call for war, and cries out "Where's my rifle! WHERE'S MY GUN!" (169). Although this part of the scene can be read as a humorous poke at machismo, the boldly indicated underlying message is that Woman must be guarded because her childbearing capabilities are represented as a valuable community resource not to be misused or exhausted.

This play also exemplifies how in early Chicano nationalist theater the symbolic and physical constructions of bodies are not entirely different. Woman is held up as a useful figure central to community building but only insofar as her procreative abilities establish her as the symbol of nationalism wherein her body reproduces culture. The explicit gendering of the national body as female encourages the conflation of the guarding of the Chicano nation itself with the guarding of an actual female body.

In Valdez's work, the female body conveniently personifies the permeability of cultural borders. In *Los Vendidos* (1967), the only female character in the play, Ms. Jimenez, stands in for the loathed figure of the "sellout," one who adopts the cultural and political values of the dominant culture and rejects both Chicano culture and its political movement. This role not so subtly invokes a mimetic relationship with the figure of La Malinche, who reputedly served as translator for Hernán Cortés, an act that is said to have led to the downfall of the Aztec people and the creation of a mixed race mothered by a cultural traitor. For Valdez, the female body marks the boundary of Chicano community because she incarnates the pattern for cultural betrayal from the inside of culture as well as attack from the outside. The La Malinche myth labels women as *la chingada,* which translates as "the fucked one."

Moreover, the myth constructs the female body as "other" to male bodies, the mouth (from which she spoke her translations) and the vagina (from which she was labeled *la chingada*) violently marked as sites of cultural shame and the most damning sources of intracultural otherness. Her sexuality is depicted as terrifying because it is made to represent seduction and violation.

While Woman is upheld as a revered figure, she is also made to represent that which is most despised in the culture, as indicated in the nomenclature used to describe those who have questioned the structure of Chicano nationalism: *vendida, pocha, malinchista, marimacha* (sellout, whitened one, fucked one, dyke). These pejorative terms reveal that the culture teaches the female position as the most despised. As illustrated in *Los Vendidos,* intracultural differences that threaten the vision of community as clearly unified and culturally coherent are systematically feminized and constituted as something that must be purged from the culture. Because Woman is made to represent the threatening nature of intracultural difference, the feminine has to be completely excised from this space. Yet this move also simultaneously purges women from the arena of nationalist political organization and public discourse.

Early 1980s Chicana Criticism and Questions of Representation

The early 1980s mark the formal emergence of a Chicana criticism that had been fomenting on the front lines since the very beginnings of El Movimiento. This was largely due to Chicanas' newly established presence in higher education that gave them an unprecedented position to enact structural changes both within academia and in various branches of the Chicano community. Feminist writers, activists, and critics began by refusing to further allow women's experiences to be subsumed under the all-encompassing masculine signifier *Chicano.* By introducing and employing the term *Chicana,* feminists sought to distinguish the cultural specificity of women's experience and politicize gender as a component integral to the understanding of a culturally based political identity.

Beatriz Pesquera and Denise Segura describe the process that helped set the stage for the emergence of a specifically Chicana mode of critical inquiry:

> Intellectual marginalization of Chicanas led to an uncritical acceptance of the discourse of the late 1960s that situated Chicanas three paces behind Chicano men in the movement to overturn race-ethnic and class systems of oppression but remained silent on the question of patriarchy.

Positioned thusly, Chicanas were largely excluded from the feminist debates of the time—a dilemma yet to be systematically reversed. (95)

Leading Chicana feminist writers, artists, activists, and scholars of the time criticized the political representation of Chicanas in various institutional and organizational spaces, questioning their exclusion by white feminists on the basis of race and class and their marginalization by Chicano men on account of gender. These discussions of political representation were quickly extended to an analysis of the ways in which literary and visual representations of Chicanas not created by Chicanas themselves served to further underscore their marginalization.

With *This Bridge Called My Back* (1981), Cherríe Moraga and Gloria Anzaldúa broke ground for the emergence of an even more pointed Chicana feminist critique by adding the dimension of sexuality to the mix. The assumptions about family, nation, and community that drove the Chicano movement were systematically deconstructed as the volume's contributors pushed for a larger critical dialogue that reached outside the Chicana/o community. *This Bridge Called My Back* broke new ground by using *differences*—of race, class, gender, and sexuality—as a foundation for forging cultural connections and (re)building political solidarity between ostensibly disparate groups. Two years later, with *Loving in the War Years* (1983), Moraga's use of poetry, prose, essay, and autobiography powerfully and frankly addressed the issues that fragment Chicana/o culture from within. Previously, Chicana feminists had outlined the sexism of the Chicano movement. Moraga's work further augmented the discussions taking place in that not only did she describe the major fractures within the Chicano community—between women and other women as well as between men and women—but she also questioned why and how those fault lines appeared at all.

Loving in the War Years: The Chicana Body as Critical Intervention

Just as Chicana feminist critics built upon the most productive elements of Chicano nationalism, Moraga works from the framework of Valdez's early vision of Chicano *teatro* in her commitment to a community-oriented theater driven by identity politics.[1] While most critical of Valdez's sexual politics, she does not discount the significance of his brand of nationalism. Rather, she sees a need for shifting the meaning of the terms, as the identities that constitute Chicano culture have themselves shifted. Moraga seeks to critique and redefine the community from the inside, negotiating a space for herself that will not only serve her emotional needs, but will also help to politically unify all Chicanas/os and revitalize a Chicano movement that speaks to the current needs of identity and community building, which often reach beyond the immediacy of *familia*. Moraga does not dismiss the importance of nationalism and the family because, in spite of their inherent and often blatant sexism and homophobia, she finds them a powerful, albeit problematic, source of identity. She appropriates these assumed symbols of community building in order to problematize them and, in the process, reformulates the terms of community by building bridges as well as demarcating borders.

The replication of patriarchal structures created fault lines that continued patterns of oppression within the culture, patterns that almost always result from an exclusion of the feminine. With the continual displacement of intracultural differences—of language and class, for example—a sense of cultural wounding inevitably results because no means exist to articulate intracultural differences outside those of gender as productive in the building of community. The strict attention to gender roles in the discourse of nationalism overcompensated for the fear that intracultural differences can only divide the community from within—a fear eventually realized.

El otro lado (the other side) typically refers to the land that lies across a geographic border, but it can also refer to the zone of queer desire that lies outside of the carefully constructed boundaries of compulsory heterosexuality that inform the discourse of national identity. Many lesbian and gay Chicana/o writers describe the pressure they feel to locate their primary sense of identity in one community over another.[2] They perceive of themselves as migrants in their own land, having to move back and forth across a border that separates familial from sexual identity and to make a choice between family as embracing their sense of cultural identity and queer community as affirming their sense of desire. It is precisely these conflicts and queries that underscore *Giving Up the Ghost*.

Recasting the Role of the Chicana

Moraga wrote *Giving Up the Ghost* while studying under the direction of María Irene Fornes at the Hispanic Playwrights Lab at International Arts Relations (INTAR) in New York City.[3] Moraga's participation reflects the changes being wrought by Chicanas during the early 1980s, when a generation of formally trained Chicana artists and writers emerged, made alliances outside the Chicana/o community, and imported into their Chicana/o communities those critically useful tools acquired in other locations. Moraga's play is significant because it signals her ongoing attempts to wage cultural critique across a spectrum of social borders always with an attentive commitment to a Chicana/o-based political struggle. First in a trilogy of plays that move from the self to the family to the community, *Giving Up the Ghost* directly confronts the ways in which the Chicana female body has been constructed in early nationalist theater and builds off of the cultural critiques that Moraga began with *Loving in the War Years*.

Giving Up the Ghost centers on Latinas in the midst of working to reimagine a female self free from the specter of culturally conditioned social roles. Marisa and Amalia are two adult women involved in a sexual relationship with each other. Corky is Marisa as she was while growing up, a child who haunts the grown woman as she struggles with her sense of self. The title of the play encapsulates the various and intersecting struggles that inform the characters' relationships as they struggle to break away from the past. One character clearly identifies herself as a lesbian, the other doesn't; one is a native Spanish speaker, the other isn't; one is profoundly tied to Mexico, the other to the United States. With their only point of commonalty being gender, the solidarity of these Latinas depends on their acknowledging intracultural differences of language, class, and culture.

The first half of the play focuses on Corky's testimony on how she has come to see herself as a woman in the culture and how the culture has come to see her as a woman through the act of rape. As a young *chola,* Corky begins by recounting those representations of the female that most influenced her sense of self while growing up, yet which also instigated a profound sense of alienation from her own gender:

> when I was a little kid I useta love the movies
> every saturday you could find me there
> my eyeballs glued to the screen
> then during the week my friend Tudy and me
> we'd make up our own movies
> one of our favorites was this cowboy one where we'd be out in the
>   desert
> 'n' we'd capture these chicks 'n' hold 'em up
> for ransom   we'd string 'em up 'n'
> make 'em take their clothes off
> jus' pretend a'course but it useta make me feel
> real tough

(5)

Through her identification with film, Corky realizes that gender is a social construction physically enacted upon the body. "Cowboys" are the social agents of action, with "chicks" clearly defined as the object of their actions, those who have their clothes taken off by "cowboys," who are invested with the power to "make 'em" do so. The male ability to command sexual subordination defines his cultural power, that which, as Corky describes it, allows one to "feel real tough." For Corky, the visual prominence and repetition of these filmic images of the female as sexually violable normalize a reading of "Woman" as sexually "other."

In order to experience the feelings of power that drive the film, Corky initially strives to identify with the male subject position as directed by the film's described narrative and directorial gaze. She soon experiences great conflict in doing so, however, because she senses inherent contradictions concerning her subject position, though she cannot at the moment directly name them:

> funny now when I think about how little I was
> at the time   and a girl
> but in my mind   I was big 'n' tough 'n' a dude
> in my mind   I had all their freedom
> the freedom to really see a girl
> kinda   the way   you see
> an   animal   you know?
>
> (5)

Corky desires the sense of agency that seems so readily available to men, yet she does not want to see herself as part of the construction of female gender represented in the filmic images. She then works to disidentify from her own sense of subjectivity as a girl and instead adopts the more powerful stance of the butch *chola*, which images the masculine subject position embodied by the Chicano *bato*/male:

> I even pack a blade   no one knows
> I never use it or nut'ing but can feel it there
> there in my pants pocket   run the pad of my thumb over it
> to remind me I carry some'ting   am sharp   secretly
> always envy those batos.
>
> (4)

Significantly, Corky does not want to *be* a man; she merely wants equal access to power. The blade she packs supplements her male posturing by serving as a phallic prop. Like the "real" men in the movies, she, too, possesses a weapon that allows her to subordinate others, notably through the threat of being able to violently mark their bodies.

In order not to be a girl as defined through visual representations of the female, Corky discerns that she must not only identify with the masculine subject position but also physically objectify other girls. The play powerfully illustrates this point when Corky and her male friend Tudy spend one summer's day going from "backyard to backyard looking for prey" until they come across a little girl named Chrissy, whom they take to a shed. They tell Chrissy she's "got somet'ing wrong with her 'down there' " and pull down her shorts in order to look at her vagina (10). The scene makes an important distinction in that Corky does not seek to deny being female but, rather, seeks to distance herself from representations of the female as she witnessed them at the movies. Her appropriation of what she considers to be masculine identity becomes a way for Corky to redirect the male gaze.

Tudy interrupts Corky's looking when he "like a pendejo goes 'n' sticks his dirty finger on it" (11). When Tudy physically interrupts Corky's moment of looking, he reminds her that the filmic gaze is male and that female identity is constructed in relationship to that gaze. Corky quickly pulls up the girl's shorts and flees the scene. Because she equates being marked as female with being made sexually violable, Corky initially perceives that she must participate in violence against girls/women in order to avoid a similar fate, that she must choose to occupy one of two roles: the one who violates (*el chingón*) or the one who is violated (*la chingada*). Yet, when Corky actually corners Chrissy, she refuses to touch her in any kind of violent way. Furthermore, she refuses to read the vagina as an orifice of shame, referring to it in terms of endearment: "it was so tender-looking / all pink 'n' real sweet / like a bun" (11).

As she did in *Loving in the War Years,* Moraga shifts the focus from casting judgment on women to exploring the possible reasons behind their participation in systems of othering the female. The scene with Chrissy calls attention to the ways in which women's bodies are used as the vehicle of homosocial bonding, and it forces readers to see such experiences through the eyes of the female whose body is being violated. Moraga effectively shifts the focus of the gaze with dialogue that forces a sense of responsibility and refuses to read the action as purely symbolic: "she has this little kid's frown on her face . . . was looking at me to reassure her / that everything was cool / 'n' regular 'n' all / what a pendeja I felt like" (11). At this moment, Corky begins to engage in a process that Yvonne Yarbro-Bejarano describes as "touching the wounds in order to heal" ("Cherríe Moraga's"

85). The cultural wounds the women discuss in Moraga's text are *literal*. Most significantly, personal wounding leads to political wounding. As the women become overburdened by a history of violence, they become disabled from being able to participate fully in a larger political struggle.

Corky's ability to name her early formative experiences of being female/feminized and identify them as social constructions are crucial to her being able to become aware of alternative cultural spaces that do not rely on the marking of the female body as "other." Corky's testimony of being raped is the play's core scene because it synthesizes the process of seeing, touching, and naming that is necessary to her characters' process of healing:

> Got raped once. When I was a kid. Taken me a long time to say that was exactly what happened, but that was exactly what happened. Makes you more aware than ever that you are one hunerd percent female, just in case you had any doubts   one hunerd percent female whether you act it or like it or not. (36)

Corky's declaration that rape "makes you more aware than ever you are one hunerd percent female" encapsulates her realization that culturally sanctioned violence against the female body is what defines her as "other," "whether you act it or . . . not." In her butch *chola* posturing, Corky denies full identification with the female subject position. As soon as her gender becomes visibly signifiable in adolescence ("getting chichis [breasts] 'n' all"), however, Corky perceives that her body marks her as a target (37). Ultimately, she cannot escape the physicality of her body. One may actively choose to perform outside of the socially constructed boundaries that constitute masculine and feminine codes of behavior—as Corky does in her tough butch *chola* posturing—but, as long as social systems are in play that enforce representations of the female as "other," for Corky there exists the very real specter of physical abuse of women that no performance of gender can fully escape.

Moraga further problematizes the staging of a coherent nationalist body by linking Corky's rape to her body, not only violently and biologically marked as female but also marked as Mexican, so both gendered and racialized as "other" to her male perpetrator. Dressed in work clothes, the rapist addresses Corky in Spanish: " 'Ven p'aca,' he says." Corky obeys his request "outta respect for my primo [cousin] Enrique cus he looks alot like him" (38). In this part of the scene, Moraga calls attention to the dangers of marginalized groups replicating oppressive structures vis-à-vis nationalist patriarchy. For example, Corky does not read the situation as unfamiliar or dangerous because she has been taught that her place as a woman, but especially as a Chicana, is unquestionably to obey male authority; that is, she obeys "outta respect" for her male cousin.

Earlier Chicano *teatro* stressed elements such as shared language and appearance in defining Chicano community, but Moraga exposes them as false markers of familial and political solidarity. Violence occurs when one *does not* question racial–cum–familial social structures. During the Chicano Movement, those Chicanas who questioned their subservient roles within a movement that claimed to serve their interests were labeled by Chicano nationalists as *Malinchistas,* fucked ones, or cultural betrayers. Any attempts to talk back were read as part of Woman's inherent nature of betrayal emblematized by the La Malinche figure. Some feminist scholars speculate that Malinche was put in the role of cultural translator because her family sold her into slavery to increase her brother's inheritance. With that in mind, one then questions what kind of allegiances Malinche actually owed to her family. Corky's testimony links the violence of rape to a history of oppression in which the female body is consistently placed under erasure through male, patriarchal, colonial authority: " 'Don't move,' he tells me. In English   His accent gone. / 'n' I don' " (40). By stressing the dangers in assuming that culturally shared language and appearance in and of themselves constitute *familia,* Moraga's dialogue confronts the nationalist myth that Chicano family and community constitute a space free from violence and oppression.

Corky's intentionally unsettling description of the rape scene testifies that the most painful experiences of violence and oppression occur within the boundaries of the Chicano family and community and that the violation of these spaces leaves the most lasting scars. When the rapist places a screw-driver against Corky's underwear, he invokes another set of memories of cultural wounding and coheres Corky's experiences of violence:

From then on all I see in my mind's eye . . .
    were my eyes shut?
is this screwdriver he's got in his sweaty palm
yellow   glass   handle
shiny   metal
the kind my father useta use to fix things around the house
remembered how I'd help him
how he'd take me on his jobs with him
'n' I kept getting him confused in my mind this man 'n' his arm
with my father   kept imagining him my father returned

come back
the arm was so soft   but this other thing . . .
hielo   hielo   ice
I wanted to cry "papá papá" 'n' then I started crying for real
cuz I knew I musta done something real wrong to get myself
in this mess.

I figure he's gonna shove the damn thing up me
he's trying to get my chonas down 'n' I jus' keep saying
"por favor señor no please don"
but I can hear my voice through my own ears
not from the inside out but the other way around
'n' I know I'm not fighting this one I know
I don' even sound convinced.

"¿Dónde 'stás papá?" I keep running through my mind
"¿dónde 'stás?"
'n' finally I imagine the man answering
"aquí estoy.   soy tu papá."
'n' this gives me permission to go 'head
to not hafta fight.

                                        (40–41)

Corky cries out to her father for help, as he is the most trusted and powerful man she can think of that might help her get out of this crisis. Chicano nationalism teaches men that their role is that of a protector from just such acts of violence. Her cry to her father can also be read as an allusion to incest ("I kept imagining him my father returned") that signifies the ultimate act of cultural betrayal in a system of patriarchy: violence at the hands of the father. If Woman is made to represent familial and communal boundaries, then it follows she must be constrained inside the culture by the father's hands. The image of the wound thus signifies a much larger cultural trauma because it describes how community is ruptured when the father figure becomes the oppressor of the norms, values, and behaviors of community members. Corky's memories reveal the painful irony of the patriarchal social structure in that the father figure is the one who betrays the community because, in the name of constructing a cohesive cultural identity, he is willing to sacrifice members of his own family. This occurs because related systems of oppression are already in place. The janitor can rape Corky because symbolic representations of Woman as "the fucked one" become an accepted discursive reference in the defining of Chicano community and, in turn, authorize acts of rape as an acceptable prerogative of male behavior. Femaleness is defined through the experience of rape as a "normal" part of the social construction of gender.

Moraga's staging literalizes the ways in which the female body was symbolically represented in early Chicano *teatro*. In doing so, she emphasizes that any acceptable othering of the female body ultimately tears apart the social fabric. The violence against Corky's body is described as the making of a hole; the tearing of her body represents cultural wounding as experienced from the inside of one's primary sense of home and community:

> there was no hole
> he had to make it 'n'
> I saw myself down there like a face
> with no opening
> a face with no features
> no eyes no nose no mouth
> only little lines where they shoulda been
> so I dint cry
> I never cried as he shoved the thing
> into what was supposed to be a mouth
> with no teeth
> with no hate
> with no voice
> only a hole. A Hole!
> (gritando) [screaming/crying out]
> HE MADE ME A HOLE!
>
> (42–43)

In contrast to Valdez, Moraga presents the social construction and the physical construction of bodies as two aspects of the same oppression. The graphic and violent image of being made a hole forces readers to confront the social construction of gender as a violent physical marking against the female body. The crying out of "HE MADE ME A HOLE!" testifies to the impossibility of escape and makes visible the destructive nature of patriarchy so easily buried beneath the normalized images of women as violable Malinche figures. Moraga's text exposes the intracultural ruptures in community building that were completely unaddressed in the early Chicano theater, which focused on disruption and violence as existing solely outside the boundaries of Chicano family/community.

After Corky proclaims that the rapist has made her a hole, she disappears from the rest of the play, a narrative shift that symbolizes how such acts of violence against women serve to erase them, literally, from the social text. In the 1995 Dartmouth production, directed by Patricia Herrera, when Corky left the stage, there was a palpable sense of loss that required the spectator to consider whether the play and the gathered community could heal the wound represented by Corky's absence.

The character of Marisa illustrates how being made a "hole" can be reworked into the process of becoming "whole." This is achieved through Marisa's building with Amalia a lesbian-identified relationship determined by their differences of race, gender, and sexuality. For Marisa, as an openly self-identified Chicana lesbian yearning for a committed relationship, lesbian desire offers the strongest possibility for healing, one found in actively loving other women and learning to love oneself as a woman through touching other women. Although Moraga presents Amalia and Marisa as different in age, appearance, preferred spoken language, and country of origin, their history as Latinas struggling against inter- and intra-cultural oppressions draws them together. The relationship, however, does not focus on any kind of essentialism; rather, they must learn to work in, with, and through their differences. While the familial model significantly informs their sense of self, it cannot serve as the foundation for their relationship. The test is whether or not new models can be made.

The process of naming exposes the constructedness of culture and allows its members to conceptualize what is needed to create new cultural spaces. By naming the wounds given to her by her own culture, Corky begins to transform the wounds into something else. Part of the power of recognizing that one is constructed as a "hole" is using that knowledge to realize that one can (re)construct absence into that which is whole and so address the need to "make *familia* from scratch" as necessary to the personal and political survival of Chicanas. Marisa/Corky searches to re-create the most fruitful emotional properties of the family, yet she/they also simultaneously engage in the process of "making" something else. Moraga's project acknowledges that family fulfills important emotional needs and, significantly, stands as a master narrative of most, if not all, social relationships. Therefore, one should not dismiss the family as an important model of community; one should instead think of it more in terms of *negotiation* and draw upon those aspects that are powerful and do work, even while discarding what is limiting and does not translate into the imagining of community as a place of liberation for *all* of its members.

In *Giving Up the Ghost,* the concept of "making *familia*" offers a way to reconceptualize family and community as socially constructed, and the very naming of a space of "making *familia* from scratch" affirms its possibilities. Not all find happy endings in their quests to make *familia;* it is a frustrating and often painful process. Yet the play affirms the making as an ongoing process that can absorb even repeated failures; note the closing lines: "It's like making familia from scratch / each time all over again . . . with strangers / if I must. / If I must, I will." In this way, *Giving Up the Ghost* honors many of the key ideals of early Chicano nationalist theater—primarily, a theater of collaboration and political activism—and introduces a much-needed critique of what does not work about Chicano nationalism, namely, its symbolic representations of women that, as Moraga's work clearly shows, have great and lasting impact on the actual experienced lives of women.

"Queer Aztlán": Continued Reimaginings of the Social Body

Giving Up the Ghost wrestles with the question of how women become vital members of community building when their bodies are continually placed under assault by the very male members they are being asked to support. In her collection of essays, *The Last Generation* (1993), Moraga responds to a question posed by poet/playwright Ricardo Bracho: "How will our lands be free if our bodies are not?" (145). In "Queer Aztlán: The Re-formation of Chicano Tribe," she attempts to reconceptualize Chicano nationalism by reimagining an Aztlán-based model of community building. Even as she critiques the sexual politics of nationalism, Moraga does not discount the significance of its terms. In a time when identities are in a constant state of flux, she fears that "nation will be lost," that Chicano community building rooted in a politicized social protest movement will disappear unless Chicanas/os are offered a revitalized, more inclusive, culturally based political movement. Working from what she sees as Chicano nationalism's most admirable qualities—"its righteous radicalism, its unabashed anti-assimilation, and its *rebeldía*"—Moraga clings to the word *nation,* advocating that Chicanos "retain our radical naming but expand it to meet a broader and wiser revolution." She thus calls for Aztlán to be reformulated as a "queer Aztlán," a Chicano homeland "that could embrace *all* of its people, including its *joteria* [gay and lesbian members]." Here, just as early nationalists used the term *Chicano* to include both men and women, Moraga uses the term *queer* as all-inclusive because she sees *joteria* as being "in a critical position to address those arenas within our cultural family that need to change" (*Last Generation* 151,

150, 147, 159). She embraces *queer* to describe a space of cultural negotiation, what other theorists hopefully view as a state of becoming, a political identity yet to be fully realized.

In reformulating the terms of Aztlán, Moraga clarifies that by *nation* she does not mean a struggle for nation-states but for "nations of people, bound together by spirit, land, language, history, and blood." In her eyes, such a described nation offers a space of community building in which "we can work to teach one another that our freedom as a people is mutually dependent and cannot be parceled out—class before race before sex before sexuality" (*Last Generation* 168, 174). The Chicano nationalist paradigm, through its emphasis on biological family, defined queers as completely outside of *la familia* because of their refusal of a model of compulsory heterosexuality—the irony, of course, being that some of the most important Chicana/o activists have been lesbian and gay: Luis Alfaro, Emma Perez, Alicia Gaspar de Alba, Francisco Alarcon, and Monica Palacios. Because Chicana/o lesbians and gays have traditionally been defined out of their families, they have had to redefine what family, culture, and community mean to them.

While I agree with Moraga's assessment that Chicana/o lesbians and gays have been placed in a position that has enabled some of the most pointed cultural critique on Chicano social and political issues, I do so with reservation, for early male Chicano nationalists also felt themselves to be in a distinct and privileged "critical position." Interestingly—or perhaps tellingly is a better word—despite Moraga's intentions to revise Chicano nationalism, she often falls into the same discursive traps as early nationalists. One of the key problems with "queer Aztlán" is that the nation cannot do what the essay asks—that is, to create a borderless community. The nation, as traditionally defined within the specificity of Chicano culture, cannot be anti-nationalist; exclusions must be made. Placing *queer* before *Aztlán* cannot erase the fact that Aztlán was originally conceptualized around the exclusion of female agency and that which does not fall within a paradigm of compulsory heterosexuality. The word *queer* removes *hierarchies* but not distinctions of nation and sexuality per se. Furthermore, without explicit definition and contextualization, *queer* reads problematically, the lack of specificity expectantly evading the dangerous terrain surrounding this vision of a community without walls.

Yet "queer Aztlán" must also be considered as part of Moraga's ongoing process as a playwright, activist, and writer committed to making Chicano community from scratch, a process full of conflict and contradiction. Moraga's critical shortcomings are instructive in that they illustrate the limits in imagining community outside of the family/nation model and the larger problem of a politics based on all-inclusive difference. Moraga does not want to, nor does she feel she can, break off with tradition completely. Therefore, she is working to reformulate the terms of Chicano community building by working *through* the most ingrained cultural discourses, and the future depends on precisely such reformulations. The fact that family or Aztlán have been one thing does not necessarily mean that they cannot become something else.

NOTES

Thanks to the following people for their insightful comments, which directed the course of this essay: Diana Taylor, Chon Noriega, Carl Gutierrez-Jones, Julie Carlson, Brenda Jo Bright, Patricia Herrera, and Lisa Nelson.

1. Yarbro-Bejarano has been the most prolific writer on Moraga's work, and her essays have helped to provide a point of departure for my own thinking about Moraga's plays.

2. For one of the most moving examples of this painful border crossing between Chicano and queer families, see Gil Cuadros, *City of God*.

3. Throughout this essay I cite the first of two published versions of *Giving Up the Ghost*, which brings together the three principal characters through a series of introspective monologues and reads very much like the poetic performance tradition that Yarbro-Bejarano describes in "Teatropoesía by Chicanas in the Bay Area: *Tongues on Fire*." The second version is substantially revised based on several professional stagings of the work and conforms more to the traditional structures of American realist playwriting. Moraga argues that the more experimental poetic structure of the original work (i.e., the sparse stage directions and introspective meditative dialogue) that so distinguishes the first version reflects her inexperience at that time as a playwright. Yet these are the very elements that I read as so forcefully challenging the representations of community established in early Chicano *teatro*. This is not to say that the second published version does not do that but that it does not do so in as artistically confrontational a manner.

REFERENCES

Cuadros, Gil. *City of God*. San Francisco: City Lights, 1994.

"El Plan Espiritual de Aztlán." 1969. *Aztlán: An Anthology of Mexican American Literature*. Ed. Luis Valdez and Stan Steiner. New York: Alfred A. Knopf, 1972. 402–6.

Giving Up the Ghost. By Cherríe Moraga. Dir. Patricia Herrera. Nuestras Voces, Dartmouth College. March 1995.

Moraga, Cherríe. *Giving Up the Ghost: Teatro in Two Acts*. Los Angeles: West End, 1986.

———. *Heroes & Saints and Other Plays*. Albuquerque: West End Press, 1994.

———. *The Last Generation*. Boston: South End Press, 1993.

———. *Loving in the War Years*. Boston: South End Press, 1983.

———. "Queer Aztlán: The Re-formation of Chicano Tribe." Moraga, *The Last Generation* 145–74.

Moraga, Cherríe, and Gloria Anzaldúa. *This Bridge Called My Back*. New York: Kitchen Table / Women of Color, 1983.

Pesquera, Beatriz M., and Denise Segura. "There Is No Going Back: Chicanas and Feminism." *Chicana Critical Issues*. Ed. Norma Alarcón et al. Berkeley: Third Woman, 1993. 95–115.

Valdez, Luis. *Los Vendidos. Early Works: Actos, Bernabe, and Pensamiento Serpentino*. Houston: Arte Publico, 1971. 40–52.

———. *The Shrunken Head of Pancho Villa. Necessary Theater: Six Plays about the Chicano Experience*. Ed. Jorge Huerta. Houston: Arte Publico, 1989. 153–207.

Yarbro-Bejarano, Yvonne. "Cherríe Moraga's *Shadow of a Man:* Touching the Wound in Order to Heal." *Acting Out: Feminist Performances*. Ed. Lynda Hart and Peggy Phelan. Ann Arbor: U of Michigan P, 1993. 85–103.

———. "Teatropoesía by Chicanas in the Bay Area: *Tongues on Fire.*" *Mexican American Theatre: Then and Now*. Ed. N. Kanellos. Houston: Arte Publico, 1983. 81–97.

Harry Elam and Alice Rayner

Echoes from the Black (W)hole:
An Examination of *The America*
Play by Suzan-Lori Parks

In the summer of 1994, the Disney Corporation considered building an American history theme park in Alexandria, Virginia, a suburb close to the nation's capital. Many American historians opposed the plan, citing the inability of a theme park to capture the reality of American history and the inappropriateness of a Disney park as a location for the racial violence and oppression in that history. In August 1994, the Op-Ed pages of the *Washington Post* became a forum for a debate on the propriety of housing a slavery exhibit in the proposed park. William Styron, author of the controversial *Confessions of Nat Turner,* wrote:

> Visitors to any Disney extravaganza do not go seeking emotional up-heaval; they go chiefly for fun and entertainment and they want quick jolts of these things. I don't believe for a moment that they want a vicarious experience of slavery that will be "painful and agonizing," which is what the Disney people promised. . . . Amid Disney's high-tech honky-tonk diversions, such gruesome displays would utterly falsify the complex tragedy of the slave experience. (19)

For the Disney corporation any and everything seems available for thematizing.

The controversy nonetheless ignored an increasingly commonplace idea, coming largely from European cultural critics of the 1970s and 1980s: Disney worlds are, in fact, paradigms for America, the American sense of history and, to some degree, the "postmodern condition." To such European writers as Louis Marin, Umberto Eco, and Jean Baudrillard, America is the land of hyperreality, where any ground for historical certainty is erased by the generation and circulation of images that have no original. Disneyland operates, according to Eco, as an economic draw that "stimulates the desire for [illusion]." As Baudrillard puts it, "Disneyland is presented as an imaginary in order to believe the rest is real. . . . It is no longer a question of false representation of reality (ideology) but of concealing the fact that the real is no longer real" (12–13).

Between the work of Hayden White, indicating the literary and rhetorical conventions of historical narrative, and deconstruction, noting the impossibility of "presence" within any representation, the idea of the "total fake" as the defining character of contemporary American culture has been gaining ground. But the condition of postmodern hyperreality presents acute political and existential questions to African Americans, whose history has been largely excluded from the governing narratives of the nation. As the incident with the Disney Corporation in Alexandria suggests, there are ways to maintain some distinction between a theme park and historical horrors. But are the postmodern ideas about history a means of further isolation of African American identities and histories from dominant discourses, or are they means of liberation from myths about the past? Is there a "real" African American history to be written? In what ways could such a history be written without the inevitable errors in the processes of representation?

In *The America Play,* Suzan-Lori Parks responds to these questions in part by situating them in a theatrical and performative medium. Theatrical performance, that is, can incorporate ideas of hyperreality without annihilating the differences between real and representational experiences. Although the real of the past may inevitably be lost, performance animates that past in the reality of the performative present. The problem for the characters in the play is how to participate in the myths of history. The problem for Parks is how to right and rewrite history in a postmodern culture that has dismantled the idea of history. *The America Play* outlines the absence of a personal and racial origin by foregrounding the performative present of theater. Parks addresses the issue of African American exclusion and inclusion in three ways: first, by exploiting the metaphors of theater, theme park, and theatricality; second, by formal innovation in the musical, spoken, and literary elements of the text; and, finally, by the resonance of the specific problem of historicity and meaning with a long dramatic tradition concerned with a dead or absent father figure. Parks's riffs on the discrepancies between writing and performing parallel the exclusions and losses between recorded history and lived experience, challenging the fundamental myths and meanings of "America" and foregrounding the role race has played in the construction of those myths.

Parks sets the first act of the play in what she calls "a great hole. In the middle of nowhere. The hole is an exact replica of the Great Hole of History" (159). The Foundling Father honeymooned with his wife, Lucy, at the "original" Great Hole, where they watched as all the "greats" of American history paraded by. "Him and Her would sit by thuh lip uhlong with thuh others allin uh row cameras clickin and theyud look down in that Hole and see—ooooo—you name it" (180). The Foundling Father ventured out West and replicated the first Hole, where he now performs "The Death of Lincoln." The Foundling Father was told he "played Lincoln so well that he ought to be shot" (164).

In a series of repeated scenes, customers enter, pay a penny, choose a gun, and shoot the Foundling Father, who immediately recovers to tell the audience more of his story. In a single image, this great hole, the exact replica of history, this theme park, conflates the "empty space" of the theater, the absence of a "real" historical scene, and the obvious theatrical presence of pretense. In his monologue the Foundling Father relates his struggle to become what Houston A. Baker calls "Black and Whole." Baker theorizes that "to be Black and Whole is to escape the incarcerating restraints of a white world and to engage the concentrated, underground singularity of experience that results in a blues desire's expressive fullness" (151–52). For Baker a "blues desire's expressive fullness" is the free and full-bodied expression of African American cultural production. It can only occur in a space uncontrolled by the hegemony of white cultural domination. His metaphor for this space is a black hole, a powerful and empowering site where time and space do not exist, where white cultural representations have been "squeezed to zero volume" (152), allowing room for uninhibited African American cultural exploration. Thus, for Baker the "rite of the black hole" is a symbolic, spiritual, and practical pilgrimage to a location where one can be Black and Whole, uninhibited by the constraints of the dominant white culture.

The Foundling Father's personal odyssey, which he retells in the first act of *The America Play* and which reaches fruition in the second act, is such a journey. The Foundling Father asks how his African American history has been included in the Great Hole of History. As he explains, he has always been a "digger." He traveled the country, he says, digging holes to construct his own history. The graves are both his own creation and the defining products of his existence. In his search, the Foundling Father seeks an identity, a meaning, and an understanding of his significance within the (w)hole of American history.

Throughout *The America Play*, Parks riffs on the concatenation between *hole* and *whole*. She muses on the symbolism of a "black (w)hole" as it led her to create the play:

You think of h-o-l-e and then of w-h-o-l-e and then black hole, and then you think of time and space, and when you think of time and space you think of history, and suddenly all these things start swirling around and things start attaching themselves to each other and suddenly you have two characters sitting in a hole digging and a guy who looks like Abraham Lincoln appears. (Pearce 26)

The relationships between whole and hole, time and space, history and Lincoln, are at once logical and illogical, sequential and nonsequential. Her complex and conflated line of reasoning underscores the complex principles of quantum physics, black holes, and morphic space in the context of a family drama. Just as the Foundling Father in the first act seeks recovery of an identity through repetition of the Lincoln scene, Lucy and Brazil, in the second act, seek recovery of the body of the dead Foundling Father.

The intersection between an actual production of the play, the Foundling Father's theatrical presentation of the assassination, and the historical fact that Lincoln was shot in a theater, all point to a sense of the theatricality in history as well as to Parks's commitment to right and rewrite history. Parks signals that "America" itself is a theatrical and performative entity. She quotes John Locke at the beginning of the script and writes in the program for the production: "In the beginning all the world was America." In her explanation for using the quotation she says, "it may encourage people to think about the *idea* of America in addition to the actual day-to-day reality of America. . . . All the world was an uncharted place, a blank slate, and since that beginning everyone's been filling it with *tshatshkes,* which we who come next receive and must do something with" (Pearce 26). The history of America and of African Americans is an "open" space, a blank at its beginning, yet filled with objects and relics: *tshatshkes* going into the hole of history.

"Where is history?" asks Parks. "I take issue with history because it doesn't serve me—it doesn't serve me because there isn't enough of it. . . . I don't see any history out there, so I've made some up" (Pearce 26). There is a gap between the constructed myths and the lived experience, between the stories told and the day-to-day detail that is excluded. The "Real" of history cannot be seen or repeated, yet it continues in experience of those who live after, like the ghost of slavery. The excluded reality, however, caught between myth and matter, constitutes the gap or blank slate that is open to rewriting. It must be "made up" or filled in with ideas, memories, imagination, and matter. As the Locke quotation suggests, "America" is a blank that is at once empty and filled with the specific, material representations of America.

The stage is a site for combining the open idea with material artifacts. In constructing the imaginary scenario of the enactment of the assassination by an African American, the Foundling Father, who is said "to bear a striking resemblance to the 'Great Man,' " Parks foregrounds the binding of the real and imaginary, history and representation. The Foundling Father's portrayal of Lincoln can be read as mimetic, but he is clearly not performing a "realistic" imitation. He is rather, Parks says, a "Faker." The idea that the Foundling Father is a faker of the Great Man underscores his distance from the myth of Lincoln and his removal from the received truths of American history. But, unlike the hyperreality of Eco's Disneyland, the fake does not stimulate a desire for further illusion. Rather, it points to the absent elements—one of which is the black body—in the myth of Lincoln and the difference between the myth and the embodied performance of the Foundling Father.

Race is never mentioned in the play. It is, instead, at once erased and foregrounded through the performance. The performer is visibly marked as black, and his performance as the historically white Lincoln demands a consideration of racial categories. Parks uses the unique power of theatrical representation to re-represent the traditional image and authority of Lincoln. The Foundling Father simultaneously comments on racialized performance and performs race. Another way to put this is that by "being" a visibly black performer portraying a white figure, the actor demonstrates the performativity of race itself. As Harryette Mullen argues, "whiteness is produced through the operation of marginalizing blackness" (74). Whiteness and its privileges depend upon the construction of the boundary that separates it from blackness.

As a black actor appropriates and performs the figure of Lincoln, he both displaces the connection of black liberation to benevolent whiteness and centers the African American in his own performance. In performance there is, to be sure, a certain comic effect. But the comedy sustains a time-honored ability of an underclass to parody privilege and, by that parody, to expose the contradictions in what appears to be the natural linkage of power to persons and race.[1] The Foundling Father's performance is correspondingly inclusive and exclusive. In his performance of Lincoln his black body is purposefully and explicitly included. Yet the performance occurs between a life-sized cutout of Lincoln and a white bust of him. Positioning the figures on stage in this way underscores the production of both blackness and whiteness, and, although marginalized in history, the performing Foundling Father is in the center of the stage.

In his seminal article, "The Fact of Blackness," Frantz Fanon writes that "not only must the black man be black; he must be black in relation to the white man" (108). Fanon then expands on this racial positioning and the resultant mythology of black inferiority and white superiority. The positioning of the Foundling Father, sandwiched between the representations of the white Lincoln, visually demonstrates Fanon's contention. Moreover, the color contrast suggests that the performance of race depends upon attributes beyond color. As the actor talks directly to an audience, he is both implicitly and explicitly performing blackness with, as he says, "a wink to Mr. Lincoln's pasteboard cutout" and "a nod to the bust of Mr. Lincoln." The black actor delivers his performance with a wink and a nod to the images of white history: undercutting them even while acknowledging them.

In the production of *The America Play* at the New York Public Theater, the actor Reggie Montgomery as the Foundling Father performed certain behaviors traditionally associated with the minstrel tradition. Montgomery's repetition of those behaviors and his tails, the costume of the minstrel players, stand as a consciously racialized performance. In addition, the inverted minstrel show of the black Foundling Father performing a white Lincoln examines what Eric Lott called the "desire" for white privilege in the black performer and the desire of the Foundling Father to insert his narrative within the history of America, again acknowledging and undercutting that history.

To the extent that the liberation of the slaves is identified with Lincoln, African Americans are marginalized in their own story. The meta-narratives that establish Lincoln as the "Great Man" depend upon a relationship to the slaves that diminishes them as the "Lesser Known." As the Foundling Father says, "The Hole and its Historicity and the part he played in it all gave shape to the life and posterity of the Lesser Known that he could never shake" (162). The perpetuation of the Lincoln myth has created real scars for African Americans. Taking on guilt for a crime they did not commit, an African American agency in history is once again erased. But in *The America Play* agency is restored even while history is being questioned. With that series of assassinations the African American actors figuratively murder the power and control of the American myth over their lives. As a woman shouts, "Liiiiiiiiiiiiiiiiarrrrrrrrrrrrrrrrrrrrrrrs!" after her shot at the Great Man, she symbolically destroys the lies that have sustained the guilt of association between Lincoln's death and African Americans.

History is nonetheless filled with gaps. As the Foundling Father seeks to understand his own history in relation to the myths surrounding the Great Man, his interest centers around holes, gaps, chasms.

What interested our Mr. Lesser Known most was those feet between
where the Great *Blonde* Man sat, in his rocker, the stage, the time it
took the murderer to cross that expanse, and how the murderer crossed
it. He jumped. Broke his leg in the jumping. (167–68)

The twenty feet between the stage and the presidential box is a precise
measurement for the immeasurable distance between theatrical illusion and
the historical fact. The "empty space" of the theater, like the black holes of
astrophysics, conflates the time and space between the mythic moment and
the performer's present. Like the Hole of History, it is a space into which
the Real of history disappears. Yet, in terms of what Peggy Phelan has called
the "disappearance" of performance, the act of imitation is the same as the
original act of assassination. Both are fundamentally unrepeatable: the repetition can only be a fake. As John Wilkes Booth jumped the gap onto the
stage, breaking his leg, history became imaginatively and concretely theatrical. Booth landed on the stage and left a real man dying and a woman
screaming. He turned the real event of murder into a theatrical event. Booth
sutured the gap between reality and stage, thus creating myth. Likewise, the
Foundling Father struggles with the gaps in this theatricalized history that
both separates and unites the Lesser Known and the Great Man, real events
and stories.

    In the second act, Brazil and Lucy dig for the Lesser Known's bones.
Out of the hole they take relics from the past, each an isolated atom of a
decaying history. This act entails a search for what might be called the body
of history: a digging for artifacts that might confirm the materiality of the
past, if not its meaning. In the hole Brazil finds a bust of Lincoln, a jewel box
with the initials *A. L.,* the teeth and bone of Washington, licked boots,
whale blubber, documents, and the medals for "bravery, honesty, trustwor-
thiness, standing straight, standing tall, standing still, advancing and retreat-
ing . . . for cookin and cleanin, for bowin and scrapin. Uh medal for fakin"
(186). Later he finds a bag of pennies (Lincoln pennies, presumably used to
pay for the "Death of Lincoln" act), and a television.

    Parks's theatrical project is to discover a particularly black wholeness
within the hole of history and to bridge the gaps by rewriting history and by
filling the hole of the stage and of history with relics. She writes:

Since history is a recorded or remembered event, theatre, for me, is the
perfect place to "make" history—that is, because so much of African-
American history has been unrecorded, dismembered, washed-out,

one of my tasks as playwright is to—through literature and the special strange relationship between theatre and real life—locate the ancestral burial ground, dig for bones, find the bones, hear the bones, sing, write it down. (5)

Lucy and Brazil, like the Foundling Father in the first act, struggle to be black and whole, in a space that is free from the "incarcerating constraints of a white world." Their actions and their liminal status in the hole, between the world of the living and that of ancestors, between the real and the imaginary, parallel Baker's articulation of "The Rites of the Black (W)hole."

The Rites of the Black (W)hole recover material items of historical production but rewrite their meanings. These items contrast, however, with the echoes of a gunshot that reverberate throughout the second act of the play. The "original" gunshot is duplicated and repeated, but it is never the "one" that shot Lincoln. And this frustrates Lucy: "Now me I need tuh know thuh real thing from thuh echo. Thuh truth from thuh hearsay" (175). Both material objects and disembodied echoes from the past limit the possibility of knowing the "real thing." The desire to know can never fully meet up with what is lost in representation.[2]

Into and out of the void, that is, everything goes and everything comes. As Brazil digs up the pennies, the yellow beard, and the television, Lucy intones her own list of recovered objects: "Thuh bees knees; Thuh cats pajamas; Thuh best cuts of meat; My baby teeth; Thuh apron from uhround my waist; thuh hair from off my head; My mores and my folkways; My rock and my foundation; My spare buttons in their envelopes; Thuh leftovers from all my unmade meals; Thuh letter R; Thuh key of G" (193–94). The hole of history penetrates all the layers of representation, from the concrete (my baby teeth) to the imaginary (the bees knees), from the radical absence behind the loss (leftovers from unmade meals) to the founding principles of language and music (the letter R, the key of G).

The bullet hole in Lincoln's head penetrated his body, but it also penetrates the discursive layers of meaning and the affective layers of experience. In distinction, then, to Baudrillard's idea of the simulacra that have eliminated any ground for a real, Parks, from a Lacanian viewpoint, finds a way of showing an interpenetration of representations and historical artifacts with a historical Real that cannot be named but nonetheless operates both materially and affectively. That is, she does not, like Baudrillard's Disneyland, conceal the fact that the real is no longer real. Instead, she reveals the performative nature of images along with the difference between those images and a historical Real. The performative becomes a space for African American history. Or, as Allen Nadel suggests, "reality is authorized for African Americans by performance" (103).

In this view the process of correcting history precludes any recovery or reanimation of the dead except by simulation, but it does come to terms with the dead in the theatrical ritual itself, in the empty space, or hole, of the theater, where fragmented, disjointed artifacts combine with the ordering principles of language and music and where, like the leftovers from all the unmade meals, radical absence is a generative source of representation in performance.

The formal innovations in Parks's play serve to engage with the hole, not with a better narrative but with the clearly material signs of an African American cultural production. The consistent use of dialect spellings, that is, provide rhythmic clues for performance, but they also disturb a reader's flow. The fact that the spellings are undetectable in performance replicates the incommensurable intersection of writing and performing, of written representations and a historical Real. The specifically literary elements in Parks's text—her footnotes, spellings, capitalizations—are not part of a performance. They come before or after, in a script or in a program. In this way Parks exploits the potentials as well as the limitations in the written text and the performance event. Each demands its own kind of reading and interpretation. What is visible on the page is not audible in performance, yet each one informs and sustains the other.

In an attempt to fill the "hole" of history or to "make some up," Parks, in a footnote, attributes the line, *"Emergency, oh Emergency, please put the Great Man in the ground"* to Mary Todd Lincoln after the death of her husband (160). The attribution of this line is an ironic nod toward the authority of scholarly or historic research to cite and record the real. According to Parks: "Most of them [footnotes] are totally made up. One of them talks about what Mary Todd *might* have said on the night her husband died. It's playing again with the form and the idea of a footnote" (Pearce 26). Academic footnotes confirm meanings, elaborate ideas, and assign authorship but are peripheral to the textual body. Parks's written text parodies these purposes, satirizes the process of critical interpretation, and points out the impossibility of determining the Real. At the same time, the footnotes play with the status of the peripheral text as a sign for marginalized experience. Where are those footnotes in performance? Like the exclusions of history, they are on the side. They ironically have the status of the "necessary and probable," more commonly associated with the fictions of plot. They are excluded from performance but illustrate what textual margins can offer that performance cannot even as they put the validity of historical records under suspicion.

Visual elements of the written text give the kind of emphasis in writing that cannot be precisely duplicated in performance even by an actor's ability to perform attitudes. Capitalization tends to turn words into metaphysical categories, and the irony is not lost on Parks. Conversely, the sonorous effects of spoken language provide musical relations that signify in ways written words cannot. Throughout the text, for example, Parks plays with rules of capitalization: "The Greater Man was by trade a President. The Lesser Known was a Digger by trade" (160). On the printed page, the capitalization of *The Lesser Known* and *Digger* are titles on a par with the capitalization of *President,* but the sound of the word *Digger* in performance is suspiciously close to the derogatory racial term *nigger,* and the proximity of the three bring *Digger, Nigger,* and *President* in relation to one another as occupational titles. The pejorative name is implied by the sound in performance just as the text implies that blackness is an occupation. The textual and performed implications are not identical yet support one another as commentary on race.

Such literary and performance devices continue in a series of puns, as when Brazil refers to both his "faux-father" and his "foe-father." The sound of the dialect, that is, allows for a many-layered meaning when it is heard, but the written text makes the punning possibilities explicit. The literary text separates single meanings from the density of the performed sound but demonstrates the complexity of the sound that is carrying its own commentary on the false and adversarial position of the American "forefathers."

Brazil's name explicitly riffs on the negatively racialized nickname for Brazil nuts, "Nigger toes." The naming of Brazil is a joke on a joke, an example of "reverse racism." With this name, the Foundling Father is "signifyin' on the signifyin'." Foundling Father reports that Brazil was "named in a fit of meanspirit after the bad jokes about fancy nuts and old mens toes his son looked like nobody" (162). This information is bracketed off in the body of the text. The history of Brazil's name is thus further removed from performance and text of American history, and Brazil "looks like nobody." The invisibility or marginalization of African American history becomes a playground for Parks to make up some history. If there is no history "present," if it is a black hole, then almost anything is possible. She allows herself footnotes that come from "authoritative" sources as well as unauthorized, imaginary facts. Historical fact joins imaginary acts in the ritual of representation, not in order to reproduce events mimetically but, rather, to give solace for loss.

The defining terms for the loss of identity, history, and meaning, however, have a long history in the Western dramatic tradition. From *Oedipus* to *Hamlet* to *Waiting for Godot,* the absent patriarch stands out as a perpetual source of struggle for meaning and identity. Representations of patriarchs suffuse American drama as well as American history. Among American realists like O'Neill, Miller, and Williams, sons struggle to reconcile their lives and desires with the authority of the father. Often these plays entail an exorcism of the father's ghost from the moral, spiritual, or psychological center of the family. In *The America Play,* Parks works in this tradition but extends the work beyond the tropes of the father found in American realism by returning formal ritual elements specific to African American cultural production. Part exorcism, part reconciliation, this play is an archaeological dig into the symbolic forms of the American patriarchs, the Founding Fathers, all of whom have fallen into the hole of history.

In one sense the staged assassinations function as an exorcism of the problematic patriarch of American history. But the figures who do the shooting also suggest the psychoanalytic aspects of this exorcism without, however, resorting to psychology. One assassination is played out by a newlywed couple on their honeymoon. Symbolically, they execute the father, replacing him with the image of a new generation. Another assassin is a "regular" who returns each week. In the New York Public Theater production a black man young enough to be the Foundling Father's son performed this role. This served as a potent visual signifier for the Oedipal conflict of father and son, and his weekly repetition marked it as a rite of passage into manhood. Both the Foundling Father and Brazil struggle to reconcile themselves with the legacy of the father, yet, like so much in the postmodern, these references are more like echoes from a lost origin. The historical patriarchy is echoed in the familial, but there is no Oedipal narrative in the play. Instead, there is Oedipal reference to the absence of the father and the foundling status of infant Oedipus left to die. Playing against the word *founders,* Parks foregrounds the orphan status of the African American. He has no parent, no origin. He is a foundling, already caught into a system of naming and representations that is not his own. The guarantor of meaning is already absent, already no more than a depthless image (the pasteboard cutout) and a bodiless head (the bust). This suggests that for an African American it is not a matter of adapting to a postmodern condition but that the condition of an absent meaning is already in operation. The space of the postmodern, however, allows the experience of the orphan to be refigured in a rite that is in the dimension of what Lacan called the Symbolic.

The postmodern absence of a Real in history enables the previously disenfranchised to construct a history through acts of writing, representing, or, as Parks notes, "making some up." Engaging the postmodern and rearticulating its discourse has the possibility of repositioning black thought and black intellectual activity in its effect on Western culture. As black British sociologist Stuart Hall proclaims, "Now that in the postmodern age, you all feel so dispersed, I become centered" (44).

"Wholeness" in Parks's play occurs as ritualized, symbolized acts of theater. The ideal of wholeness, as Ellie Ragland points out, protects limited human consciousness from its own vulnerabilities, its own limits and its own losses (82). In Parks's work generally, wholeness occurs not as a coherent narrative structure but in the ritualistic, if fragmentary, performance. Signifiers, minus the object of signification, perform in her theater. Those signifiers are material. They are found in the sound and rhythms of the spoken language as well as the literary performances of the text.

The reconfiguration and reclamation of African American history come from the conscious manipulation of those signifiers, and that manipulation provides a mode for the cultural production of blackness. As a cultural production both the scene "The Death of Lincoln" and *The America Play* itself are means of entering into the circulation of cultural images and gaining economic advantages. One irony of the Foundling Father's production of the "Lincoln Act" is that he makes money from it. It enables him to live in an economic system that ideologically precludes him, and both Lucy and Brazil are part of the act, so they, too, profit from "fakin."

> "This is how youll make your mark, Son" the Father said. The Son was only 2 then. "This is the Wail," the Father said. "There's money init," the Father said. On what he claimed was the 101st anniversary the Father showed the son "the Weep" "the Sob" and "the Moan." How to stand just so what you do with the hands and feet (to capitalize on what we in the business call "the Mourning Moment"). Formal stances the Fatherd picked up at the History Hole. The Son studied night and day. By candlelight. No one could best him. The money came pouring in. (182)

The showmanship in acting out mourning parodies rituals from the performative black church tradition as well as from the minstrel tradition of stereotype, exaggeration, and exploitation. But the other side of the minstrel show and showmanship is that it gave African Americans a unique place in the history of American theater. The performance space was a space of divisive, subversive agency. African American minstrels could both mock and profit from the dominant culture. Brazil's skill in imitating kept the money pouring in.

The principle of appropriation, furthermore, works both ways. While white minstrels appropriated—indeed, created—African American stereotypes through blackface, Parks has African American actors in the roles not only of Lincoln but the actors in the play *Our American Cousin*. This reversed appropriation denaturalizes historical whiteness. It allows the visible markings of racial difference and the power of theatrical performance to cross racial lines. It foregrounds the flexibility and the mutability of theatrical enactment without avoiding the material aspects of race. According to Parks:

> I'm working the theater like an incubator to create "new" historical events. I'm re-membering and staging historical events which, through their happening on stage, are ripe for inclusion in the canon of history. (4–5)

Brazil's training in the fakin' of mourning is a way of crossing the boundaries between the absence grounded in death and the presence of performing signifiers. But this is not the same as the Disney production of American history or Baudrillard's sense of the simulacra. The absence of an origin is, by contrast, a generative absence. History both falls into the hole and emerges from it as memory. In *The America Play,* the significance of the historic remembrance is both visually and aurally reinforced through repetition and revision. Several times in the first act of the play the Foundling Father repeats the cry, "Emergency oh, Emergency, please put the Great Man in the ground." Thus, in the second act of the play, when the deceased Foundling Father reappears as ancestral spirit, he again cries, "*Emergency,* oh, *Emergency,* please put the Great Man in the ground." Lucy points to the coffin on stage and responds to the Foundling Father: "Go on. Get in. Try it out" (197). Now the Foundling Father has in effect become the Great Man. His legacy, his place in history, is reaffirmed. He has become Black and Whole. He is at rest.

The entire play becomes a ritualized performance of mourning and laying the past to rest in the hole of history. The Foundling Father has assumed a place within the Hall of Wonders, and his son, Brazil, recounts his history. The orphan, too, has become an image. Now the Foundling Father is "One of thuh greats Hisself!" (199). His son recuperates and re-members the father. The father's particularly African American history is passed on through this theatrical ceremony. In a distinctly postmodern pastiche of the imaginary and concrete, of historical record and reconstruction, Parks confronts history without nostalgia. She refuses exclusion without denying loss.

NOTES

The authors would like to dedicate this essay to the memory of Sherifa Edoga, an extraordinary student who "danced to the rhythm of her own definitions."

1. In a chapter from *Bodies That Matter* on Nella Larsen's *Passing,* Judith Butler discusses how the character Bellow could be construed as performing whiteness:

> This suggests one sense in which "race" might be construed as performative. Bellow produces his whiteness through a ritualized production of its sexual barriers. This anxious repetition accumulates the force of the material effect of a circumscribed whiteness, but its boundary conceded its tenuous status precisely because it requires the "blackness" that it excludes. In a sense a dominant race is constructed (in the sense of *materialized*) through reiteration and exclusion. (275n. 4)

2. The Lacanian Real is, Ragland says, that which makes "holes" in discourse; it is made up of

> disjointed, fragmented pieces of our "selves"—unsymbolized meaning—that appear as *jouissance* effects. . . . [P]arceled-out, broken-up, separated pieces of body, language, thought comprise the subject in the real. And so Lacan says the subject's cause is always already loss, a lost cause. . . . [H]e viewed all human activities and systems of thought as idealized fantasies of wholeness we invent or create to give ourselves the comfort of believing in a Oneness of resolutions within consciousness. The anxiety attendant upon the human reality of loss (and its remainders) is not physically bearable, except intermittently. But it is theoretically bearable and even helpful in understanding our texts, our poetics, our politics, and our lives. (82)

REFERENCES

Baker, Houston A., Jr. *Blues, Ideology and Afro-American Literature: A Vernacular History.* Chicago: U of Chicago P, 1984.

Baudrillard, Jean. *Simulacra and Simulation.* Trans. Sheila Faria Glaser. Ann Arbor: U of Michigan P, 1994.

Butler, Judith. *Bodies That Matter.* London and New York: Routledge, 1993.

Eco, Umberto. *Travels in Hyperreality.* Trans. William Weaver. New York: Harcourt Brace Jovanovich, 1986.

Fanon, Frantz. "The Fact of Blackness." *Black Slave, White Masks.* Trans. Charles Lam Markmann. New York: Grove, 1967.

Hall, Stuart. "Minimal Selves." *The Real Me: Postmodernism and the Question of Identity.* ICA Documents 6. London: ICA, 1987.

Lott, Eric. *Love & Theft: Blackface Minstrelsy and the American Working Class.* New York: Oxford UP, 1993.

Mullen, Harryette. "Optic White: Blackness and the Production of Whiteness." *Diacritics* 24.2–3 (Summer–Fall 1994): 71–89.

Nadel, Alan, ed. "Boundaries, Logistics, and Identity." *May All Your Fences Have Gates: Essays on the Drama of August Wilson.* Des Moines: U of Iowa P, 1994.

Parks, Suzan-Lori. *The America Play and Other Works.* New York: Theater Communications Group, 1995.

Pearce, Michele. "Alien Nation: An Interview with the Playwright Suzan-Lori Parks." *American Theater* (March 1994): 26.

Phelan, Peggy. *Unmarked: The Politics of Performance.* London and New York: Routledge, 1993.

Ragland, Ellie. "Lacan, the Death Drive, and the Dream of the Burning Child." In *Death and Representation.* Ed. Sarah Webster Goodwin and Elisabeth Bronfen. Baltimore and London: Johns Hopkins UP, 1993. 80–102.

Styron, William. "Too Big for Disney." *Washington Post* 16 August 1994: A19.

Robert H. Vorlicky

Marking Change, Marking America: Contemporary Performance and Men's Autobiographical Selves

I

> Whether we like them or not, Franklin, Whitman, Douglass and Henry
> Adams . . . have been leading architects of American character. They have
> built the house in which many of the rest of us have lived. But all of them
> address, primarily, men, or men and boys. . . . To tell the rest of the
> story—of what went on *in* the House—will be a challenge for the years
> ahead.
> —Robert Sayre, "Autobiography and the Making of America"

In seventeenth- and eighteenth-century American autobiographical writing, the authorial male "I" characterized not only a literary genre but a nation. With what Robert Sayre calls "the preeminent kind of American expression," this voice emerged as early as 1608 in Captain John Smith's narration of his travels and "adventures" and is traceable in a range of prose from Jonathan Edwards's diary and correspondence to John Woolman's *Journal* and Ben Franklin's *Autobiography*. This distinctly gendered "American expression" aggressively sought to clarify an otherwise complicated (if not contradictory) relationship between the "I" voice and the community. The tension between the "individual" and "group" (or nation), continued to evolve as a vital, necessary topic in the autobiographies, personal essays, poetry, and journals of such eighteenth- and nineteenth-century luminaries as Jefferson, Emerson, Whitman, and Thoreau. Writing on the connection between autobiography and the making of America, Sayre concludes, "Commencing before the Revolution and continuing into our own time, America and autobiography have been peculiarly linked" (147). Expressed differently, "America" and the autobiographical "I" voice have been thought of, historically, as one and the same, and they have been perpetually linked as such in American men's writings.

Sayre suggests that the authorized, representative male subject voice "address[ed], primarily, men and boys," yet one might argue that they also severely restricted the range of *topics* related to men's lives that they would engage. Nonetheless, this voice, usually white and heterosexual, presented itself as foundational. Upon it rested the challenges set forth by issues of personal identity and nationalism that could be untangled, constructed, and set forth as the "ideal," the "universal," and the "representative." The solution offered by the voice was relatively simple: one must demonstrate trust in the present voice through, as Sayre argues, either mimicry or emulation. Through this action, one builds upon the virtues of the voice in order to create a shared sense of (national) character with all others. After all, the singular, autobiographical voice presumably spoke for the nation, and the author's experiences were presumably the experiences of other Americans. His story was to be read and to be heard as the life of an American; his life was to be read and to be heard as the story of America. From this perspective, male autobiography functioned early on as a literary equivalent to the budding myth of America—a myth that, as Jeffrey D. Mason argues, is "exceptionally powerful because it creates and wields fictions in an attempt to transcend the personal and particular and to convey the experience of an entire culture" (11).[1] Central to most myths of America is the influential, albeit problematic, American masculine ethos.

Recent attention to previously marginalized autobiographical writing has effectively disrupted conventional notions of what constitutes works of personal, literary, and even "national" worth. Gender, race, ethnicity, and sexuality are among the features valued today when the specificity of the "I" voice is ascertained and located. Indebted to the pathbreaking scholarship in autobiography theory from the mid-1950s through the 1970s, critics since the 1980s have once again altered the landscape of autobiography studies. Focusing their research in areas of gender, race, ethnicity, and colonialism, contemporary critics are unearthing, reclaiming, and recognizing hitherto undervalued or absent autobiographical texts written by women, lesbians and gays, and heterosexual men of color. These texts have been positioned within/against the previous autobiographical paradigms and the conflation of American and white male identity. Quite dramatically, therefore, the stories of "the American" and of America, captured in the first-person singular, have changed in the last quarter of the twentieth century.

Unlike their eighteenth- and nineteenth-century American (male) counterparts, few contemporary "I" voices presume universality (or representativeness), since the "I," or self, has come to be conceived in relation to others. In this way, the subject/object begins to take on subject/subject (or self to self) dimension or awareness, approximating what Jessica Benjamin calls "intersubjectivity" (19–24). No "I" can infer a coherence that overcomes the deeper fashioning that its postmodern pieces constitute. "The postmodern subject—the split, multiple, or contradictory 'I,' " according to Deborah Geis, "is thus a decentered one" (34). The sites suggested by the "I," therefore, remain hotly contested, as challenges are continually waged over the idea, the meaning, and the body of the "individual." Contextualizing this particular interest in the relationship among the individual, the "I" voice, and autobiography as genre, Paul John Eakin suggests that the masculinist bias in our understanding of *individualism* needs correction. Whether we like it or not, autobiography is a product of the culture of individualism and "individuation is decisively inflected by gender" (66). Thus, clarity about the context in which the "I" is framed remains critical to a discussion and an understanding of how to read, see, and hear the historic and contemporary American "I" voice.

In terms of theater practice, autoperformance derives from the convergence of autobiographical material, the physical presence of the individual, and the authorial "I" voice of the speaker. Richard Schechner draws a significant distinction in relation to autoperformance: "I don't mean monologues in the traditional sense of a one-person show, but in the more radical sense of using the person who is performing as the source of the material being performed. Compressed into a single presence is author-director-performer" (44). Geis locates the source of America's interest in monologue in the experimental theater of the 1960s and 1970s. Its "postmodern revisioning of subjectivity," argues Geis, "inspired new approaches to the portrayal of characters' 'inner lives,' and this obviously had a significant impact upon the role of monologue." This same experimental theater contributed to the development of performance art and, in particular, of autoperformance (37). According to Peggy Phelan: "Performance Art's most radical and innovative work often involves a thrillingly difficult investigation of autobiography. By rejuvenating the possible ways of presenting and representing the self, Performance Art has changed the notion of theatrical presence and widened the methods by and through which the self can be narrated, parodied, held in contempt, and/or made to be the source of revelatory vision and thought" (28).

Performance art and specifically feminist autoperformance were among the original "new approaches to the portrayal of characters' inner lives" that Geis regards as having evolved out of American experimental theaters. Performances in this mode "underscore monologue's unique status as both theatrical (i.e., containing boundaries that designate performance) and personal (i.e.,

the first-person narrative as a point of departure for autobiography or subjectivity), granting it a narrative flexibility that makes it succeed initially where
other types of theater activity may not" (Geis 153). Explaining the impact of
this vigorous representation of women's subjectivity in performance art,
Jeanie Forte claims that, "rather than masking the self, women's performance is born from self-revelation as a political move"; the artists "challenge
the symbolic order by asserting themselves as 'speaking subjects,' in direct
defiance of the patriarchal construction of discourse." Since the 1960s, according to Forte, "the intensely autobiographical nature of women's performance has evidenced the insistence on a woman's ability to 'speak' her
subjectivity" (224).

One feature of this subjectivity, in many cases, has been an attempt "to
tell the rest of the story," as Sayre requests, "of what went on *in* the House."
Among the self-consciously autobiographical performers are Holly Hughes,
Deb Margolin, Marga Gomez, Susan Miller, Ntozake Shange, Blondell Cum-
mings, Robbie McCauley, Beatrice Roth, Leeny Sack, Cherríe Moraga,
Rachel Rosenthal, Darci Picoult, Camryn Mannheim, and Karen Finley.
Collectively, these voices capture a range of women's experiences marked by
racial, sexual, ethnic, age, and class features. Each self-consciously acknowledges that her voice is both connected to and separate from "other" women;
that is, each effectively dismisses any arguments of essentialism. They "represent themselves," as solo artist Lenora Champagne remarks, "in images created as alternatives to or comments upon the traditional images and roles they
had inherited." Often, their alternatives or comments are criticized as "confessional," but, as Champagne concludes, "this view overlooks the difference
between confession and revelation" (xi). It is on the level of personal "transformation" that contemporary female and male performers intersect with one
another when they engage autobiographical material. This transformation, as
it relates to this essay's focus, is stimulated by one's rejection of a self-identity
based upon cultural codings of gender.

When contemporary autoperformers "transcend" cultural codings of
gender, they present historically unique first-person singular Americans, a
diversity of voices and faces that challenges the myth of a universal, paradigmatic American identity; as such, they are markedly different from their
white male predecessors. For this reason, one can consider the performance
of America in terms of the performance of gender—that is, who and what
Americans can be when captured on stage through (gendered) portraits of
American male and female (fictional or experienced) lives. In turn, the
dramatized characteristics of Americans conveniently comment upon the
contradictions that arise between the fictions and truths about America. In

the latter twentieth century, American culture has duly acknowledged the undeniable impact of gender socialization on the construction of people's lives. The semiotic of gender codings that determines (i.e., constructs) representation—most noticeably revealed through dialogue codes (i.e., what characters do and don't say to one another vis-à-vis the "gaze" of the author)—has been successfully challenged in the monodramatic form by the solo performer over the last thirty years.

For the contemporary American autoperformer, the primary agent for individualized transformation and the location of difference is personal language usage emanating from the present, visible body of the speaking subject. This dramaturgical feature characterized the earliest radical work by feminist performers. Paradoxically, their mutated, mainstream offspring can now be found, for example, in the hybrid personae of today's female television talk show hosts. The media has constructed a generalized image of the female host as one who casts herself and her spectators as mutual confidantes. The female host, in effect, mimics the conservative agenda of female representation circulating in and perpetuated by mass culture. Confronting this representation are pioneering female solo performers in the theater, who, like Anna Deavere Smith, challenge female archetypes in order to push (or perhaps to blur) the boundaries of representation, meaning, and the politics of performance through their exploration of the relationship among autobiography, fiction, documentary, and performance technique.

In present-day theater and performance, however, this dynamic movement of representation galvanized by autoperformers is unfolding nowhere more unexpectedly than in the contemporary performance of men's autobiographical selves. This is noteworthy simply because the public has not seen and heard men represented in a form of autoperformance that displays them as individuals who experience their own range of marginalizations.[2]

The current transitional period for men's autoperformance, starting in the late 1980s, owes its greatest debt to feminist performance artists. Male autoperformance would not exist without feminism and the artistic, political legacy of confrontational, subversive, nonphallocentric women's art. From this perspective, Forte's analysis of women's performance art since the 1960s connects them in spirit to the transitional wave of men's autoperformance: "Their disruption of the dominant system constitutes a subversive and radical strategy of intervention vis-à-vis patriarchal culture" (217). In making this link between feminist performance art and male autoperformance, some continue to view gender solely as a binary system, one that fixes "Woman" as a category and will always privilege men. This view, however, dismisses outright the notion that gender can also be considered performative, let alone that its socially constructed roots are not impervious to personal or cultural change. Essentialists may have difficulty recognizing and respecting the differences among men's individual, lived experiences when confronted with a de-essentializing male subjectivity in performance—one that moves beyond stereotypes, clichés, and the myth of American male identity. To some spectators it may appear (and deliberately so) that certain male performers incorporate the strategies of female autoperformance into their work. After all, women performance artists, according to Forte, use "the condition of their own lives to deconstruct the system they find oppressive, and their performative practice shares concerns with recent theory interested in unmasking the system of representation and its ideological alliances" (219). Certain emerging male autoperformers, however, also share with women artists the desire to "unmask" American systems and their ideology. Their tactic is less an appropriation of feminism or women's cultural production than it is a man's embrace of feminism into his personal thought, emotions, and behavior, which, in turn, becomes a "given" in his artistic representation of self.

The oppositional strategy most often implemented in recent male autoperformance displays two striking features: (1) language usage that disrupts the semiotic of maleness that otherwise restrains men's dialogue vis-à-vis rigid cultural codes of masculinity; and (2) the inclusion of references to diverse relationships, particularly those between and among members of the same sex (e.g., family, friends, lovers, or acquaintances). Male solo performance that specifically explores the subject's connection to and separateness from other men consciously seeks to redefine in language the engendered power structures that otherwise contextualize and restrain these relationships. In this way, a man, present in his body and talking in a personal voice about other men, constitutes a radical act of representation. He shatters the otherwise conventional paradigm of male representation and the traditional, essentialist features of the male "I" voice.

This technique has led to the critique of male autoperformers for being too confessional, if not outright self-indulgent.[3] Marked accordingly (as a firm cliché of heterocultural values), men are not supposed to speak too personally, or so dictates the myth of (anticipated, desired) male behavior in America. The personal itself has traditionally been coded as female and therefore devalued. What happens to our understanding of American autoperformance—the theatricalization of the personal, "of the self rather than of a character" (Geis 155)—when the personal is linked to the female? Is autoperformance a "female" form (in the manner, for example, that realism has been marked as "male" by numerous feminist theorists) or possibly an "ungendered" or "omnigendered" form? If so, why is it so popular now with male soloists? More important, perhaps, are such distinctions or categories even useful to delineate?

Enter Spalding Gray—the man who, through popular recognition, grounded male autoperformance as a viable artistic choice in American theatrical production. Gray's work "exemplifies the 'cross-over' from avant-garde to mass cultural status," remarks Philip Auslander, "that many performance artists of the media generation seem to hope for" (59). Gray's commercial success has not been matched, however, either by men of color autoperformers or by female autoperformers. A crucial question arises, therefore, the response to which may suggest the outline of popular cultural and commercial "success" for the male autoperformer: where are Gray, the man, and America, the idea and the actual place, situated when the "person/personal," linked to the "female," enters the critique of male autoperformance? And what is the relationship between Gray's autoperformance and the performance of the myth of the American male ethos?

II

> I realized that I could not, and did not want to, reduce others to that object, that study for the stage. I wanted to explore myself as other. I wanted to investigate my actions. I no longer wanted to pretend to be a character outside myself. The streets where I encountered this other were in my body and mind. The "other" was the other in me, the constant witness, the constant consciousness of self.
> —Spalding Gray, "About *Three Places*"

Much has already been written about Spalding Gray—his collective and solo endeavors, from his participation in the Performance Group and Wooster Group to the works based upon his life from *Sakonnet Point* (performed in 1975) to *Gray's Anatomy* (published in 1994). Praising Gray's most recent autoperformances, William Demastes emphasizes how Gray "creates a sophisticated theatrical persona, who himself reenacts an awakening on-stage designed to sensitize the audience to its own awareness" (75). I propose to consider briefly the place that the personal occupies in Gray's autoperformances, or what John Gentile calls Gray's movement from his "own particular life story to address themes of social and historical significance" (149). Specifically, what are the boundaries that define the personal for Gray; does the framework of his "particular life story" achieve a balance between depth of insight and his duly recognized sense of irony? And how have the critics responded over time to the critical discourse that has come to define the culture's perceptions of Gray's autoperformances, of his personal life? In turn, I will amend Demastes's position on Gray's so-called awakening on-stage by starting to qualify exactly what Gray does and does not talk about, what he does and does not "awaken" to.

David Savran argues that "for Spalding Gray, all performance is autobiographical, not because it recreates the performer's past, but because the performer can play only himself, can project only the diversity within. . . . He used the 'method' to find an alternative to it and become a creator of autobiography (using the self as text) rather than a re-creator of someone else" (63). Schechner concludes, however, that in Gray's performance style a "path toward self-transcendence is through a thicket of ever more complicated self-remembering—complicated psychologically, even metaphysically, but not theatrically; his theatrical progress is toward minimalism" (48).

Gray is an entrancing performer, an affable, talented individual whose storytelling has the charm and comfort of someone familiar, someone with just the right touch of challenge and authority to engage our attention and imagination. A study of Gray's autobiographical pieces reveals that something quite predictable occurs in the structure of the stories, something that may begin to explain why we do not find in his work what Phelan calls a "shar[ing of] selfhood" or perhaps a particular dimension or feature of "selfhood" that is revealed in what Gray will or will not express in language (29). Yet it is on this level of the "autobiographical"—Spalding Gray as speaking subject and as text—that Gray remains, paradoxically, engaging and frustrating. What he omits is any contextuality of selfhood as an American male, despite the fact that this is his ostensible subject. Even more perplexing is his choice (conscious or not) to narrate the self with little or no reference to other men, particularly any who might help shape a context of the personal. Ironically, that which is absent from his master plot just might contribute to his cultural success as a man telling "his" story—from an otherwise (culturally and dramaturgically) authorized American male point of view.

Like nearly all playwrights of male-cast plays, Gray is trapped, to some extent, in a semiotic of maleness that reveals itself structurally in the author's restricted (i.e., limited) choices of topic selections. In *47 Beds* (1986), he refers to his father, his brother, and certain male friends, but in later pieces he frames his stories through his interaction with men in positions of authority (those with whom he comes into contact because of a service being rendered or professional advice being sought) and women. Such figures quite often initiate his self-disclosing remarks or reflections. In *Monster in a*

Box (1990) and *Gray's Anatomy* he depends upon his companion Renee or a representative of an institution—his eye doctor or psychiatrist, for example, or a person with whom he conducts business—to prompt his self-disclosures. He speaks of no male friends as confidants, as individuals with whom he engages in personal dialogue. His "life as art" performance has become peculiarly conventional and formulaic in its choice not to represent man as capable of, let alone desirous of, personal, nonprofessional interaction and dialogue between men.

This narrative choice does not appear, at first, to be a deliberate performative strategy of the kind Demastes praises: "While Gray's work may appear supportive of the status quo, it presents a persona who ironically utilizes an empowered naivety to undermine itself and the authority it seems to uphold" (86). What catches my attention is not Gray's reliance upon irony, but rather the stark omission in content, throughout his numerous autoperformances, of male relationships. If, as Savran suggests, Gray projects the "diversity within" himself, what kind of self-censoring occurs—especially for one who professes his own "constant consciousness of self"—when Gray fails to address these relationships, even if finally to dismiss them? In their absence from the story what, then, is absent from the portrait of selfhood that is revealed in language? How is one, finally, to measure what Schechner calls Gray's "self-transcendence"? Whether on stage, on screen, or in print, Gray rarely addresses or speaks to the dynamics or the details of his relationships with men—their successes and failures or their existence. It is not useful to fracture his voice into person or persona, author or performer-director; rather, it is crucial to stay with his language, with what is and is not spoken—to stay *inside* his story.

Gray ends the stage version of *Swimming to Cambodia* by telling about a dream, according to Demastes, "in which [Gray] witnesses a straw boy consumed by flame. The dream takes place in Hollywood, where Gray wanders the streets trying to tell the event to anyone who will listen," but, in particular, he seeks out the boy's mother (amid no mention of his father [92]). Gray's final words are: "And I knew all the time I was telling this story that it was a cover for the real story, the Straw Boy Story, which, for some reason, I found impossible to tell" (127). Demastes, referring to Gray's non-story, concludes:

> The text, finally, avoids the central issue, never even announces the issue, and thus the validity of the performer's presence is undermined as is the entire text itself. Finally, *Swimming to Cambodia* strives to group itself in some "other" that it cannot present because it *cannot* be

presented. To fill the void, Gray has presented exactly what is *not* to be valued. (93)

I am struck by the intimacy of the (gendered) image and action in the dream-story: two men in relationship to each other—one who is dying and silent, only to be regenerated as a silent straw boy effigy while the other watches in silence. If, as Demastes argues, Gray "fill[s] the void" for us in the theater with a story that "is *not* to be valued," then we are left wanting to *hear* the "real story" behind this dream of male self-destruction.

In 1982, Theodore Shank suggested that Gray's "monologues are the most literally autobiographical work that has been presented in the theatre" (179), a remark that many might still accept, fifteen years later, as accurate. At stake here is the value one gives to the evolving sense of what constitutes material for "autobiography." Whereas Gray was among the first men to engage in autoperformance in the early 1980s, his narratives appear little affected by the wave of feminist autoperformance surrounding him. He constructed boundaries that defined male autoperformance for the 1980s, boundaries that contemporary male performers are continually challenging, since autobiography, for them, expands into more deeply personal, self-identifying territory. That which is noticeably absent—same-sex relationships are a case in point—calls into question the extent to which the autoperformer truly explores his "diversities within," which can lead to other identifications connected to various communities. Geis convincingly argues that Gray's work "resists an identification with a 'community' " (158).

In characterizing Gray's narrative style, Auslander argues that it is "like the television series [that] remains static and essentially conservative in that it permits no change in the characters or their basic relations" (76). Yet, remarkably, in *It's a Slippery Slope* (1996), Gray included several striking features that distinguish this work from his other fifteen solo pieces since 1979.[4] Peter Marks describes the piece as using an "ideal metaphor"— Gray's efforts to learn to ski—"for a great monologist's art: a meandering journey with a few bumps, thrills and surprise turns." Gray noticeably includes and articulates in uncharacteristic detail the "deeper pains and consolations of his life over the last several years: the death of his father, the breakup of his relationship with his wife and collaborator, Renee Shafransky, and the birth of his first child, a son, by another woman" (11–12). In personalizing his work to the point where the closest relationships in his life are actual, vital elements to the construction of his narrative, and not just fillers tagged on to serve metaphoric conceits, Gray appears to be deepening his vision as an artist and person. In searching for an unironic voice, albeit at infrequent moments, Gray presents us with his own flesh and blood, which has the power, however briefly, to startle and to humble all who share in the theatrical moment. The piece also demonstrates a broadening of topics for the artist, an exploration of the relationships between other men and himself on a personal level. For Gray, the "ideal" place to start is to reflect upon his own dad and his newly born son. Gray's engagement with these topics suggests that the autoperformer is now more deeply tempted by and responsive to time and to mortality. He seems poised to reposition himself—partially due to his articulated desire to explore complicated, intimate personal issues not only with the women but with the men in his life as well—amid the evolving, post-Gray era of male autoperformance.

Indeed, current autoperformers in this post-Gray era have clearly differentiated themselves from this most visible male artist. In contrast, these newer male solo performers engage more fluid forms and contents, taking their signal from feminist performance art in order to break the gendered codes of stage dialogue and startle audiences with the articulation, theatricalization, and physicalization of a range of male subjectivities and hitherto taboo topics. What these performers have to say and how they say it are challenging the conventional parameters of representation in male autoperformance. Their efforts are marking changes not only in how men are presented on the public stage, but also in the "I" voice that for generations presumably spoke for (male) "America."

III

I was a boy who thought he was white.
. . . .
I was a boy with Olympic dreams.
I was a boy with so much potential.
I was a boy trying too hard.
I was a boy nobody knew—nobody knew—nobody knew—nobody
    knew—nobody knew.
I WAS A BOY IN EVERY WAY.
                              —Dan Kwong, *Monkhood in 3 Easy Lessons*

Early American writers valorized a kind of "self-made" individualism that helped establish them as the representative men among men. Contemporary male autoperformance, on the other hand, has transformed this traditional presentation of a "universal" subjectivity into a kind of "self-identified" individualization, or personalization, that recognizes a man's public, articu-

lated perception of his "diversity within" (Savran 63). In turn, this individualized self is connected to a range of outer "communities," those with which
the speaker also associates at multiple points of intersecting identifications.
Male voices are starting, at last, to acknowledge the range of subjectivities
that constitute the definition of what it means to be a man—or, rather, what
it means to be male—in America; they do so in terms that surface from
within their own stories and that are situated amid, but are not wholly
determined by, the culture's gender codings. Their stories are different from
the culture's mythic renderings that have traditionally framed male master
narratives. Their work offers a revision of America's patriarchal narrative
while disputing the assumptions that inform the narrative's codings. By
theatricalizing the autobiographical self, some male performers create an
immediacy through which their voices and bodies occupy or share the space
that hitherto had been marked, in its most glaring manifestation, "for
women only" in the culture's gendered eyes and ears.

Men's autoperformance provides the critical, performative hinge on
the closet door of male subjectivities. By staging publicly a representation of
their own lives and by putting into words a man's private self, these
autoperformers necessarily challenge the monolithic semiotic of maleness
that otherwise inhibits or prohibits personalized discourse. Their works
expand our notion of male subjectivities as they position their voices within
a frame that values and relates to the authority and presence of female
subjects and "other" men while addressing their own diversities within.

One of the most revealing male autobiographical voices and engaging
performers to surface during the post-Gray era is Dan Kwong. Performing
across America since 1989, he premieres most of his work at the Highways
Performance Space, a not-for-profit organization in Santa Monica that provides opportunities for alternative theater to be performed for the diverse
communities that constitute southern California. Kwong has nurtured an
evolving autoperformative style that is increasingly complex in its thematic
content and production values. Beginning with *Secrets of the Samurai Cen-
terfielder* (1989) and *Boy Story* (1990)—the latter, an allegorical piece about
the gender war between "real" boys and "non-boys" (i.e., girls and sissies)
that makes soldiers, eager for war, out of real boys—Kwong continues to
focus his narratives on what it means to be a "hybrid" (his mother is Japanese
and his father Chinese), an Asian American, straight, and male. His stories
take him across the vast terrains of racism, sexism, homophobia, violence,
abuse, disease, crime, and sexual compulsion, yet he centers his narratives at
"home" through his interactions, both serious and comic, with family,
friends, lovers, neighbors, school mates, or anonymous Angelenos. Enliven-

ing these stories in performance, Kwong employs a range of multimedia, theatrical techniques and simple, symbolic props: hand puppets, shadow play, suggestive costuming, prerecorded musical scores (from American rock to European classical and Asian traditional folk), energetic movement (from tai chi to erotic dancing and child's horseplay), film, interactive video, projected photographs, and voice-overs.

While these theatrical elements enhance the vitality of Kwong's narrative, they do not detract from the performer's main objective: to present selected personal stories that convey both his uniqueness from and his sameness to others and to explore artistically the ways in which his experiences both are and are not grounded in conventional notions of America. Perhaps his greatest link, besides physical theatricality, to other contemporary male autoperformers—from groundbreakers Tim Miller and Keith Antar Mason to Luis Alfaro and Carl Stokes—and what distinguishes such artists' work from Gray's, is a deliberate foregrounding of relationships to men, to masculinity, to what it means to be a man in America. Kwong's narrative strategy integrates these issues into his performance, and, consequently, his work presents a bold departure from the narrative style of Gray's autoperformance.

Kwong divides his full-length performances into sections, each related thematically to the others. Thirteen sections constitute *Tales from the Fractured Tao with Master Nice Guy* (1991), which Kwong summarizes as the story of his "dysfunctional family, Asian American style." Mapping out the early innocence of his childhood as a hybrid member of an "over-achieving" Asian American family, Kwong moves to the traumatic family rupture when his parents, Sam and Momo, divorced. Interacting with a wizened apparition called "Master Nice Guy" (the performer appears in a bearded getup on a prerecorded video), Kwong hears the fatherly advice that he must not allow his "secret" pain to be "locked up inside too long." "It's bad for you, makes you crazy," warns Master Nice Guy. "That's old-country stuff, boy. You're an *American* Asian. Might as well take advantage of it!" (8). Kwong presents one's access to the personal/confessional in order to relieve "pain" as an American trait or luxury. America is also framed, however, as a geographical *place* and a psychological *location* for release.

The majority of the remaining sections in Kwong's performance either allude to or directly address his secret: the depth of the pain and dislocation created by the absent father that Kwong had not expressed, hitherto, in words. Announcing in Brechtian fashion a section toward the end of the performance, "To Myself," in which Kwong recalls a dream in which his dad humiliates him, the overhead text sign ("This is our silence, between father and son—the history of Asian men" [16]) is countered by Kwong's angry shouts at his father. In order to break that silence and thereby to have the chance *not* to repeat the father's story of domestic violence, isolation, and eventual loneliness, Kwong moves through anger to recognition and, finally, to compassion toward his dad. Within the performance's final sections, Kwong recalls, in snippets of dialogue, a phone call he had with his father, after he had moved to Chicago when he was nineteen. Sam, after nearly a decade, was breaking the silence that had suffocated his own past as well as his relationship with his son: "I'm sorry," the father repeats several times, words that "spoke for many years" (18). Crying, which he had never done before his child, Sam "went on as if he had to finish emptying his heart"; finally, father and son were able to express their love to each other. Later that night, as Kwong says, "I cried for the first time in eight years . . . like a young child whose broken heart had finally been seen" (19).

Kwong continues to open up new territory in *Monkhood in 3 Easy Lessons* (1993). He addresses his relationship to his maternal and paternal grandfathers amid his exploration of Asian American male identity, the absence of Asian American heroes from American history, current violent racial bashings, the internment camps, and the wish to be a stud, not "some wimpy CHINK" (18). He eventually encourages us to "transform ourselves and society as a whole" (16). This transformation begins *within* as he realizes that, while he "wanted *so much*" to find "courage," "dignity," and "spirit" within his paternal grandfather, his *own* life's "meaning" was to be mirrored in his grandfather's songs (18):

> I remember a man who delighted in the sound of his own spirited voice, completely uninhibited. A man who . . . allowed himself to sing out loud. . . . Songs that had never been sung before and would never again be repeated!
> And I thought: How many could do that very same thing? How many of us are willing to sing our song, even in the face of ridicule? . . . Because the moment calls for a song. Because your life is a song. (19)

In *The Dodo Vaccine* (1994–95), Kwong internalizes the power of the generational "song of life"—a kind of recognition of the value of one's diversity within and without that was passed on to him by his grandfather—in order to move freely between himself as an individual and as part of various communities. Questions related to sexuality and sexual behavior intersect with those centered on Asian American identity as the storyteller confronts issues of HIV and AIDS in the heterosexual community. Behind his own fears resides his guilt over lingering homophobia; as a straight man,

Kwong was enculturated to "despise one group: Queers" (11). Invoking his ancestors in earlier performances, Kwong now connects what he has learned about compassion and dignity from his own "family" to the extended community composed of "others":

> It is said that behind every straight man's homophobia is the fear, the dread, the blood-curdling terror that he too might be gay, might be thought of as gay, might be accused of being gay, mistaken for gay, curious about being gay. If I, as a heterosexually-identified male dare to even think about these ideas I can feel the ominous rumble of gay oppression under *my* feet, feel the earth shudder in revulsion from that hateful schism—like a faultline marching down my spine, threatening to smash me with the same mindless cruelty I have participated in and tolerated upon my gay brothers and lesbian sisters. And how terrifying to consider wearing the shoes of victim when you know the fit of the oppressor's boot so well. (12)

In speaking boldly and personally about his life, thereby addressing the breadth of his relationships to both women and men, Dan Kwong represents in his autoperformance the kind of passion that marks the best of men's solo work in the post-Gray era. His is a voice of generosity, committed to apprehending the vital interaction of all kinds of cultures and subcultures from within and without. His work, likened to Alfred Stone's "cultural narrative," pursues the links among "individualism, democratic pluralism, and autobiography" (9). For us, because all are marked by race, sexuality, ethnicity, gender, and class, Kwong wipes clean the mirror of cultural codings in order to transform it; in doing so, he insists that his image, his selfhood, remains in full view with all its diverse features present. Yet this sharpening of perspective, of personal point of view, could not have occurred if Kwong had not broken the code of male speech that inhibits such personalization.

As a straight man, Kwong chooses to speak personally to "share his selfhood" with those who will listen to his intimate yet expansive voice (Phelan 29). He chooses to begin "to tell the rest of the story," the challenge set before future generations by Sayre, by beginning to explore "what went on *in* the House." He is also marking the change in the "architects of American character"—in the storytellers of American male characters.

This shift, as captured in male autoperformance, from the myth of a monolithic American male ethos to the representation of diverse male subjectivities, follows on the heels of feminist performance art that has long subverted gender myths through its dramatization of female subjectivities. Together, for the first time in American theater history, female and male autoperformers seem to be appearing on the same, but different, stage—one that, like the country within which it is located, remains "a process, or a phenomenon in a state of constant formation" (Mason 20).

NOTES

I am grateful to the National Endowment for the Humanities for a stipend to attend the 1995 Summer Seminar on autobiography, which provided the time and resources to begin this essay. I want to thank Nancy K. Miller, the director, and my colleagues in the seminar for their critical input during our discussions on autoperformance.

1. Mason's argument frames the broader power of myth, approaching a definition of myth. I see this structure at work particularly strongly in the American context.

2. Increasingly, women have activated autoperformance in the theater as a self-defining strategy for subverting the codes of the dominant culture and ideology. Men have not, traditionally, employed this mode, perhaps because men presumed, or were presumed to be, the embodiment of dominant culture and ideology. For this reason the works of contemporary autoperformers such as Luis Alfaro, Scott Carter, Wayne Corbett, Richard Elovich, Josh Kornbluth, Dan Kwong, Keith Antar Mason, Tim Miller, and Carl Stokes function at the forefront of this revolutionary male solo theater. Their performances are redefining and enlarging the breadth of representations available to men in live art.

3. Champagne has observed that "these 'confessional' women found it ironic that the same form was praised when male colleagues began performing monologues" (xi). While the autoperformative "form" may have been the same for both sexes, women autoperformers brought a more radical content to that form, addressing reflectively, for instance, their relationships to other women. Because Champagne does not mention any specific male autoperformers in her general remarks, I can only assume that she may be referring to Gray as the most visible autoperformer at the time of her published comments.

4. I have been able neither to see nor to read "It's a Slippery Slope." Gray presented it in a limited, sold-out run in New York, and, as of June 1997, it remained unpublished. My remarks about the play are a response to Peter Marks's review of the performance. As this collection goes to press, however, Gray's solo is now in print (*It's a Slippery Slope* [New York: Noonday P, 1997]).

REFERENCES

Auslander, Philip. *Presence and Resistance: Postmodernism and Cultural Politics in Contemporary American Performance*. Ann Arbor: U of Michigan P, 1992.

Benjamin, Jessica. *The Bonds of Love: Psychoanalysis, Feminism, and the Problem of Domination*. New York: Pantheon, 1988.

Champagne, Lenora. Introduction. *Out from Under: Texts by Women Performance Artists*. New York: Theatre Communications Group, 1990. ix–xiii.

Demastes, William. "Spalding Gray's *Swimming to Cambodia* and the Evolution of an Ironic Presence." *Theatre Journal* 41 (1989): 75–94.

Eakin, Paul John. "Relational Selves, Relational Lives: The Story of the Story." *True Relations: Essays on Autobiography and the Postmodern.* Ed. G. Thomas Couser and Joseph Fichtelberg. Westport, Conn.: Greenwood, 1998. 63–81.

Forte, Jeanie. "Women's Performance Art: Feminism and Postmodernism." *Theatre Journal* 40 (1988): 217–35.

Geis, Deborah. *Postmodern Theatric[k]s: Monologue in Contemporary American Drama.* Ann Arbor: U of Michigan P, 1993.

Gentile, John S. *Cast of One: One-Person Shows from the Chautauqua Platform to the Broadway Stage.* Urbana: U of Illinois P, 1989.

Gray, Spalding. "About *Three Places in Rhode Island.*" *Drama Review* 23 (1979): 31–42.

———. *It's a Slippery Slope.* Unpublished script, 1996. Vivian Beaumont Theater, New York. November 1996.

———. *Swimming to Cambodia.* New York: Theatre Communications Group, 1985.

Kwong, Dan. *The Dodo Vaccine.* Unpublished script, 1994. Spitalfields Market Art Project, London. April 1994.

———. *Monkhood in 3 Easy Lessons.* Unpublished script, 1993. Japan American Theater, Los Angeles. June 1993.

———. *Tales from the Fractured Tao with Master Nice Guy.* Unpublished script, 1991. Highways Performance Space, Santa Monica. January 1991.

Marks, Peter. "Negotiating the Twists in Skiing and Life." *New York Times* 11 November 1996, late ed.: C11–12.

Mason, Jeffrey D. *Melodrama and the Myth of America.* Bloomington: U of Indiana P, 1993.

Phelan, Peggy. "Spalding Gray's *Swimming to Cambodia:* The Article." *Critical Texts* 5 (1988): 27–30.

Savran, David. *Breaking the Rules: The Wooster Group.* New York: Theatre Communications Group, 1988.

Sayre, Robert. "Autobiography and the Making of America." *Autobiography: Essays Theoretical and Critical.* Ed. James Olney. Princeton: Princeton UP, 1980. 146–68.

Schechner, Richard. *The End of Humanism: Writing on Performance.* New York: Performing Arts Journal Publications, 1982.

Shank, Theodore. *Alternative American Theater.* New York: Grove Press, 1982.

Stone, Alfred E. *Autobiographical Occasions and Original Acts: Versions of American Identity from Henry Adams to Nate Shaw.* Philadelphia: U of Pennsylvania P, 1982.

David Savran

Queering the Nation

America, not just the nation, but an idea alive in the minds of people everywhere. As this new world takes shape, America stands at the center of a widening circle of freedom, today, tomorrow and into the next century.
—President George Bush, State of the Union Message, 31 January 1990

We will be citizens.
                    —Tony Kushner, *Angels in America, Part Two: Perestroika*

At the end of World War II, the United States staked both its identity as a nation and its plans for global economic dominance on its opposition to communism as an economic, political, and ideological system. In the early 1990s, however, the dissolution of the Soviet empire and the fall of communist parties from East Berlin to Moscow were greeted with something other than unalloyed jubilation. Behind the giddy triumphalism of George Bush's State of the Union Messages, one may detect the sense of a national identity crisis in the making. A reluctant president admitted in his 1992 address that "there's a mood among us. People are worried. There has been talk of decline" ("Transcript" A17). To redress this "mood," and the possibility that the national security state might need to be dismantled, Bush, with the support of both Republicans and Democrats, accelerated the production of a new and threatening other to substitute for communism: the terrorist, or rogue, state. In an attempt to counter the dire threat of peace to military Keynesianism, they engineered deadly imperialist spectacles in Panama and Iraq. But these shows of force, in Paul Piccone's estimation, were not in themselves enough to shore up the "collective values and aspirations whose heterogeneity had hitherto been conveniently fused into a national *group* . . . by the external mediation of the threatening communist other" (9). A diffuse network of international terrorism was unable to produce the same relatively secure sense of national identity that the communist menace provided. What was needed was a compelling ideological fix, and the president's vision of the United States as the "freest," "kindest," and "strongest nation on earth" provided the basis for a renewal of nationalist ideology ("Transcript" [1992] A17). Yet his speeches of the early 1990s did not merely recycle a rhetoric of freedom (which, coincidentally, celebrated the unrestricted international flow of capital); taking on the mantle of the sage, Bush noted in his 1992 address that "in the past 12 months, the world has known changes of almost biblical proportions" (A16). This address, like many of his messages of the early 1990s, overflows with an almost apocalyptic discourse of progress and transfiguration, repeatedly referencing "democracy's advance," "a new world order," and "a dramatic and deeply promising time in our history" ("Transcript" [1990] D22; "Transcript" [1991] A12; "Transcript" [1992] A16). Attempting to revive U.S. nationalism and place the nation at the very center of history, they redefine "America" as "the beacon of freedom in a searching world" ("Transcript" [1991] A12).

During this national identity crisis one theatrical event stands out. Since its first workshop production in 1990, Tony Kushner's *Angels in America: A Gay Fantasia on National Themes* has changed the face and scale of the American theater. Having amassed the Pulitzer Prize, two best-play Tonys, and other prestigious awards, it has proven, against all odds, that a play can tackle the most controversial subjects—including politics, religion, and sex—and yet be a hit. As a meditation on "national themes," *Angels* (more provocatively than any other recent cultural text) explicitly engages questions of national history, identity, and mission by reenvisioning both what has been and what could be. At the same time, the play insistently links the nationalist project to an antihomophobic one by demonstrating the crucial importance of gay men in the construction of a national subject, polity, and literature. *Angels* queers the idea of America by reimagining the heavens and the earth, by producing hermaphroditic angels, an AIDS-stricken prophet, and a "flaming" God (2:49).

This essay represents my own meditation upon these disparate phenomena: the end of the Cold War identity crisis, the new (and old) nationalisms of the 1990s, and the success of *Angels in America*. I hope to demonstrate that by tapping into a number of diverse and contradictory narratives about the constitution of the nation, *Angels* manages to reinvigorate a fantasy of America that reaches back to the early nineteenth century and simultaneously to hold out the possibility of a new, and even revolutionary, queer nation. Before detailing the play's relationship to a new social movement, Queer Nation, that emerged as the play was being written, I will briefly sketch the play's appropriation of Mormon ideology. I want to emphasize, however, that I do not intend by this structure to contrast one progressive idea of the nation with a reactionary one (the ideological positions are by no means so clear-cut). On the contrary, what intrigues me is how the play activates the regressive and radical ideas embedded in both movements.

Millennium Approaches

That the consolidation of a nationalist ideology in the United States during the 1830s and 1840s (rather than at the time of the Revolutionary War) coincided with the invention of Mormonism is no accident. For a political unit is quite different from a nation that, in Benedict Anderson's celebrated formulation, is "an imagined political community . . . imagined as both inherently limited and sovereign" (6). With the success of Jacksonian democracy and the development of Manifest Destiny, an imagined community of Americans finally began to solidify. Simultaneously, on many different fronts a national culture was in the process of being constructed that would, in Frantz Fanon's words, make both "the totality of the nation a reality to each citizen" and "the history of the nation part of the personal experience of each" (200). The composition of American histories and the popularity of American writers in the years following the War of 1812 were crucial in producing the fantasy of a nation of boundless opportunity whose imaginative geography stretched from the quickly growing cities of the Northeast to the beckoning frontier. With the emergence of the so-called American Renaissance in the 1830s and 1840s, the idea of America, or what Lauren Berlant designates as the "National Symbolic" ("the order of discursive practices" that interpolates subjects into "a collectively-held history"), finally crystallized "under widespread pressure to develop a set of symbolic national references whose possession would signify and realize the new political and social order" (20, 29).

The production of a national subject and culture during the first half of the nineteenth century was thus a decisive step in aligning the state with the nation (at least in fantasy) and ensuring both the stability of the body politic and its suitability for industrial capitalism. It is far more than coincidence that the birth of modern America coincided with what is often called the Second Great Awakening (the first culminated in the Revolutionary War). During these years, as Klaus J. Hansen explains, "the old paternalistic reform impulse directed toward social control yielded to a romantic reform movement impelled by millennialism, immediatism, and individualism." This movement, in turn, "made possible the creation of the modern American capitalist empire, with its fundamental belief in religious, political, and economic pluralism" (49–50). For those made uneasy (for a variety of reasons) by the new individualism, this pluralism authorized the growth of alternative social and religious sects, including new communities such as the Shakers, the Oneida Perfectionists, and, most prominently and successfully, the Mormons (see Sandeen 42–58). As Hansen emphasizes, "Mormonism was not merely one more variant of American Protestant pluralism but an articulate and sophisticated counterideology that attempted to establish a 'new heaven and a new earth.' " Moreover, "both in its origins and doctrines," Mormonism "insisted on the peculiarly American nature of its fundamental values" and on the identity of America as the promised land (52).

With its four Mormon characters and quasi-Mormon Angel, *Angels in America* maintains a very close relationship to the epistemology of Mormonism, at least as it was originally articulated in the 1820s and 1830s. Many of the explicitly hieratic qualities of the play—the characterization of prophecy, the sacred book, as well as the Angel her- or himself—owe far more to Mormonism than to any other source. Even more important, the play's conceptualization of history as progress, its millennialism, and its idea of America bring it startlingly close to the tenets of early Mormonism. Providing Calvinism with its most radical challenge during the National period, early Mormonism was deeply utopian in its thrust (and it remains so even today). Its concept of time is identical to the temporality for which *Angels in America* polemicizes. Like *Angels,* Mormonism understands time as evolution and progress (in this sense it is more closely linked to Enlightenment epistemologies than Romantic ones) and holds out the possibility of unlimited human growth: "As man is God once was: as God is man may become" (qtd. in Hansen 72). As part of a tremendous resurgence of interest in the millennium between 1828 and 1832, Mormonism went far beyond the ideology of progress implicit in Jacksonian democracy (just as *Angels'* millennialism goes far beyond most contemporary ideologies of progress [see Bushman 170]).

In many ways, early Mormonism presented a significant challenge to the principles of individualist social and economic organization. Being communitarian in nature, it proposed a kind of ecclesiastical socialism that represented a repudiation of the principles of laissez-faire and an attempt "to restore a more traditional society in which the economy was regulated in behalf of the larger interests of the group" (Hansen 124–26). This nostalgia for an earlier period of capitalism (the agrarianism of the early colonies) is echoed by Mormonism's conceptualization of the continent as the promised land. Believing the Garden of Eden to have been sited in America and assigning all antediluvian history to the Western Hemisphere, early Mormonism believed that the term " 'New World' was in fact a misnomer because America was really the cradle of man and civilization" (27, 66). So, as in *Angels,* history is tied to theology and the privileged character of the nation to its sacred past. At the same time, this essentially theological conceptualization of the nation bears witness to the "strong affinity," noted by Anderson, between "the nationalist imagining" and "religious imaginings" (10–11). As Timothy Brennan explains it, "nationalism largely extend[s] and modernize[s] (although [does] not replace) 'religious imaginings,' taking on religion's concern with death, continuity, and the desire for origins" (50). Like religion, the nation authorizes a reconfiguration of time and mortality, a "secular transformation of fatality into continuity, contingency into meaning" (Anderson 10–11). Mormonism's spiritual geography was perfectly suited to this process, constructing America as both *arche* and *telos,* both origin and meaning of history.

This conceptualization of America as the site of a blessed past and a millennial future remains a powerful and compelling image even today (and one exploited by neonationalists of every stripe), giving meaning to history, making sense of the catastrophes of the past, and assuring Americans that the end will be triumphant. It also represents a repudiation of the ideologies of individualism and acquisitiveness that underwrite the Jacksonian marketplace. Yet, as Sacvan Bercovitch points out, this contradiction was at the heart of the nationalist project. Like the writers of the American Renaissance, Mormonism "adopted the culture's *controlling* metaphor—'America' as synonym for human possibility" and then turned it against hegemonic values. Both producing and fulfilling the nationalist dream, it "portray[ed] the American ideology, as all ideology yearns to be portrayed, in the transcendent colors of utopia" (642–43, 645). A form of dissent that ultimately—and contradictorily—reinforced hegemonic values, Mormonism reconceived America as the promised land, the land of an already achieved utopia, and simultaneously as the land of promise, the site of the millennium yet to come.

Despite their radically different political orientations, both George Bush and Tony Kushner are deeply indebted to the millennialism exemplified by early Mormonism. And although Kushner's vision of America does not, like Bush's, erase the histories of genocide, imperialist aggression, slavery, racism, and homophobia, *Angels* remains profoundly ambivalent as a cultural text. It can be—and has been—accommodated with stunning ease to a project whereby the theological is not only enlisted in the aid of the political and the historical but is constructed as a transcendent category into which the political and the historical finally disappear. For all its commitment to a historical materialist method, for all its attention to political struggle and the dynamics of oppression, *Angels,* like the ideology of early Mormonism and other millennialist discourses, finally, I believe, sets forth a liberal pluralist vision of America in which all, not in spite but because of their diversity, will be welcomed into the new Jerusalem (see Savran). Like other apocalyptic discourses, from Joseph Smith to George Bush, the millennialism of *Angels* works in part to reassure an "audience that knows it has lost control over events" not by enabling it to "regain . . . control" but by letting it know "that history *is* nevertheless controlled by an underlying order and that it has a purpose that is nearing fulfillment." It thereby demonstrates that "*personal* pain is subsumed within the pattern of history" and resuscitates a vision of America as both promised land and land of infinite promise (Brummett 37–38). Yet Mormonism is not the only source of the play's nationalism, and George Bush does not provide the only lens through which to read the play's utopian longings. Just as important and much more elusive (because open-ended) is the play's relationship to Queer Nation, a political movement that coalesced just one month before *Millennium Approaches'* first workshop production.

Queer Nationalism

In April 1990, members of ACT UP, the AIDS activist group, angered at the recent escalation of violence against lesbians and gay men as well as more generalized "visibility issues," met at the Lesbian and Gay Community Services Center in New York City (Trebay 34). Out of their impromptu meeting emerged a new movement, Queer Nation, which would adopt a broader social and political agenda than ACT UP and which was quickly consolidated in New York, San Francisco, Boston, and other major U.S. cities. Inspired by diverse sources, including ACT UP, the civil rights and black power movements, the post-Stonewall gay and lesbian liberation movement, the feminist movement, the countercultural action theater of the Yippies, and the antiwar and nuclear freeze movements, Queer Nation represented one of the so-called new social movements. Unlike most pre-1960 forms of social and political activism in the United States, the new social movements serve primarily a middle-class rather than working-class constituency and are, in the main, less concerned with economic oppression than social injustice. Turning their attention to civil society, they are dedicated to mobilizing not just around political issues but cultural ones as well, ranging from broad questions of enculturation and socialization to specific issues relating to the media, the construction of identity, and the effects of various discriminatory practices (see Gamson).

Queer Nation, representing a heterogeneous and shifting constituency (like most new social movements), brought together a number of contradictory agendas without offering theoretical coherence. Ideologically, it was aggressively antiassimilationist and "nonestablishment" ("Queer" 20). Eschewing both political process and any hint of reformism in favor of direct confrontation, it staged militant and highly theatricalized actions (such as kiss-ins, zaps, and the occupation of heterosexualized spaces such as suburban shopping malls and straight bars) that, Henry Abelove points out, expressed "a felt need to create a wholly non-domestic site of excitement, outrage, and interest" (25). In the words of Allan Bérubé and Jeffrey Escoffier, "Queer Nation takes to the street wearing 'QUEER' stickers and badges on their jackets, fighting to keep queer turf safe from bashings." Like "queer urban street gangs," Queer Nationalists practiced a kind of guerrilla warfare against "straight" culture (which had the same highly negative ambience that "establishment" did for the New Left). Being the products of a mediatized and commodified culture, they (unlike their 1960s forebears) did not reject consumerism but "embrace[d] the retrofuture/ classic contemporary styles of postmodernism." Committed to a style that is "slick, quick, anarchistic, transgressive, [and] ironic," it exemplified the new "politics of cultural subversion" (which became so popular both in the streets and in the academy during the 1980s) that invert, or more properly, *queer* the normative (12–14). As described by Lauren Berlant and Elizabeth Freeman, "its tactics are to cross borders, to occupy spaces, and to mime the privileges of normality—in short, to simulate 'the national' with a camp inflection" (196).

Yet what was perhaps most remarkable about Queer Nation was its expropriation of the discourse of nationalism in an era when, at least for most self-identified leftists, nationalism was (and remains) deeply suspect. Rooted in a strong sense of communitarianism that insists that "whenever one of us is hurt we all suffer," Queer Nation affirmed, as Esther Kaplan explains, that "we are a *nation* of queers" (36). Like *Angels in America,* Queer Nation represented an attempt to queer America, to produce a counterhegemonic patriotism that militates for a redefinition of the nation and simultaneously for the recognition of the always already queer status of American culture (from Whitman to Madonna). Like *Angels,* it was tied not just to a national identity crisis induced by the end of the Cold War but also to the various nationalist projects of the Reagan-Bush years: the ostentatious spectacles of nationhood (including, most prominently, the Statue of Liberty centennial and the 1984 Los Angeles Olympics), the controversies over flag burning and the Pledge of Allegiance, and the imperial muscle-flexing in Grenada, Panama, Libya, and Iraq. In the face of such extravagant—and

murderous—spectacles of empire, Queer Nation and *Angels in America* offered a relatively benign nationalist counterexample.

As Bérubé and Escoffier point out, however, even the name Queer
Nation is oxymoronic, asserting both difference and sameness. Insofar as
queer designates a perverse or marginal positionality and *nation* an affirmation
of commonality and centrality, Queer Nation necessarily combined "contradictory impulses" (12). Yet each part of the designation is itself contradictory. Historically, *queer* represents a stigmatizing term for lesbians and gay
men that, like the pink triangle, has been reclaimed, inverted if you will, as a
form of resignification. Its widespread usage during the 1990s among self-
identified queers is indicative of at least an implicit rejection of the notion of
"internalized oppression" that characterizes so much post-Stonewall discourse. Unlike many women and men who came of age politically during
the 1970s (the heyday of lesbian and gay identity politics), queers recognize
the difficulty in trying to distinguish between a stigmatized and a positively
inflected identity. The disdain felt by some queers for the terms *lesbian* and
gay—and for the ethos of the 1970s—is thus symptomatic of a generational
split. Inevitably, in the discourse of many queers, lesbians and gay men are
constructed as older, more *embourgeoisé,* and thus more conservative and
assimilationist than queers (see Abelove, "Queering"; and Hennessy).

Yet *queer* is not only the symptom of generational and class-based
conflicts, it also represents a different way of conceptualizing sexual identity and, more specifically, a means of destabilizing the binary oppositions
homosexual/heterosexual, sex/gender, gay/lesbian, masculine/feminine,
and male/female. As Eve Sedgwick observes, it "can refer to: the open
mesh of possibilities, gaps, overlaps, dissonances and resonances, lapses and
excesses of meaning when the constituent elements of anyone's gender, of
anyone's sexuality aren't made (or *can't* be made) to signify monolithically"
(8). Unlike *lesbian* and *gay,* it is an exorbitant signifier, designating a wide
range of sexual and gender dissidents, including those (like leatherfolk,
masturbators, or transgendered subjects) who may not be easily accommodated to the prevailing binary logic. *Queer* also enjoys the distinction of
being—at least theoretically—gender neutral, so that it can describe both
male- and female-sexed bodies. *Queer,* in other words, represents an attempt to problematize the older style of identity politics of the 1970s and
the minoritizing discourses that are associated with lesbian feminism and
gay liberation. To this extent, it is part of a new universalizing discourse
that is able to include under its umbrella anyone willing to renounce the
claims and prerogatives of heteronormativity. Not unlike the idea of America, it is a deeply utopian designation, opening up a vista of multiple,

shifting, and gloriously polymorphous bodies and pleasures. Yet, as so often happens in mass-movement politics, Queer Nation never completely realized these utopian hopes, and many Queer Nationalists complained that the organization and the functioning were dominated—yet again—by the persons, agendas, and styles of white, gay men (see Maggenti; and Trebay). This fact, perhaps more than any other, was responsible for its virtual disappearance by the mid-1990s.

Like *Angels in America,* Queer Nation combined different—and contradictory—concepts of subjectivity, identity, and nationhood. Practicing a postmodernist identity politics that simultaneously asserts and destabilizes identity, it epitomized the turn in new social movements away from an economic and class-based—which is to say, Marxist—reading of oppression in favor of an ideological and cultural one. As Berlant and Freeman note, "Queer Nation's nationalist-style camp counterpolitics . . . shift[s] between a utopian politics of identity, difference, dispersion, and a specificity and a pluralist agenda in the liberal sense that imagines a 'gorgeous mosaic' of difference without a model" (197). Like *Angels,* its commitment to demarginalizing the queer subject meant in practice the privileging of white, gay men (women in the play tend to be pathologized and/or marginalized). Yet in this case the contradictions inherent in these cultural productions result, I believe, not just from the contradictory class positionality of the actors involved (a dominated fraction of the dominant class, to borrow Bourdieu's formulation) but from the specific situation of white, gay men, many of whom, as individuals, possess a great deal of economic and cultural capital but who, as a class, remain relatively disempowered politically (see Bourdieu 29–73).

Perestroika

Rather than dismiss Queer Nation and *Angels in America* (and the queer cultural moment of the early 1990s that they instantiate) as being as reactionary as George Bush and consequently of little use in imagining a progressive politics, I want to put pressure on the concept of queer nationalism implicit in these productions. For it is my belief that Queer Nation failed less because its theory of nationalism was faulty than because it was never able to actualize it. As Neil Lazarus notes, "mainstream scholars have characteristically deplored 'new' nationalisms wherever they have been mobilized, on the grounds that they foment revolution, or that they are totalitarian, or that they result only in an intensification of already existing social division" (69). They forget, as Benedict Anderson emphasizes, that "since World War II every successful revolution has defined itself in *national* terms" (2).

As Aijaz Ahmad points out, from the late 1940s until the late 1970s "anticolonial nationalism—both in the form of nationalist ideologies . . . and in the form of revolutionary wars and post-revolutionary states of the socialist Left—was a constitutive element of the global configuration" (32). And nationalism, in turn, was often supported by a variety of first-world activists and intellectuals (usually inspired by Fanon) as well as a broad range of cultural nationalists, especially (in the United States at least) black and Chicano nationalists. It was not, however, until the late 1970s—coincidentally with the rise of poststructuralism—that first-world literary and cultural theorists marshaled their forces against nationalism. Since then, the critique of anticolonial nationalism launched by Homi Bhabha, Gayatri Chakravorty Spivak, and Christopher Miller (among others) has been appropriated by and disseminated widely among the American poststructuralist elite (see Lazarus and Brennan). Ahmad offers an acute reading of this development:

> The newly dominant position of poststructuralist ideology is the fundamental enabling condition for a literary theory which debunks nationalism not on the familiar Marxist ground that nationalism in the present century has frequently suppressed questions of gender and class and has itself been frequently complicit with all kinds of obscurantisms and revanchist positions, but in the patently postmodernist way of debunking *all* efforts to speak of origins, collectivities, determinate historical projects. The upshot, of course, is that critics working within the poststructuralist problematic no longer distinguish, in any foregrounded way, between the progressive and retrograde forms of nationalism with reference to particular histories, nor do they examine the even more vexed question of how progressive and retrograde elements may be (and often are) combined within particular nationalist trajectories; what gets debunked, rather, is nationalism *as such,* in more or less the same apocalyptic manner in which cultural nationalism was, only a few years earlier, declared the determinate answer to imperialism. (38)

It may be objected that the queer nationalism of both Queer Nation and *Angels in America* is, in essence, radically different from the anticolonial nationalisms about which Ahmad is writing. Not only did queer nationalism, from the outset, prove to be primarily a white, middle-class, male phenomenon (what Fanon would call a production of the national bourgeoisie), but its locus was not, as *Angels* demonstrates, the so-called Third World at all, but rather the imperial center, the metropole itself. Queer nationalism militates for a nation very different from, say, the Algerian or Vietnamese nation insofar as it targeted only a portion of the populace. For the most minoritizing of nationalists, straights were emphatically excluded from the Queer Nation. Moreover, because the United States is only one of many states that shelters a queer minority, queer nationalism could have represented an internationalist nationalism (although, as Fanon points out [213–14], this hardly makes it unique: Arab nationalism, to name only one, is also internationalist).

Yet it seems to me that this very incommensurability between the anticolonial nationalisms of the post–World War II period and queer nationalism could have proven potentially more productive than disabling. Seen through the lens of Fanonian national consciousness, queer nationalism offered (and still offers) a powerful tool for reimagining America. First, as *Angels* suggests, in America queers—however minoritized or universalized one's definition—unquestionably represent a colonized population, one insistently pathologized, criminalized, and subjugated by the ubiquitous and violent claims of heteronormativity. Like the category "native," which, for Fanon, is brought into being and perpetuated by the "settler," the queer does not have an autonomous or pre-subjected being (36). He or she is the construction of a system of oppression. To this extent, a Queer Nationalist like Prior Walter or Belize, in Kushner's play, can never return to a nonexistent authentic self that preexists subjection, but rather can only work toward producing a different kind of subject, which in Fanonian terms can only be produced by a different kind of social and economic organization. For Fanon that new subjectivity must first and foremost be a collective one based on the idea of "the people." According to Fanon, the struggle must be "to teach the masses that everything depends on them . . . that the demiurge is the people themselves and the magic hands are finally only the hands of the people" (197). Like Queer Nation, *Angels in America,* and even early Mormonism (which, after all, has its roots in "Rousseau's concept of the collective personality of the 'people' "), Fanon recognizes that revolution cannot take place without the complete participation of all who constitute the nation (Brennan 52). In all three of these cultural productions, this means first redefining family and kinship. For Queer Nationalists, it entailed changing the designation "family" so that it was "inclusive" of all those whom one calls queer, those whom one chooses to call one's kin ("Queer" 16). In the epilogue to *Perestroika,* in one of *Angels'* most radical moves, family is redefined as the chosen and diverse few gathered to hear Prior's call to arms: "We will be citizens" of a new nation that exists (as every nation does) only in fantasy (2:148).

The construction of a queer minority that makes claims for citizenship and nationhood immediately evokes the history of black nationalism in the United States. During the late 1960s and early 1970s, many African Americans, disillusioned with both electoral politics and the civil rights movement, and inspired by anticolonialist wars (in Cuba, Algeria, Vietnam), came to believe that nationalist struggle provided the best chance for radical change. In their 1967 book, *Black Power,* Stokely Carmichael and Charles V. Hamilton explain that "black people in this country form a colony" that, because "it is not in the interest of the colonial power," cannot be liberated without a struggle. For them "institutional racism" is synonymous with "colonialism," and, pointing to patterns of economic exploitation, they compare the United States to South Africa (5–6). In their discourse, black nationalism functions to form a historical link connecting not only race with nation but also the subjugation of African Americans with the dynamics of a European imperialism that violently expropriated their ancestors as slaves from the African continent. Because of its diasporic character, it is also, like queer nationalism, a form of internationalism. A history of forced migration, however, distinguishes black nationalism from queer nationalism, and the latter does not problematize the ideas of home, exile, and ancestry in the same way. For most black nationalists, the United States remains the once and future land of slavery. Unlike Queer Nation, which was intent on reclaiming (that is to say, queering) America, black nationalism characteristically finds the historical construction of America utterly irredeemable. To this extent, Belize's declaration that he "hate[s] America," that "it's just big ideas, and stories, and people dying," serves to position him more closely to black than queer nationalism (2:96).

Yet, as *Angels in America* suggests, the question of America also remains vexed for queer nationalism. In *Angels,* the idea of America is inextricably bound up with questions of identity, migration, and progress. A queer identity, in particular, remains an elusive construction. As Eve Sedgwick's gloss on the word *queer* makes plain, sexuality, when understood as the primary determinant of identity, is highly unstable and polyvalent, more an "open mesh of possibilities" than a fixed structure of desire. Moreover, identity is always multiple, overdetermined, hybridized, which is to say, always being produced by a complex array of different (and contradictory) social and psychic factors. Kobena Mercer's elaboration of hybridity as the distinguishing mark of the work of certain black lesbian and gay artists also, I

believe, describes more generally the production of identity in Queer Nationalist discourse and *Angels in America*. Rather than constructing a nation
with inflexible borders, the latter inevitably (and ironically) "operates on the
borderlines of race, class, gender, nationality, and sexuality, investigating the
complex overdetermination of subjective experiences and desires as they are
historically constituted in the ambivalent spaces in between" (201).

In *Angels,* identity is produced in the borderlands, those multidimen-
sional sites that traverse and deconstruct the difference between center and
margin, the normative and the perverse. Like the subjects who embody it, it is
constantly on the move, constantly unmaking and remaking America. In so
foregrounding the problematics of migration, both forced and voluntary
("some of us didn't exactly *choose* to migrate," notes Belize), the play insistently demonstrates the instability not just of the borders, but also of the very
idea of America (2:55). The first scene constructs America as a land that was
invaded and settled by diasporic peoples but which, perversely, cannot exist,
which remains a site of absence. The eulogy that Rabbi Chemelwitz pro-
nounces over Sarah Ironson constructs her as one "who crossed the ocean"
and brought "to America the villages of Russia and Lithuania." But the nation
to which she immigrated, "this strange place," is "the melting pot where
nothing melted," a land that can never be home, never be more than a point
of intersection for people on the move. "You do not live in America," he tells
the assembled, "no such place exists." Rather, all his listeners (and the scene
deftly conflates assembled mourners and theater audience) have their feet in
the "clay" of "ancient culture[s] and home[s]," in other histories. As if to
remind his listeners that Jews, blacks, and Mormons are diasporic peoples, he
declares (in Yiddish-ified English) that "every day of your lives the miles that
voyage between that place and this one you cross. . . . In you that journey is."
In other words, migration is the way that history is inscribed in the human
subject, and the details of that migration produce not just identity but also the
nation that isn't. The rabbi's final admonishment—"You can never make that
crossing that she made, for such Great Voyages in this world do not any more
exist"—is spoken precisely to be refuted (1:10–11). If nothing else, the play
shows that "you" are always in the process of making a "Great Voyage,"
which is to say, that history and identity are always in process in the queer
nation that does not yet exist. And at the very end of *Perestroika,* as if to
underscore the pivotal status in the play of the struggle for national liberation,
the final exchange of dialogue (that fades out under Prior's benediction) is the
debate between Louis and Belize about the status of another national entity
that does not yet exist, the state of Palestine.

The play's commitment to the idea of history as progress—and to

Enlightenment epistemologies—has the effect of producing migration as the spatial analogue to the temporal concept of progress. "Migration" is figured as a form of "Forward Motion," which "shakes up Heaven" and violently disturbs the Angel, that "cosmic reactionary" (2:50, 55). Linking migration and hybridity with progress, *Angels* imagines the queer nation as multiracial and multicultural, the future product of a ceaseless diaspora and crossing of identities and histories. And its citizens, moving from one nation that does not exist to another, are always in exile, living their lives, like Americans, "in a state of perpetual landing" (Jehlen 9). This linkage between migration and progress has the effect not just of radically problematizing the idea of a fixed homeland, but also of indefinitely deferring the production of the queer nation. In so doing, the latter is reimagined (once again) as a utopian site, which, like Oscar Wilde's utopia, is "the one country at which Humanity is always landing. And when Humanity lands there, it looks out, and, seeing a better country, sets sail" (Wilde 207). Faced with devastation, with the violence of heteronormativity, the Queer Nationalist is a perpetual exile who does not, unlike the black nationalist or Zionist, even have the fantasy of an ancestral homeland on which to fall back. Instead, the Queer Nationalist has what Fanon calls "a national culture"—including the American theater from Tennessee Williams and Edward Albee to Maria Irene Fornes and Tony Kushner—that can "rehabilitate" the nation and "serve as a justification for the hope of a future national culture" (210).

At the same time, the lack of a queer homeland in an America that does not exist speaks to the necessarily internationalist character of queer nationalism. Every nation is potentially a queer nation, less because every nation harbors a queer minority than because of the internationalist character of desire itself. Functioning as a kind of world language, and refusing to honor boundaries (both national and otherwise), desire cunningly and unpredictably undermines the distinction between the homosocial and the homosexual, producing subjects who finally defy even as they insist upon a sexual categorization. The Queer Nationalists produced by this contradictory process are both particularized and universalized by their desires. They are made, as Monique Wittig notes of Proust, "the axis of categorization from which to universalize," the perverts who prove the inadvertent lesson of Freud's theory of sexuality: that all desire is perverted. The nation they constitute "could be described," to quote Wittig again, "as being like Pascal's circle, whose center is everywhere and whose circumference is nowhere" (61–62). So imagined, the epilogue to *Perestroika* becomes the occasion for the deconstruction of the categories "queer," "nation," and "citizen" and for the calling into question of the boundaries implied by each designation. In so doing, it provides a possible model for an anti-imperialist struggle that, as Fanon emphasizes, must always proceed by way of the national. *For "it is at the heart of national consciousness that international consciousness lives and grows"* (247–48; emph. added). As history has demonstrated, it is only by means of the nation that a new definition of community and of the human subject has been produced.

As *Angels in America* suggests, for a queer nationalism to function as an internationalism, it must also ensure that "queer" denotes more than just a particularized, if universalized, form of sexual dissidence. It must also look to the construction of racialized, gendered, class-based, and (post)colonial positionalities. Yet I don't believe that it is simply a matter of making "queer" a more inclusive or pluralist category. For queer nationalism to have become an internationalism, it would have had to go beyond the principles of identity politics as they have been constituted until now. Its most anti-assimilationist proponents never recognized that Queer Nation was founded upon what remains a *strategic* essentialism, an essentialism that, although indispensable, in Gayatri Spivak's words, for defining "a scrupulously delineated 'political interest,' " is in the end "theoretically non-viable" (207). To be viable, in other words, queer nationalism must finally call into question the very categories of identity that have authorized its production in the first place. For an identity politic, however catholic or universalizing it may seem, remains indentured (in one way or another) to a theory of the humanist subject as agent of history and, as a result, even at its most collectivizing, tends to hypostatize a kind of bourgeois individualism and to protect capitalism from critique. It may attack the pieties of humanism, but it tends to reify a political subject uncomfortably similar to the one that has produced—and is produced by—a liberal pluralist politic. As Elisa Glick argues, it "has valorized a politics of lifestyle—how we dress or get off—that fails to engage with institutionalized systems of domination" (13).

More important, the identity politics that has flourished in the United States since the late 1960s, with a few exceptions (most notably, the Black Panthers, the Redstockings, and the Gay Liberation Front), has been if not downright hostile then at least indifferent to socialism. Like the new social movements to which it is linked, it has historically privileged a particular axis of identity while more often than not ignoring the relationship between the construction of identity categories and the functioning not only of American capitalism but, more important, of capitalism as a world system. Operating within a bourgeois *imaginaire,* it has only infrequently forged coalitions with working-class movements or addressed itself to the fact that the United States since 1980 has become "the most economically stratified of industrial nations" (Bradsher A1). Characteristically reformist rather than revolutionary in its strategies, it tends to reimagine the nation in liberal pluralist terms as a resplendent mosaic in which diversity is celebrated and consumed. Usually selecting culture as its primary target, it tends not to consider the material bases for cultural production. As a result, it inadvertently falls prey to the cultural logic that conceptualizes difference as a commodity rather than a political tool. This is the politics of "lifestyle," which, Rosemary Hennessy notes, obscures "social hierarchies by promoting individuality and self-expression but also a more porous conception of the self as a 'fashioned' identity" (58).

As a mere glance at *Vanity Fair* or the "Styles" section of the *New York Times* will reveal, the marketing of queer culture—not least of all in the phenomenon of *Angels in America*—has increasingly come to resemble the commodification of black music (whether jazz, funk, disco, hip-hop, or rap), which at least since the 1960s has usually functioned as a *substitute* for an engagement with an antiracist politic. During the 1990s, controversies over lesbians and gay men in the military and the drive to repeal local statutes guaranteeing their equal protection have made lesbian and gay rights *the* civil rights issue in the United States. Yet the visibility of queer artifacts and the success of queer or queer wannabe cultural productions (including *Angels,* Madonna, k. d. lang, and lesbian chic) have too frequently replaced a commitment to fighting either for equal protection under the law or for more radical kinds of political and social change. And, although one of the most provocative aspects of Queer Nation was its all too postmodernist exploitation of corporate strategies—its construction of a flagrantly and defiantly queer consumer culture—it, like *Angels,* did not explicitly question the linkages between homophobia and economic exploitation.

One of the most problematic aspects of both Queer Nation and *Angels* is their ambivalence around the question of an alliance between a queer (inter)nationalism and other anti-imperialisms, in particular, the struggle—as attenuated as it may be at the present moment—against the system of global circulation for which national boundaries remain an impediment: capitalism. Comrade Prelapsarianov seems extremely skeptical of the idea that socialism might provide an answer both to imperialism and to the genocidal force of various bourgeois nationalisms (resuscitated most distressingly in the former Soviet bloc). Searching for a "beautiful Theory," he would not agree with Ahmad that socialism is "the determinate name for [the] negation of capitalism's fundamental, systemic contradictions and cruelties" (2:14). Ahmad emphasizes that socialism, by abolishing differences in economic class, remains "essentially universalist in character," insofar as its goal is the dissolution of all social classes and the international division of labor. Thus, "even as a transitional mode," it "cannot exist except on a transnational basis." At the same time, however, "the *struggle* for even the prospect of that transition presumes a national basis, in so far as the already existing structures of the nation-state are a fundamental reality of the very terrain on which actual class conflicts take place." A queer (inter)nationalism would have to agitate to overturn the existing bourgeois state apparatuses that have adjusted all too well to the exigencies of capital (even in the Third World). It would have to strive for a massive restructuring not just of the cultural relations that support a pluralist identity politics but also of those international mechanisms, most notably the World Bank and International Monetary Fund, that work to consolidate and strengthen the circulation of capital and the international division of labor. For it is only "at the level of popular political forces, which are by the very nature of things in conflict with the state, that a nationalism can actually *become* an anti-imperialism" (316–18). Without popular and mass-movement resistance, transnational capital will only strengthen and extend the mechanisms of the bourgeois state.

One of the most intriguing proposals for restructuring was put forth by Mikhail Gorbachev in his 1987 book, *Perestroika,* which is also, by no mere coincidence, the title of part 2 of *Angels in America.* Gorbachev's project for restructuring (the literal meaning of *perestroika*) was regrettably short-lived, having been precipitously smothered by an upsurge of consumerism and the deeply reactionary bourgeois nationalisms that led to the collapse of the Soviet Union. His book, however, written in one of those rare historical moments during which, to borrow Harper's phrase, a kind of "painful progress" is possible, calls for a wide-ranging and fundamental recon-figuration not only of the Soviet economy, but also of its politics, society, and culture (2:144). Being a utopian manifesto, it does not look greedily at capitalism but envisions a different kind of socialism as the answer to the crises that engulfed the Soviet Union in the mid-1980s. Time and again, Gorbachev insists that perestroika does not signal a turn away from socialism or from Leninism, but rather its fulfillment: "More socialism means more democracy, openness and collectivism in everyday life, more culture and humanism in production, social and personal relations among people, more dignity and self-respect for the individual" (37). Committed, like *Angels,* to reclaiming Enlightenment epistemologies, Gorbachev's *Perestroika* recognizes that "progress" remains "the product of the Revolution" and "the fruit of socialism" (17–18).

In their extremely disparate ways, Kushner's *Angels in America,* queer nationalism, Fanon's national liberation, and Gorbachev's perestroika all speak to the desirability of what Neil Lazarus refers to as "a 'new' humanism, predicated upon a formal repudiation of the degraded European form, and borne embryonically in the national liberation movement" (93). The deeply problematic nature of the old European (and American) humanism—epitomized by the murderous policies of George Bush—with its championing of individualism, autonomy, and the "free" market and its inextricable connection with the imperialist project, is all too obvious (it has, after all, served historically as the rationale for colonialism). But *Angels* suggests that humanism as an idea—no less than America as an idea—is by no means irredeemable (this seems to me to be crucial to its success). In his consideration of humanism, Ahmad usefully distinguishes between "the epistemological and the practical (i.e., political and ethical) issues involved" in the concept. He points out that while Marx clearly broke with a liberal humanist epistemology, "Marxism recoups its humanist energy" with regard both to the "constructedness of history (unauthored but humanly made) and the ethical life of the species-being (the struggle from necessity to freedom)" (327).

Understood in this sense, then, a Marxist humanist notion of freedom—from want, from necessity—differs radically from the liberal humanist idea of freedom, tied as it is to the exigencies of the capitalist marketplace. So, too, a Marxist humanist notion of universalism, which is linked to the transnational character of socialism as the answer to imperialism and the international division of labor it leaves in its bloody wake, must differ from Bush's universalism, which is connected both to the globalization of capital and to the universalist currency of the commodity form. Finally, a Marxist humanist egalitarianism, rooted in "the ethical life of the species-being," must differ both from a liberal humanism that promises equal opportunity but delivers only economic and social inequality and a liberal pluralism that celebrates cultural difference but covertly reinforces the murderous subordination of margin to center, black to white, woman to man, queer to straight, and the human subject to the unimpeded flow of capital. The (inter)national crisis precipitated by the end of the Cold War thus represents an opportunity to imagine radical perestroika. By attempting this impossible project, *Angels in America* aims to reconceptualize and reclaim humanism and to take up Fanon's challenge in the name of a queer internationalism:

> Let us consider the question of mankind. Let us reconsider the question of . . . all humanity, whose connections must be increased, whose channels must be diversified and whose messages must be re-humanized. (314)

REFERENCES

Abelove, Henry. "From Thoreau to Queer Politics." *Yale Journal of Criticism* 6 (1993): 17–27.

———. "The Queering of Lesbian/Gay History." *Radical History Review* 62 (1995): 44–57.

Ahmad, Aijaz. *In Theory: Classes, Nations, Literatures*. London: Verso, 1992.

Anderson, Benedict. *Imagined Communities: Reflections on the Origin and Spread of Nationalism*. London: Verso, 1991.

Berlant, Lauren. *The Anatomy of National Fantasy: Hawthorne, Utopia, and Everyday Life*. Chicago: U of Chicago P, 1991.

Berlant, Lauren, and Elizabeth Freeman. "Queer Nationality." *Fear of a Queer Planet: Queer Politics and Social Theory*. Ed. Michael Warner. Minneapolis: U of Minnesota P, 1993. 193–229.

Bercovitch, Sacvan. "The Problem of Ideology in American Literary History." *Critical Inquiry* 12 (Summer 1986): 631–53.

Bérubé, Allan, and Jeffrey Escoffier. "Queer/Nation." *Out/look* 11 (Winter 1991): 12–14.

Bourdieu, Pierre. "The Field of Cultural Production, or The Economic World Reversed." *The Field of Cultural Production: Essays on Art and Literature*. Ed. Randal Johnson. New York: Columbia UP, 1993. 29–73.

Bradsher, Keith. "Gap in Wealth in U.S. Called Widest in West." *New York Times* 17 April 1995: 1+.

Brennan, Timothy. "The National Longing for Form." *Nation and Narration*. Ed. Homi K. Bhabha. London: Routledge, 1990. 44–70.

Brummett, Barry. *Contemporary Apocalyptic Rhetoric*. New York: Praeger, 1991.

Bushman, Richard L. *Joseph Smith and the Beginnings of Mormonism*. Urbana: U of Illinois P, 1984.

Carmichael, Stokely, and Charles V. Hamilton. *Black Power: The Politics of Liberation in America*. New York: Vintage, 1967.

Fanon, Frantz. *The Wretched of the Earth*. Trans. Constance Farrington. New York: Grove Weidenfeld, 1968.

Gamson, Joshua. "Silence, Death, and the Invisible Enemy: AIDS Activism and Social Movement 'Newness.'" *Ethnography Unbound: Power and Resistance in the Modern Metropolis*. Berkeley: U of California P, 1991.

Glick, Elisa. "Genderfuck and Other Fashionable Utopias: Challenging the Politics of Pro-Sexuality." MS.

Gorbachev, Mikhail. *Perestroika: New Thinking for Our Country and the World*. New York: Harper and Row, 1987.

Hansen, Klaus J. *Mormonism and the American Experience*. Chicago: U of Chicago P, 1981.

Hennessy, Rosemary. "Queer Visibility in Commodity Culture." *Cultural Critique* (Winter 1994–95): 31–76.

Jehlen, Myra. *American Incarnation: The Individual, the Nation, and the Continent*. Cambridge: Harvard UP, 1986.

Kaplan, Esther. "A Queer Manifesto." *Village Voice* 14 August 1990: 36.

Kushner, Tony. *Angels in America: A Gay Fantasia on National Themes. Part One: Millennium Approaches*. New York: Theatre Communications Group, 1993.

———. *Angels in America: A Gay Fantasia on National Themes. Part Two: Perestroika*. New York: Theatre Communications Group, 1994.

Lazarus, Neil. "Disavowing Decolonization: Fanon, Nationalism, and the Problematic of Representation in Current Theories of Colonial Discourse." *Research in African Literatures* 24 (Winter 1993): 69–98.

Maggenti, Maria. "Women as Queer Nationals." *Out/look* 11 (Winter 1991): 20–23.

Mercer, Kobena. "Skin Head Sex Thing: Racial Difference and the Homoerotic Imaginary." *How Do I Look?: Queer Film and Video*. Ed. Bad Object-Choices. Seattle: Bay Press, 1991. 169–210.

Piccone, Paul. "The Crisis of Liberalism and the Emergence of Federal Populism." *Telos* 89 (Fall 1991): 7–44.

"Queer." Interviews by Steve Cosson. *Out/look* 11 (Winter 1991): 20.

Sandeen, Ernest R. *The Roots of Fundamentalism: British and American Millenarianism, 1800–1930*. Chicago: U of Chicago P, 1970.

Savran, David. "Ambivalence, Utopia, and a Queer Sort of Materialism: How *Angels in America* Reconstructs the Nation." *Theatre Journal* 47 (May 1995): 207–27.

Sedgwick, Eve Kosofsky. *Tendencies*. Durham: Duke UP, 1993.

Spivak, Gayatri Chakravorty. "Subaltern Studies: Deconstructing Historiography." *In Other Worlds: Essays in Cultural Politics*. New York: Routledge, 1988. 197–221.

"Transcript of Bush's State of the Union Message to the Nation," *New York Times* 1 February 1990: D22.

"Transcript of Bush's State of the Union Message to the Nation," *New York Times* 30 January 1991: A12.

"Transcript of President Bush's Address on the State of the Union," *New York Times* 29 January 1992: A17.

Trebay, Guy. "In Your Face." *Village Voice* 14 August 1990: 34.

Wilde, Oscar. "The Soul of Man under Socialism." 1891. *Intentions and Other Writings*. Garden City, NY: Dolphin Books, n.d.

Wittig, Monique. "The Point of View: Universal or Particular?" *The Straight Mind and Other Essays*. Boston: Beacon Press, 1992. 59–67.

Jeffrey D. Mason

American Stages (Afterpiece)

At bottom, the study of American culture rests on questions of boundaries. Where do the "American" borders lie? Do they present harsh barriers, simple demarcations, or vague buffer zones? Are they as thick and high as a rampart, or are they pliantly permeable, mere suggestions of a transition from one perspective to another? How do they frame the territory and give it shape? Do they suggest a passage from one space into a distinct other, or do they float on the fringes, dissolving and re-forming between ambiguous margins on both sides? Most important, how do they determine questions of allegiance, responsibility, and identity? How do these boundaries shape the behavior of people and their institutions? Who belongs? Do the boundaries define the people, or do the people dominate the boundaries?

Since this collection treats the *performance* of "America," another set of questions clamors for attention. How does one signify American status? Josephine Lee suggests that some consider "Americanness" as necessary of proof; one must establish longevity of residence, a certain relationship to the land, an acceptance of values (probably selected reflexively in order to set up the validation of one's claim), a significant contribution to the economy, or some other basis for a claim. Ann Larabee traces the transition that an immigrant might make between her traditional heritage and a probably universalized "American" identity and so reveals the difficulty of locating a juncture or a boundary that one might clearly cross. If such a transformation were possible, or feasibly recognizable, how would one then perform it? By what external show does "American" shine?

The very concept of nation implies homogeneity; as Charlotte Canning writes, "Community is the way in which the nation is imagined." The Chautauqua tradition rested on a vision of America as so homogeneous that the same tent show would play equally well in every town across the land. Similar presumptions of homogeneity appear in the totalitarian uniformity of Levittown, in the mass-marketing success of Wal-Mart, and (to move closer to the notion of performance) in the nationwide simultaneous release of blockbuster motion pictures and the broadcast of network television series. Such strategies work from a comprehensive model of "America."

Yet, as Tiffany Ana López observes, community is a matter of exclusion as well as inclusion, so the formation of community must involve negotiation over membership. Her discussion of Moraga raises the questions of whether we can conceptualize the notion of community apart from the models of "family" and "nation" and of whether it might be possible to reinterpret those terms. The idea of "family" suggests, powerfully, common interests and experiences, but, as we extend "family" into "clan" and on by increments to reach "nation," the theoretical imperative of commonality exerts an increasing degree of pressure on the expanding unit. Questions of signification and performance rise again, for the underlying presumption of a performance event is that all involved form a community to a degree that they can at least understand one another; in this sense, a community shares a sign system and probably also the experiences and understandings that contribute to the evolution of the signifying vocabulary.

Larabee's discussion of community theater suggests that a community can find its identity only "as a subculture, an alternative territory that is always defined by a larger geography." That is, the community performs itself only in relation to an "other," just as the Neighborhood Playhouse positioned "its subjects in the dominant culture's symbolic exchange." In this context, a culture exists only in a comparative sense, a postulate that threatens the American grip on egalitarianism, for our traditions and even our laws display skepticism that equality can thrive where there is no uniformity. Diversity renders equality problematic.

If we are not one, then we are many, perhaps a certain nation by very virtue of our diversity. In that case, does "America" as a unitary concept simply dissolve? Ginger Strand clarifies that even as early as the Federalist period in Boston, the theater provided a site for struggle over competing views of "America." López, building on the tradition of Aztlán, observes that the notion of Chicano nationalism suggests either a nation within a nation or two overlapping, coterminous nations, an idea that seems to represent the actuality accurately—the southwestern United States was once part of Mexico, and that border between two such disparate nations belies the degree to which the entire region shares cultural traditions—while at the same time subverting the very notion of nation and encouraging, in some minds, xenophobia. David Krasner offers polyphony as a metaphor for the co-operation of the constituents of African American culture, but we might expand the chorus to include voices from all American traditions, optimistically fastening our hopes on the figure of music as the performative art that most effectively blends solo lines to form a harmonious whole. By contrast, Robert H. Vorlicky's study of autoperformance implicitly suggests the troubling implications of attempting to perform "America" through one individual's sensibility rather than through a collective.

Beyond ethnicity, performing "America" is partly a matter of the evolving politics of gender and sexuality and of how much room "alternative" views have been able to claim on American stages. Vorlicky writes, "Early American writers valorized a kind of 'self-made' individualism that helped establish them as the representative men among men," so one can infer that the male voice first defined those qualities and institutions still assumed to "be" "American," such as individualism, competition through free enterprise, opportunity, and a contentiously participatory democracy. This straight white male priority has become the object of challenge; for example, David Savran describes America as the field of an ongoing contest between the queer and the straight.

"American" as a gendered vision or concept is not restricted to the white mainstream. Lee suggests that "the masculinist and heteronormative propensities of Asian American cultural nationalism seem incompatible with women's empowerment and self-determination." She also reminds us that in *Paper Angels,* Genny Lim presents the land as female and the farmer as male, evoking similarly gendered constructions in such canonized mainstream plays as *Desire Under the Elms* and *Death of a Salesman*. López identifies the father as the accepted source of nationalistic power and authority and then proposes Pancho Villa's disembodied, shrunken head—maleness bereft of male biology—as evidence of the hollowness of patriarchy. She presents Corky, the woman who perceives her rape as proof of her femaleness, in order to raise the question of to what extent "America" defines the "other" through violence; the most disturbing implication in her analysis is that the "other" can be someone who should be embraced as part of "America," in this case, the rape victim, or *la chingada* ("the fucked one").

La chingada might represent the fundamental antithesis of the paradigmatic "American": the "American" is a victor, while *la chingada* is implicitly expelled as a loser, one who was not strong enough, one who ostensibly allowed herself to become a victim. The American experience offers many examples of aggressive and appropriative behavior. Rosemarie K. Bank traces the antebellum appropriation, classification, and commodification of artifacts, and she analyzes the strategies by which both serious-minded and "humbug" museums reduced and consumed, in particular, American Indian culture; she asserts that "it is in the reproduction of those disenfranchised in

U.S. society in the antebellum decades that cultural authenticating processes are most exposed." Her discussion inspires questions of how America today processes experience in terms of its nationalistic agenda. Krasner indicates that American colonialism seeks to homogenize the world, and Leigh Woods suggests that American culture and its materials become means to transform the entire planet into "America." These colonial and imperialist patterns resonate closely with hallowed notions of competition and achievement. *Las chingadas* do not seem to "belong" (to use the word as in O'Neill's *The Hairy Ape*) in an American ideology that gives paramount place to the expectation (not merely the hope) of success; note Savran's analysis of *Angels in America* in the context of Mormonism as a preter-American movement, fascinated with growth, oriented toward progress, and driven by a vision of an available utopia. Yet the staging of success can also involve its interrogation. Pointing to Augustin Daly's rise, Kim Marra observes that becoming an American can, for many immigrants, involve a struggle aimed at joining a desirable group or rising to a coveted status. Yet Lee cites Frank Chin's perspective on Maxine Hong Kingston to ask whether success in the mainstream must inevitably indicate that one outside of it (in this case, an Asian American) has betrayed and forsaken her background. In wider frameworks, Marra wonders whether success must operate through imperialism and capitalism, and Larabee interrogates the conflation of class with regard to the formation of cultural identity. In other words, the American imperative seems to suggest that the poor as well as those who do not join in the parade are, due to their own inadequacies, *las chingadas*.

La chingada complements the image of the hole that plays a fundamental role in two of our essays. In *Giving Up the Ghost,* Corky cries out that the rapist made her into nothing more than a hole, and López asserts that the social construction of gender can constitute an attack on the female body, arguing that if we build community on patriarchy but allow the father figure to act as an oppressor, then we sanction a wounding. Harry Elam and Alice Rayner develop the image of the hole from Parks's Great Hole of History and its replica, the latter acting as a metaphor for the "empty space" of the theater. Both essays reveal notions of emptiness, vacancy, evacuation, and incomprehension as well as the idea of the violation that transforms something into nothing. Such a hole might be the dark consequence of the American enterprise; the revealed glory is a function of the covert excavation. López condemns violation as inherently heinous, but while Elam and Rayner agree, they also cite Houston A. Baker to interpret the hole as offering limitless opportunity, a new version of the tabula rasa where those demeaned as *las chingadas* might create their own experience and write history anew, an Edenic vision that recycles one of the oldest American traditions.

The struggle over boundaries that pervades the performance of "America" comes down to making claims and denying them, or to establishing "American" and "other." This contest can lead to a negativist strategy for asserting one's "American" status by displacing, relocating, or actually erasing the adversary. This exclusionary project leads to rejecting rivals as not white (see Krasner, Lee, López, and Elam and Rayner), not heterosexual (see López and Savran) or not male (see Larabee, Marra, Lee, and López). To cast such people as "not-Americans" is somehow to define them as foreigners, to claim "American" can become a defense against being branded a "foreigner," and to damn "foreigners" can by reflection valorize "Americans." If that which is "foreign" is whatever does *not* reflect an "American" quality, wish, or strategy, a "foreigner" can quickly become the agent or repository of evil, of "not-American." By extension, whoever does not satisfy a certain conception of "American," no matter his actual origin, is therefore a foreigner and must be banished. Yet, inasmuch as we are a nation of immigrants, citizenship and even residency are matters not of nativity but of simple presence, and "foreigner" becomes a slippery term, perhaps a vague and feeble means of referring to someone in transition, someone who might, at any time, become an American, while "American" is a contingent title. Indeed, everyone in America has lost some portion of cultural inheritance; with reference to the loss of style, custom, and idiom, literary and cultural critic Philip Fisher argues, "In every American personality there exists a past history of erasure" (73). The trajectories between "American" and "foreigner" trace fears and anxieties that flared during an episode that transformed the entire nation, through the proscenium arch of its news media, into a stage, and which reinforces my suggestion, early in the first portion of this essay, that the drama we enact in the playhouse is only one manifestation of the more widespread culture wars.

I am writing this passage in May 1997, just two years after the Oklahoma City bombing, and the jury in Denver has retired to deliberate on the matter of Timothy McVeigh. As news of the bombing suffused the media on the morning of 19 April 1995, an early theory described the perpetrators as fundamentalist Islamic terrorists, fanatics bringing the jihad to the heartland of America and transforming the plains community into an unwilling counterfeit of Beirut. CNN reported that investigators sought to question several men, Middle Eastern in appearance, who had been seen driving away from the building shortly before the blast. To so construct the putative agents of the calamity—dark, foreign, and elusive—was to condemn them as outlaws from American conceptions of decency, law, and compassion. As cold rain turned the Murrah Federal Building's dust into muck, outraged citizens cast themselves as protectors of the innocent victims and instruments of bitter retribution against the imagined invaders, the aliens, the demons from beyond the space—geographic, spiritual, psychological, cultural—that some cherish as "America."

When the most likely suspect turned out to be an American, a white man, a Gulf War veteran later linked with the ultra-right militia movement, the sensibility that had so precipitously constructed the erstwhile villains met itself driving around the corner. If McVeigh were the bomber, then he had shattered more than the Murrah Building: he had played a role that no "real" American should have been able or willing to undertake and so had shaken the very idea of American identity. When the FBI raced to the Noble County Jail, they found an angry mob demanding the death of the "baby killer." The roughnecks hated the man, hated him not only for what they believed he had done, but also because he might seem to be one of them. Anxious to separate themselves from the crime and to affirm that "America" does not callously crush its children, they gathered in the street to cast McVeigh out. The newspapers and television networks presented him not as a cowboy, a poet, a maverick lighting out for the territory ahead of the rest, or even a Rambo sacrificing himself to correct American history gone awry, but rather as a pariah, a zealot who had twisted the American ideology of liberty and individualism beyond the accepted limits. Yet, while the public could have accepted—even embraced, with relief—menace if inflicted by outsiders, McVeigh's alleged complicity turned the collective gaze inward, and beneath the shift from Islamic terrorists to the crewcut partisan lay a quick, forced revision of the American sense of self, a galvanic, choking moment of recognition. "America" now undeniably encompassed a paramilitary counterculture, one as genuine and American as the woods where its troopers, costumed in camouflage fatigues and smearing war paint over their self-righteously grim expressions, rehearsed for the coming Alamo.

All of this is the stuff of the stage, even of cheap theatrics: a confection of extravagant rhetoric and anguished posturings. McVeigh came to light embedded in a mise-en-scène that could have been borrowed from a Sam Shepard play: a farm in rural Michigan, a body shop on the outskirts of town, a nine-millimeter semi-automatic pistol, a handful of Black Talon bullets, a battered GMC pickup, a bumper sticker reading "American and Proud," the Dreamland Motel, and a bar called Club Yesterday. Above the sad, dogged routine—arrest and arraignment, rescue and internment—

crackled the unpredictable electricity of a performance but one not restricted to the apparent confines of the playhouse. The melodramatic trappings remind us how closely the public display of national identity can
resemble the staged performance of a role.

The drama of the bombing brings together three issues that have
helped to give *Performing America* its shape: boundaries and membership,
"American" behavior, and the politics of success. The blast ripped a hole in
the American turf and instantaneously transformed all of us into *las chingadas,*
but the crime carried troubling contingencies regarding our claim of injury.
If one of us perpetrated this violation, we cannot displace our outrage. If the
bomber "belongs," then the "American" community hardly reflects the
vision of Chautauquan hopes. If violence is an American means of appropriating and asserting power, then the bomber has turned one of our strategies
against us. During that brief, happy moment of misinformation shortly after
the blast, we jumped at the chance to define the calamity as alien, but since
then, the nation has struggled to accept the catastrophe as revealing an
element, however unpleasant, of "America."

Perhaps the bombing represents a psychotic extreme in the national
identity crisis. If "America" is a construction constantly rebounding and
multiplying in the freeplay of discourse, then how *can* one perform it? One
might embrace the contest over the notion as well as its constant shifting and
so raise the artistic risks while encompassing theoretical subtleties. On the
other hand, one might try to establish a fixed, certain vision, either claiming
to be able to paralyze freeplay for a moment or presupposing a given, a
center, a transcendental signified—"America" as a paradigmatic monu-
ment—in relation to which to describe spaces and peoples. In either case,
performance involves struggle, and some production of American iconogra-
phy, perhaps in desperation, has moved toward obscuring and displacing any
assumed actuality. Elam and Rayner pursue "the idea of the 'total fake' as
the defining character of contemporary American culture," specifically in
the context of Disneyland as a paradigm for America, which, building on the
work of Umberto Eco and Jean Baudrillard, they present as "the land of
hyperreality, where any ground for historical certainty is erased by the
generation and circulation of images that have no original." In other words,
signification—including performance—can create an imaginary "America"
of its own, so the project of searching for "America" must also include the
attempt, perhaps vain, to locate and establish a grounding in some putative
actuality. In this sense, performance becomes a means of arguing a case, of
presenting a vision and trying to assert its validity. One hopes to find the
reality through the performance of it.

I shall close by returning to one of my original points, that we cannot and should not regard the theater as distinct from its nation. We, as artists, should attend not only to *how* we perform but to *what* we perform. If this remark seems condescending or pedestrian, I suggest that the relentless reduction of the National Endowment for the Arts provides ample proof that the daring, the challenging, and the political receive little encouragement from the well-established institutions of the culture that claims freedom as its cornerstone. I wish to urge the ideas of performance as an irresistible impulse (a compulsion to find shape in experience and to do so in a variety of venues, a way of claiming the cultural narrative) and of the theater as a cultural phenomenon, not merely in the sense that it involves aesthetics and cultivation, but more that it grows out of the life of the people. Savran asks whether "America" can survive without migration, progress, or, more fundamentally, an accepted concept of normativity. The question itself reveals the difficulty of the problem in that it presents as commensurate alternatives both visions of change and retreats to stasis. Elam and Rayner suggest that culture is something that its adherents seek to nurture and even recuperate; one might point to such a preservationist posture in order to explain the conservative visions conveyed in the most obviously flag-waving plays and at the same time to understand why the mainstream public reacts with such confusion and outrage to those plays that sing America discordantly and in minor keys. When Savran closes his essay with challenges to liberal humanism, pluralism, individualism, autonomy, and the free market, all by way of promoting Marxist notions of freedom and internationalism, we see that one can yearn for "America" in ways that seem strange to others but which involve a revisiting of its most fundamental principles. The danger of fear and tyranny is that if one person can shrivel into *una chingada,* then we are all in jeopardy. America may require boundaries, but we need not mark them with barbed wire.

REFERENCE

Fisher, Philip. "Democratic Social Space: Whitman, Melville, and the Promise of American Transparency." *Representations* 24 (Fall 1988): 60–101. *The New American Studies: Essays from* Representations. Ed. Philip Fisher. Berkeley: U of California P, 1991. 70–111.

Contributors

Rosemarie K. Bank has published in *Theatre Journal, Nineteenth-Century Theatre, Theatre History Studies, Essays in Theatre, Theatre Research International, Theatre Studies, On-Stage Studies, Journal of Dramatic Theory and Criticism, Women in American Theatre, Feminist Rereadings of Modern American Drama, The American Stage,* and *Critical Theory and Performance.* She is the author of *Theatre Culture in America, 1825–1860* (Cambridge) and is currently preparing *Staging the Native, 1792–1892.* She is a recent National Endowment for the Humanities (NEH) Fellow and serves on a number of editorial and executive boards and is Associate Professor of Theater at Kent State University.

Charlotte Canning is Associate Professor in the Department of Theatre and Dance at the University of Texas at Austin. She is the author of *Feminist Theaters in the USA: Staging Women's Experience* (Routledge) and has published on theater, history, and feminism in *Theatre Journal, Theatre, Lit: Literature, Interpretation, Theory,* and *Theatre Annual.*

Harry Elam is the Christensen Professor in the Humanities at Stanford University. He is the author of *Taking It to the Streets: The Social Protest Theater of Luis Valdez and Amiri Baraka* (Michigan) and coeditor of *Colored Contradictions: An Anthology of Contemporary African American Drama* (Plume). He is currently completing a critical study on August Wilson and is coeditor, with David Krasner, of the forthcoming *African American Theatre History and Performance Studies: A Critical Reader* (Oxford).

J. Ellen Gainor is Associate Professor of Theatre Studies at Cornell University. She is the author of *Shaw's Daughters: Dramatic and Narrative Constructions of Gender* (Michigan) and the editor of *Imperialism and Theatre* (Routledge). She is currently completing *The Plays of Susan of Glaspell: A Contextual Study* and will be one of the editors for the first *Norton Anthology of Drama.*

David Krasner is Director of Undergraduate Theater Studies at Yale University, where he teaches theater history, acting, and directing. His book *Resistance, Parody, and Double Consciousness in African American Theatre, 1895–1910* (St. Martin's) received the American Society for Theatre Research's 1998 Errol Hill Award. He is coeditor, with Harry Elam, of the forthcoming *African American Theatre History and Performance Studies: A Critical Reader* (Oxford) and editor of the forthcoming *Method Acting Reconsidered: Theory, Practice, Future* (St. Martin's). He has published articles and reviews in *African American Review, Theatre History Studies, Theatre Research International, Theatre Studies, Theatre Journal, Theatre Survey, New England Theatre Journal, Modern Drama, Nineteenth-Century Theatre,* and *Text & Presentation.* He is currently at work on a history of African American theater, drama, and performance in the Harlem Renaissance.

Ann Larabee is Assistant Professor of American Thought and Language at Michigan State University. Her essays on women playwrights Susan Glaspell and Djuna Barnes have appeared in *Modern American Drama: The Female Experience,* ed. June Schlueter, and *Silence and Power: A Reevaluation of Djuna Barnes,* ed. Mary Lynn Broe. Her work has also appeared in *American Studies, Literature and Medicine, Postmodern Culture,* and *New England Theatre Journal.*

Josephine Lee is Associate Professor of English at the University of Minnesota, Twin Cities. She is the author of *Performing Asian America: Race and Ethnicity on the Contemporary Stage* (Temple) and a coeditor, with Imogene Lim and Yuko Matsukawa, of the forthcoming *Re/Collecting Early Asian America: Readings in Cultural History.*

Tiffany Ana López is Assistant Professor of English at the University of California, Riverside, where she teaches American drama and Latina/o literatures. She edited the anthology *Growing Up Chicana/o* (William Morrow). Recent publications include "Imaging Community: Video in the Installation Work of Pepón Osorio" in *Art Journal* (Winter 1995); and "A Tolerance for Contradictions: The Short Stories of María Cristina Mena" in *Nineteenth Century American Writers: A Critical Reader* (forthcoming from Blackwell). She is currently completing her book *Bodily Inscriptions: Representations of the Body in U.S. Latina Drama.*

Kim Marra is Associate Professor of Theatre Arts at the University of Iowa. Her publications include *Passing Performances: Queer Readings of Leading Players in American Theater History,* coedited with Robert A. Schanke (Michigan), and articles in *Theatre Survey, Theatre Annual, Journal of Dramatic Theory and Criticism, New England Theatre Journal, ATQ: Journal of 19th Century American Literature and Culture,* and *Staging Difference: Cultural Pluralism in American Theatre and Drama* (Lang). Her essay in *Performing America* is part of a book-in-progress analyzing relationships between autocratic male producer-managers and iconic female stars in United States theater from 1865 to 1930.

Jeffrey D. Mason is the author of *Melodrama and the Myth of America* (Indiana), of various articles and papers on American theater and drama, and of a novel entitled *Cousin Jack* (Alexander Associates). He has directed forty-six productions, including his own translation of *La Dame aux Camélias*, and acted in nearly thirty, most recently as Cassius in *Julius Caesar* and Monostatos in *The Magic Flute*. He teaches theater studies and performance at California State University, Bakersfield.

Alice Rayner is Associate Professor of Drama at Stanford University. She has published *Comic Persuasion* (California) and *To Act To Do To Perform* (Michigan) as well as articles in *Journal of Dramatic Theory and Criticism, Theatre Journal, Theatre Quarterly,* and *Discourse.*

David Savran is Professor of English at Brown University. His essay in this collection is an abridged version of a chapter in his book *Taking It Like a Man: White Masculinity, Masochism, and Contemporary American Culture* (Princeton).

Ginger Strand is an independent scholar who writes about contemporary and historical American theater. Her publications include pieces on Sophie Treadwell, Eugene O'Neill, Edward Harrigan and Tony Hart, Edwin Forrest, Augustin Daly, and pamphlet plays of the American Revolution. She would like to thank the Mellon Society of Fellows at Columbia University and the Council of the Humanities at Princeton University for postdoctoral fellowships that made this piece possible.

Robert H. Vorlicky is Associate Professor of Drama at Tisch School of the Arts, New York University. He is the author of *Act Like a Man: Challenging Masculinities in American Drama* (Michigan), *Tony Kushner in Conversation* (Michigan), and a forthcoming book on Asian American performance artist Dan Kwong (Cassell). He is the president-elect of the American Theater and Drama Society, the editor of performance and film reviews for *The David Mamet Review,* and the recipient of numerous awards, including fellowships from the National Endowment for the Humanities, Fulbright

Foundation, Karolyi Foundation for Creative Writing, and the Wisconsin Arts Board.

Leigh Woods is Professor of Theatre and Drama at the University of Michigan. He has essays on acting and performance in a variety of journals and has appeared as an actor in new plays by George W. D. Trow and Wendy Wasserstein as well as in American premieres by Heiner Müller and Mikhail Shatrov. His books include *Garrick Claims the Stage, On Playing Shakespeare, Public Selves, Political Stages: Interviews with Icelandic Women in Government and Theatre,* with his wife, Ágústa Gunnarsdóttir, and *Playing to the Camera: Film Actors Discuss Their Craft,* which he coedited with Bert Cardullo, Harry Geduld, and Ronald Gottesman.

Index